Astrological Predictions
for the Age *of* Light

THE UNITED STATES, CHINA & JAPAN

Michael Mercury

Copyright © 2018 Michael Mercury
Astrological Predictions for The Age of Light
The United States, China and Japan
ISBN: 978-0-9981842-0-3

Published by
Elephantsdance Publishing
P.O. Box 3239 #306
La Pine, OR 97739
www.ElephantsDance.org
info@elephantsdance.org

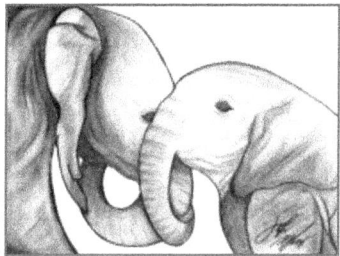

Elephants Design: Joshua McCann

Editors:
Frieda Kodl
Brian Elsasser
Carolyn Daughters
Linda Martin
Rebecca Woolston

Consultant: Jack Koulbanis

Graphic Designer: Thom Vallance, ThomVallance.com

Preface By: Maria J. Mateus

Cover Designers: Ahrynn McCann, Julie Rosen

All rights reserved. No part of this book may be reproduced or used in any form, including Photo-stat, microfilm, xerography or other means, or incorporated into any information-retrieval system, electronic or mechanical, without written permission from the copyright owner.

First Edition – April 2018
Printed in the United States of America

Dedication

To my mother and father,

Lieutenant Colonel Ardyth E. Cochran
and
Carmen T. Vazaquez Cochran,

The most loving and wisest teachers,
by example, I have ever known.

Contents

Dedication 4

Foreword 7

Preface 10

Chapter 1: Eternity = Present 12
The World: Eternal Implications...
The Age of Light Evolves into the Age of Aquarius

Chapter 2: The Four Directions of Light 42
The Present Future: United States, China and Japan
The Ascending Light

Chapter 3: Awareness 68
Heaven or Hell?
The I Ching: Universal Wisdom for the Age of Light
Change, Constantly Arriving
As Above, So Below

Chapter 4: The Age of Light 90
The Dawning of the Age of Aquarius
Quetzalcoatl, a Messenger from Eternity
Wake Up!

Chapter 5: United States Sibly Chart and Japan's Meiji Chart
Astrological Synastry Interpretation 106
Astrological Synastry Analysis

Chapter 6: Japan Meiji-USA Sibly 138
Astrological Synastry Analysis

Chapter 7: Japan Understanding China 150
Neighbors for Life

Chapter 8: Japan's Relationship with China 164

Chapter 9: Transit Chart of Tokyo 176

Epilogue: All is Light 188

Aknowledgements 196

TimeSpace
Creation
The Transparent Mirror
Eternal Light
from
No Where.

★ ★ ★ ★ ★ ★ ★   ★ ★ ★ ★ ★ ★ ★   ★ ★ ★ ★ ★ ★ ★

Astrology is a living language.
It illuminates the Inexplicable through conscious awareness.
Astrology is a beacon for understanding the events that unfold
in the Age of Light, as the world navigates the Present
beyond the Mayan Prediction and into
the Age of Aquarius.
The end of ignorance but not the end of the world is upon us.

Foreword

Astrology studies the synchronicity of life experiences. Why it emerged at the dawn of civilization is unknown, its history deep and complex. But its influence throughout the ancient world is undeniable. Introduced to the Greeks by the Babylonians in the 4th century B.C., astrology was elevated to the science of astronomy, 'the law of the stars.' And from Greece, it spread to the Roman and Arab worlds.

In the early days of astrology, astrologers were viewed as messengers of the gods, explaining human behavior through their observations of the lights in the sky. Astrologers were sought for their understanding of the mysteries of life and provided guidance for communities to harmonize with nature and be in tune with their many gods. Over the centuries that followed, astrology continued to grow and evolve, shaping and defining fulfillment for humankind.

The Latin root of the word "religion" is religiō, which means "to link back." Religion is of the past. The Present is where God resides. Now for the second time we have mentioned the word God, not spoken in ancient times, let us agree or agree to disagree, depending on your point of view, the word God is a relic. In ancient times, if you knew the name God, then you possessed magical power. It represents the past, and the word has been so abused and misused by religions and organizations, it has lost the clarity it may have once had. Of course, to personalize the name God as if it were a person is the first and last mistake. We examine the concept of God throughout the book. A female Muslim medical doctor once said to me, "Man needs God, God does not need man." Truth, truth, and truth is all there is!

Throughout this book, I implement various metaphysical techniques developed in Western astrological traditions to illuminate the future for the world as the Mayan Prediction manifests itself into the Age of Light. As we observe creation through the prism of these analytical tools, the footprint of the Divine becomes evident right before our eyes! Let us observe together and see the world as it is, not as we wish it to be.

I have spent a lifetime on the edge of Eternity, studying the ways of astrology and metaphysics, learning both 'to be' and 'not to be 'in the present moment. And, this is how I approach my reading of astrological charts: to be still and meditative, to let the charts reveal themselves, and to use the language of astrology to interpret, navigate and explain the inexplicable (to whatever degree possible). So it is with this methodology that I have written a book which in part offers a glimpse into the role we all play through the process of self-discovery in shaping the world of tomorrow.

There are so many people who have guided, loved and supported me in my journey through life. I'm so humbled and grateful. To be alive and to love are the greatest gifts of all, and I embrace them with everything that I am.

I dedicate this book to you, my friends and readers. Thank you for letting me into your lives.

It was the best of times, it was the worst of times, it was the age of wisdom, it was the age of foolishness, it was the epoch of belief, it was the epoch of incredulity,

it was the season of Light, it was the season of Darkness,

it was the spring of hope, it was the winter of despair,

we had everything before us, we had nothing before us,

We were all going direct to heaven, we were all going direct the other way—in short, the period was so far like the present period, that some of its noisiest authorities insisted on its being received, for good or for evil, in the superlative degree of comparison only.

~ Charles Dickens, A Tale of Two Cities

Preface

By Maria J. Mateus

Eschatological scenarios and a belief in the end of time have been around since antiquity. Every culture and religion at one time or another has believed their time was uniquely giving way to a global crisis that would usher in a new, better era. Prophets have often proclaimed the arrival of messiahs, and doomsday seers frequently predict the destruction of civilizations.

Yet, we are all still here. They were wrong, and perhaps we have been foolish to listen to them. Or have we? Perhaps we simply did not understand the nature of the changes in their appropriate scale.

In this book, Mercury tells us December 21, 2012 was a day just like any other day. Nothing of any major importance was going to happen. The world was certainly not going to end. It is important to place these words in their proper context because anyone with a minimum amount of global sensitivity and awareness who has been alive the last couple of years has noticed that something unique is indeed occurring since December 21, 2012.

The earth constantly reminds us of its abuse and agitation. Nations and governments are in the midst of turmoil; one minute economies are growing, the next they are contracting at unprecedented rates. People seem caught up in a state of frenetic urgency and crisis.

Why? What are these changes we are experiencing, and what do they mean in the larger scheme of human existence?

Preface

I first met Mercury many years ago when we were both students at Kepler College of Astrological Arts and Sciences. On one occasion we were sitting at the same table listening to Robert Hand lecturing about Neoplatonism. This teacher had a special interest in the subject and was speaking beautifully on the nature of God. I looked to my side and saw tears rolling down Mercury's face. This was the first of many instances when I would get a glimpse into Mercury's extremely sensitive soul. As an astrologer, and just like the Mayans he discusses, Mercury understands the cyclical nature of time. Further, he understands what we are experiencing, when seen within a historical perspective, is not unique. But what is most important is he senses that, when seen within the perspective of a human lifetime, something unique is indeed happening that needs to be discussed and understood.

For many years, modern astrology has taken refuge in personality analysis to avoid making predictions that may turn out to be erroneous. But as he is a traditional astrologer interested in the destiny of nations, Mercury understands personality analysis is not an option.

I value Mercury's courage to make specific predictions about the outcome of the changes we face as a society. In this work, and because of his special connection to the Japanese people, Mercury examines how global changes will impact the island nation of Japan. By examining the transits concerning two charts he establishes for Japan and Tokyo, Mercury makes predictions about the economic, political and ecological changes that nation can expect to undergo.[1]

In keeping with good empirical astrological practice, some of these transits are analyzed with respect to historical manifestations of the same cycles. For example, the extremely potent current Uranus entry into Aries has occurred previously and is best understood within the historical context of the worldwide Great Depression of 1930.

For Japan, Mercury courageously foresees many specific challenges, such as economic austerity measures followed by a period of growth and expansion; the increasing prominence of women in politics and policymaking, and possible natural disasters occurring in Tokyo in 2018 and/or 2023. But overall, according to his astrological interpretation, he says Japan is the New-Old Shangri-La of the Age of Light, which prepares the world for the Age of Aquarius. This work is, indeed, the product of a sensitive's gaze at the soul of the Japanese nation, the United States, China and the world.

---

[1] Examining astrological transits of two charts is a technique used to forecast future trends and developments based on a natal chart and planet locations at various times, years and dates in relationship to the natal chart.

Chapter

Eternity = Present

The World: Eternal Implications…

The Age of Light Evolves into the Age of Aquarius

What you are is what you have done, and what you will be is what you do now.
   ~ Siddhārtha Gautama, the one who woke

The World: Eternal Implications…

"We live on the edge of Eternity. While the world as a whole appears to be in the midst of imbalance with ignorance, representing the Dark Ages, I unexpectedly discovered a New Age is dawning.

Many centuries ago, astrologer-priests of the Mayan Empire in Central America devised a calendar to not only mark the passage of time but also predict the future for all humankind.

Based on this astrological calendar, the Mayan Prediction indicated December 21, 2012 would be the demarcation point at which every human being on the planet would experience a *"vibrational shift."* This extraordinary evolutionary transformation of consciousness would be unprecedented in recorded history. The approach to this auspicious date would be punctuated with natural disasters—typhoons, hurricanes, tornadoes, tsunamis, earthquakes, volcanic eruptions, mega droughts, historic wildfires, record floods and more—signs, the Mayans predicted, the demarcation point had come to "the end of time but not the end of the world." Recent geological weather events around the world before and after December 12, 2012 have proven accurate. The worst air pollution in the world is in China and India, and it is now affecting the health of the people of both countries. That same pollution in China is affecting the air quality in Japan and has been detected as far as the United States. China is experiencing major landslides, more frequent earthquakes, historic floods, hurricanes and sandstorms, which are happening around the world.

Just prior to the Mayan point of arrival on March 11, 2011, Japan experienced the end of time but not the end of their world. Since this historic moment took place in Japan, it has brought into question the public's trust and confidence in their authority with the tribe. The ramifications of Fukushima are going to change the basic cultural structure of Japan and its relationship with authority.

In 2012-2013 and throughout 2017, record tornadoes wreaked havoc on homes and led to the loss of life across the Midwestern United States. Hurricane Sandy hit the state of New York. Flooding in the state of Colorado, the kind not seen in more than 100 years took lives and almost destroyed communities.

After the Mayan point of departure, a world-record typhoon named Haiyan hit the Philippines in 2013, while earthquakes off the coast of Japan reminded the Japanese of the dangers lurking below. And in Japan, more floods, landslides, earthquakes and tsunamis are waiting in the wings.

In this century, the United States and China culturally implode, and the Japanese people begin to understand how to live an enlightened life. This is a result of the Fukushima disaster, which is far worse than the Japanese government has revealed. For livingkind to survive in the Present, we need to live in harmony with nature and end our current destructive lifestyle, which has the potential to eliminate the wondrous forms of life we currently take for granted.

This book examines how and why the Japanese people will express their tribal self-consciousness to the world. It also examines how the United States and China are going to change and adapt by learning how to live peacefully and in harmony with nature and each other with the dawning of the Age of Light, which is the preamble to the Age of Aquarius. The rest of the world may follow or they, too, will suffer the consequences of ignorance.

I am reminded of a lecture in Ascona, Switzerland, in which Joseph Campbell shared a quote concerning the Bible. D. T. Suzuki stood at the front of the room, his hands on his hips, his eyes peering through round-rimmed spectacles at the audience before him. He started his lecture as follows: **"God against man, man against God, man against nature, nature against man, God against nature, nature against God— very funny religion."**

This book examines the fact the United States and China have major obstacles to overcome based on their lack of tribal awareness. The two largest economies in the world are losing a sense of unity within their own cultures, which has been co-opted by greed and corruption. Japan also has some housecleaning to do in regard to corruption in business and government. As a tribal culture, the Japanese people learn to lighten up their cultural bias towards the rest of the world, as the Age of Light disinfects the world of its ignorance in preparation for the Age of Aquarius.

★ ★ ★ ★ ★ ★ ★   ★ ★ ★ ★ ★ ★ ★   ★ ★ ★ ★ ★ ★ ★

The ancient Mayan astrologer-priests based their calendar on meticulous celestial observations. Another culture also recorded predictions concerning the time of transformation we are now experiencing. This enlightened culture and seers included the Hopi Indians of the American Southwest.

The Mayan Prediction and Hopi vision appear to provide the most accurate details regarding the dramatic events associated with the aftermath of December 21, 2012, which unfolds in many directions. I associate my analysis of the Mayan Prediction and Hopi awareness in terms of the Present-future of the United States, China and Japan from the perspective of the Western mundane astrological tradition. At its height, the Mayan civilization was both brutal and enlightened. The Maya created the most advanced civilization in the Americas before the arrival of Columbus in 1492. Of all the great Mesoamerican civilizations that fell to the Spanish conquistadors, the Maya held out the longest. Even today, their descendants have preserved their language, their cultural consciousness and, most crucially, the calendar upon which the Mayan Prediction is based. At the peak of Mayan development, between 600 A.D. and 900 A.D., Mayan linguists formulated an advanced system of writing in the form of hieroglyphs with which the history of their civilization was recorded on monuments throughout their cities and lands. The Mayan astrologer-priests' celestial observations and mathematical research rivaled the achievements of ancient Egyptian astrologers. Unfortunately, few written versions of the Mayan calendar survived the Spanish conquest. Catholic priests burned any Mayan religious documents they found.

The surviving calendar manuscripts indicate the date of December 21, 2012 the beginning of the fifth cycle of 5,200 years. These surviving calendar manuscripts were called "Calendar Round," "Tzolkin" (Count of Days) and "The Long Count." The Mayans called the fifth cycle measured by all these calendars "Job Agaw," which translates into English as the Fifth Sun. Other tribal sources I have researched refer to the Job Agaw as the "Sixth Cycle" or the "Fifth Cycle of the Sun." For continuity's sake, I will refer to this fifth 5,200-year cycle.

The first four "Suns," or Mayan calendar cycles, represent the four corners or compass points of the Earth: east, west, north and south. On the surviving Mayan calendars, images of the first four Suns are represented as enclosed or limited by the Earth's four corners—boxed as it were, by the compass frame. However, in the Fifth Sun, the Mayan Prediction indicates humankind will begin evolving beyond limitations of artificial frameworks, measurements, and definitions imposed externally by ignorance and culture.

★ ★ ★ ★ ★ ★ ★   ★ ★ ★ ★ ★ ★ ★   ★ ★ ★ ★ ★ ★ ★

Chapter 1 Eternity = Present

Prophecies of the Elders of the Hopi Indian Nation of North America are remarkably similar to the Mayan Prediction. According to the Hopi Elders, we are coming to the end of an era during which time has been measured externally by clocks. Simultaneously, the Age of Aquarius is dawning with the promise of sustained, timeless peace and harmony. In other words, the fixed, mechanistic perception of time will begin to unfold into timelessness that flows more in rhythm with nature infused by human consciousness. To accommodate prophecies of the Hopi and others in line with the Mayan Prediction, the Age of Light is preparing the way for the Age of Aquarius to arrive by 2150. The next 150 years is the turning point for humankind. The choice of walking towards heaven or descending into hell is now before us.

The Hopi nation, some scientists theorize, are descendants of the Anasazi or Ancestral Pueblo, who flourished from approximately 100 A.D. until 1600 A.D. in the American Southwest. The Hopi call their ancestors *Hisatsinom* or "Ancient People." In Hopi mythology, the *Hisatsinom* climbed upward through sacred underground chambers called kivas into this world and lived in many places on the planet. Scientists have not been able to identify their precise geographic point of origin. The Hopi eventually settled on lands that now make up part of their present- day reservation, overlapping the modern U.S. states of Arizona, New Mexico, and Utah here in their Fourth World.

Like the Mayan Prediction, prophecies of the Hopi Elders mention a numbered sequence of succeeding worlds or "Suns." The Hopi and Maya agree we are now living in the Fifth World or Sun.

According to the Hopi prophecy, the end of the Fourth World would be marked by tragic, gigantic upheavals in both the natural world and human civilization. Specifically, in our time human-caused disasters would poison vast swaths of the planet. Corruption, class warfare, injustice and revolutions in thinking and consciousness would convulse human relations. Extreme weather and geological disasters, occurring independently of direct human influence, would signal the transitional period beginning the Fifth World or Sun. Currently, one can observe the media to see these examples playing themselves out each day around the world, from the Middle East to weather-related disasters in the United States, South America, China, Europe, India, the Philippines, Pakistan, Thailand, New Zealand, Australia and Japan. The list goes on.

The planet Pluto in Capricorn historically supports the transformation of the *status quo* by dismantling it and stripping away the lies and corruption of authority. The spotlight on India in 2013 and again in 2017 when Ram Rahim Singh, a spiritual leader with strong political connections was convicted and sentenced for twenty years for rape, that occurred many years earlier. Also, the problem with bribery and political corruption had the public citizenry in India challenging the government, as well as the global public challenging their own governments in countries around the world like Syria and Egypt, Venezuela. And, this list goes on as well. This kind of change will increase around the world from country to country as the Age of Light exposes the evil humankind does unto itself, especially towards females globally, a topic we discuss later in the book.

The Hopi prophesied an epoch marked by such interesting changes taking place just prior to and after the vibrational shift, an epoch in many respects very similar to the one in which we all live now. The Hopi described the four Worlds that had existed previous to the current transition as the "growth of time." The World we are entering, the Fifth World, will be essentially characterized as the Hopi prophets said, as existing "beyond time."

In speaking of leaving the Fourth World and entering the Fifth World during our current time of transition, the Hopi prophecy is uncannily similar to the Mayan Prediction. Essentially, the similarity lies in the ordinal numbers—the movement of humankind from a "Fourth" to a "Fifth" plane of existence. The four worlds of the past are Möbius Flowing as the Present.

The Hopi foretold the ending of the Fourth World would be accompanied by a series of catastrophes they called "the three great shakes." The first two great shakes have already occurred: World Wars I and II. "Shakes" may seem a relatively mild term for wars that led to millions of deaths, but the Hopi Elders nonetheless got the timing right.

In my opinion, the 2011 earthquake in Japan (and the following Fukushima Daiichi nuclear power plant disaster) is the third shake. National Aeronautics and Space Administration (NASA) reported the Japanese earthquake influenced the Earth to rotate just a little bit faster, shortening the length of the day by about 1.8 microseconds (a microsecond is one-millionth of a second). I speculate this very small shift, combined with trashing the home we live on, is affecting our Jetstream, which has been unstable compared to its previous patterns prior to the Fukushima earthquake. We live in a delicate balance with nature, which is being affected by our waste and garbage, and in turn is affecting the atmosphere we take for granted.

In 2013, Japan's NHK world report noted several leaks in the plant's reservoirs have occurred since the disaster. Radioactive contaminated water has been leaking into the ground and the ocean. It is estimated 120 tons of contaminated water have leaked into the soil. In 2015, I could not find the estimated tons of contaminated water since it has not been disclosed to the public. Also in 2013, up to 400 tons of groundwater seeped into the cracks of the plant daily, mixing with the radioactive material there. In my opinion, the extent of these threats to the land and ocean is being largely withheld from the Japanese public. The fact is they don't know the consequences of the Fukushima damage to the ocean and landmass surrounding the nuclear disaster. Then in October 2013, a 7.2 earthquake occurred in the ocean hundreds of miles off the coast of Japan near Fukushima. The Japanese authorities' decision to withhold a great deal of information concerning radiation was probably made in an attempt to prevent chaos and fear. Regardless, truth cannot hide, and as the truth becomes known, a shift in world consciousness will result. Around the globe, before the end of this century, people will demand their governments forego dangerous forms of energy use in the future.

To that end, the Hopi Elders also mentioned the Blue Star Spirit, most dreaded of all the evil personages in their spiritual pantheon. The Hopi Elders predicted the appearance of the Blue Star Spirit would manifest at any time in the period between 2012 and 2063. In my estimation, however, the predicted return of the Blue Star Spirit, commonly thought to be a precursor of disaster, will be a blessing, ushering in a god-like consciousness that will thrive in the world. The Blue Star is Us, we're the genesis of the Light to become.

Chapter 1 Eternity = Present

South of the Hopi tribal lands, across hundreds of miles of desert and dense jungle, the Maya in Central America were also aware of the Blue Star Spirit. In Mayan mythology, this dangerous apparition is called Quetzalcoatl or the "Plumed Serpent." Indeed, according to Edward Herbert Thompson, the Maya are also known as People of the Serpent.

The Maya revered Quetzalcoatl as, among other things, the patron of priests and calendars. Quetzalcoatl was also identified with the planet Venus. In this guise as the morning and evening star, Quetzalcoatl symbolized both death and resurrection, which we associate with Pluto. However, the Mayan priests never offered Quetzalcoatl human sacrifices—only birds, butterflies and snakes.

✶ ✶ ✶ ✶ ✶ ✶ ✶   ✶ ✶ ✶ ✶ ✶ ✶ ✶   ✶ ✶ ✶ ✶ ✶ ✶ ✶

On the Hopi reservation in Arizona, there is a sacred monument known as Prophecy Rock. To the Hopi, this monument represents hope for the future of humankind. On Prophecy Rock are drawings and images depicting people walking two paths. Along one path, humans proceed toward a life of peaceful prosperity. At the end of the other path, humankind is shown suffering through the darkness of war and human-made disasters.

I meditated on the symbolism of Prophecy Rock while also taking into consideration the thousands of astrological charts I have read over the years. It became clear to me the Hopi imagery may specifically be applied to moments in life during which each one of us makes continuous personal choices to experience heaven or hell. By being Present, I discovered choiceless observation, the journey beyond time, beyond heaven and hell: bliss.

Such Biblical concepts may seem quaint and irrelevant in our modern age. But whatever you personally call these concepts, the reality is the choices you make on a daily basis add up to determine the quality of your life. Choices do not occur in a vacuum; they are not isolated from consequences. It has taken me a lifetime to learn choiceless observation as a middle way of living.

> *People pay for what they do, and still more for what they have allowed themselves to become. And they pay for it, very simply, by the lives they lead.*
> ~ James Baldwin, *No Name in the Street*

Imagine the consequences of such choices in your life applied to the macroscope in which tribes, nations and even worlds rise and fall.

> *If we do not now dare everything, the fulfillment of that prophecy, re-created from the Bible in a song by a slave, is upon us: God gave Noah the rainbow sign, No more water, the fire next time!*
> ~ James Baldwin, *The Fire Next Time*

Let us embrace the fire Baldwin refers to and call it the Age of Light rather than the fire of destruction. According to my research based on the mundane astrological tradition, we are now seeing the approach of a vibrational shift very similar in many ways to the transitions from Fourth to Fifth Sun or World the Mayan calendar-makers and Hopi prophets respectively described. In other words, the Mayan Prediction describes what essentially will be an opportunity for each individual to choose to continue existence in heaven or hell (or the appropriate cultural equivalent) or to change the beliefs and concepts governing their quality of life. In my estimation, the fire Baldwin alluded to may be some form of destruction, which brings forth a birth that delivers the Present Lightness of being.

The Age of Light Evolves into the Age of Aquarius

Before ushering in the Age of Aquarius, the Age of Light was the bridge from the Age of Pisces, which extended approximately from 250 B.C. until 1900 A.D., according to many professional astrologers. The Birth of Christ marks the *conception* of the Age of Pisces, seen as the divine point of Light sparkling to life in the womb of the entire world. Can we acknowledge, the Universe is its own organism, alive and evolving…!?

The Birth of Christ is generally accepted as occurring 250 years after the beginning of the Age of Pisces. The moment when a Zodiacal Age begins is, by definition, mysterious. The unknown nuances of humankind's consciousness in a Zodiacal Age are now becoming manifest in the world, thus ascending us all from the Dark Energy into the Age of Light. Thus, the birth of Jesus, a representative of the Age of Light, was little noted during the Age of Pisces. In fact, no one—historian, Biblical scholar or astrologer—can say with certainty the exact date of his birth.

The birth of every child reminds one of the Godhead in all of us. In spirit there is Light, and Light is conscious as spirit in body. Saint Athanasius of Alexandria spoke in the 4th Century to the idea that "God became man so man might become a god." Truth=God

The year 250 B.C. saw upheavals, including the retreat of long-established cultures and patterns of perception. The Greek civilization was in retreat and decaying as the legions of Rome advanced. The Battle of Corinth in 146 B.C. effectively ended Greek independence. In due time, the Roman Republic was overthrown and replaced by the Roman Empire, which subsequently collapsed in 455 A.D. when the Vandal tribes of northern Europe sacked the city of Rome. The dark horrors of that human-made disaster, in which thousands of Roman citizens died as their city burned, was truly an experience of hell on Earth. It was a descent steep and terrible indeed from the lofty heights of idealism and heavenly harmony among humans that had animated the original Roman Republic and the Greek city-state of Athens, the cradle of democracy. The cultural Lights of philosophy, art, drama, poetry and literature had burned brightly—and still form the templates of many Western traditions. Nevertheless, the Greek and Roman people had turned away, had given up the spiritual cohesion that supported those enlightened accomplishments. Think of the enormity of violence and killings from the beginning of so-called civilization; blood wasted, for what?

The march of history is always marked by the ebb and flow of power and its institutions, like waves advancing and receding down a beach. History appears to have war and peace trading places looking for a place to rest. Such rhythms of form and dissipation represent the spiritual duality of conqueror/master and victim/slave that hold sway under the astrological sign of Pisces, depicted symbolically as two fishes. Since the symbol of two fish is the sign of Pisces, could this be Jesus was born in March, the sign of Pisces? The Bible makes many positive allusions to fish that transcend this duality. In the time beyond the Mayan Prediction, humankind will move beyond these separate roles into a "wholeality." This is the practical perception that will liberate those who are able to adapt to the end of time as we have known it—but it is not the end of the world, by being Present.

> *Jesus Said,*
> *"Recognize what is in your sight, and that which is hidden from you will become plain to you. For there is nothing hidden which will not become manifest."*
> http://gnosis.org/naghamm/gthlamb.html

✦ ✦ ✦ ✦ ✦ ✦   ✦ ✦ ✦ ✦ ✦ ✦   ✦ ✦ ✦ ✦ ✦ ✦

Light is the way to love, truth and the Present. Light liberates humankind rather than capturing and enslaving humankind. Light liberates the totality into the **Present wholeality**.

Some astrologers suggest the conjunction of the planets Mars, Jupiter and Saturn, positioned within 7° of each other in 6 B.C., combined to form the Star of Bethlehem that guided the three Magi to Christ's birthplace.

> *Jesus was born at Bethlehem in Judea during the reign of Herod. After his birth, astrologers from the east arrived in Jerusalem, asking, "Where is the newborn king of the Jews? We observed the rising of his star, and we have come to pay him homage." ... Then Herod summoned the astrologers to meet him secretly, and ascertained from them the exact time when the star had appeared...After hearing what the king had to say they set out; there before them was the star they had seen rising, and it went ahead of them until it stopped above the place where the child lay. They were overjoyed at the sight of it, and entering the house, they saw the child with Mary his mother and bowed low in homage to him; they opened their treasure chests and presented gifts to him: gold, frankincense and myrrh. Then they returned to their own country by another route, for they had been warned in a dream not to go back to Herod.*
> ~ Matthew 2: 1-12

It is interesting to note the Magi, the three Kings of the Orient, were also knowledgeable astrologers and aware of the significance of the celestial conjunction they had so carefully observed.

A thousand and many more years passed until suddenly, at the height of the Age of Pisces, Western Europeans began to perceive and value bodies of water differently than they had since the time of Christ. With new eyes, European monarchs, scientists, politicians, mapmakers, sailors and merchants looked toward horizons wider than those surrounding the landlocked Mediterranean. The apparently limitless Atlantic beckoned beyond the Pillars of Hercules, also known as the Rock of Gibraltar. Around 1425 A.D., the first sailing expeditions ventured south into the Atlantic. Their dual mission was to bring organized religion to the heathens and pursue the slave trade along the western coast of Africa. The sailors navigated by carefully observing the stars.

Once energy was directed outward, it was only natural for the Portuguese to be the first to venture west and south from their westernmost edge of the European continent. They hopped from island to island—the Canaries, Cape Verde and southward along the western coast of Africa. The success of these early voyages led, of course, to longer and longer ventures, eventually south to India and west to America. There are discoveries still being verified, which indicate the Chinese, Vikings or others may have found the Americas before Columbus.

The unknown world, represented on medieval maps as vast blank spaces labeled "Here There Be Dragons" became crisscrossed with sea lanes, watery roadways along which to conduct trade and return plunder to their European homelands of the 15th and 16th centuries. Rather than a medium of miracles during the Life of Christ—when, according to the Bible, Christ rebuked stormy seas and walked on water—water became reduced to two-dimensional extensions of commercial empires at the height of the Age of Pisces. The watery roadways led to and returned from treasure troves beyond the wildest imaginations of Medieval Europeans.

Returning triumphantly to their homelands in their sailing ships loaded with stolen gold, silver and precious gems, the Spanish conquistadors shifted the balance of power in Europe. Based on the exploitation of resources, capitalism came into its own, replacing feudalism; the ancient arrangements of power relationships based on family ties and fixed amounts of inherited wealth. Suddenly, the predictable, constant world of Medieval Europe experienced a vibrational shift into the constantly innovative capitalist economy managed by a rising merchant class that profited magnificently. We are now in the beginnings of the Mayan and Hopi vision where the acceleration of the vibrational shift demands great change. It begins and ends with exploitation, resources, capitalism, socialism, communism, terrorism, corruption, dictators, oligarchies, plutocracies, wealth, money, politicians and distribution, which all are going to adhere to Climate Change before the end of the century.

The Present Is All That Exists

Think about this: Jesus and Buddha shared the bond of love as the foundation for their teachings. They taught eternal laws that speak to the heart and soul of humankind—if only we can filter out the noise of modern life to hear their prescient voices. They spoke of the sweet fragrance that is forgiveness, which in Buddha's words was "letting go." They based their teachings on the fact there is no permanence in this world. Change is the Kingdom of Heaven as defined by Christ in *The Lord's Prayer*: "Thy Kingdom come, Thy will be done, on earth as it is in Heaven." There in plain, simple words, Jesus pointed to the same spiritual dimension of which Buddha spoke: Now, the Present!

Buddha said it this way: "What you are is what you have done, and what you will be is what you do now!" With the deepest respect, I take that to mean the following for today: If you are here now, you have always been here, and you will always be here or you could not be here now.

During Christ's historical lifetime, the Jews of Israel could not accept this concept of heaven in the Now. It was too alien. Making the effort to understand the message Jesus shared would have meant they would have to shift their consciousness and perceive new ways of doing things. With the Age of Pisces dominating the vibration of their minds, that change was too much---Jesus' words overloaded their mental circuits. Light is always present, and it is Consciousness. Thus Jesus and Buddha both asked their followers to turn away from materialism and look within!

In the context of the materialistic and brutal times in which those Enlightened Ones lived, their messages were indeed revolutionary. And, what is a revolution after all but a vibrational shift—a shift in our earthbound perspective on the celestial sphere and the meanings we may find there. The enlightened ones' messages, if responded to mindfully and with open hearts, could provide the guidance and direction all of us will need to find our way to survival and harmony during the turbulent times to come. Buddha and Jesus understood all of us in the Age of Light have a choice: love or fear.

Japan's Unique Role in the Future

Let us consider Japan and what the Mayan Prediction has in store as the world evolves into the Age of Light.

> *Too many people approach the problem of Japanese uniqueness by looking for what went wrong to make the Japanese the way they are. The answer is that nothing made the Japanese different. They are basically the norm. It is other societies which underwent change to make them different. What is unique about Japan is that it didn't change.*
> ~ Gregory Clark, Australian diplomat and author[2]

Gregory Clark, an expert on Asian history and cultures, disagrees with the popular opinion that Japan was "reshaped" by contact with the Chinese. Clark asserts there is a vast gulf between China, which concentrated for centuries on developing ideas and ideologies, and Japan, which "developed its tribal values to a high, sophisticated degree on the national level."[3] Japan is unique because, unlike modern cultures and countries around the world, her people did not forget. They continue to celebrate and manifest their tribal origins far back in the mists of time when their ancestors felt vital links between everyday life and nature.

> *The idea that one, and only one ideology is correct, does not get much of an audience in Japan. Your average Japanese are born into a basically secular society. They will have a Shinto wedding. Shinto is the animistic, tribal religion of Japan. In any other society these animistic religions died out as the society progressed. Japan is a unique example of a society which has held to, and developed the animistic religion of its origins.*
> ~ Gregory Clark[4]

---

2 David Tharp, Contributing Editor, "Japan as a Tribe," Interview with Gregory Clark, *Mainichi Daily News*, February 26, 1977.
3 Ibid.
4 Gregory Clark, "The Japanese Tribe: What Makes It Work?" *QUADRANT*, January/February 1992.

Gregory Clark goes on to describe what he considers the "benchmark" of being uniquely Japanese, a member of the Japanese tribe: "In Japan, even if you become a Christian, you often retain your original Shinto/Buddhist beliefs. To me, this lack of absolutism is a very important cultural benchmark. It identifies Japan as being radically different not only from our Western culture, but different from Korea, different from China, different from India, different from the Middle East. In this sense, at least, it is unique."[5]

★ ★ ★ ★ ★ ★ ★   ★ ★ ★ ★ ★ ★ ★   ★ ★ ★ ★ ★ ★ ★

Western cultures once were populated by tribes much like Japan is today. All humans have two sides, the intuitional-instinctive-emotional side, open to connection with others, and the rationalistic side, which is used to create highly developed political states and economic engines.

> *In the daily life of the Japanese there's a constant emphasis on feeling, on sentiment, on the heart.*
> ~ Gregory Clark "The Japanese Tribe"

In Japan, no law says one must behave honestly and with courtesy toward others or make personal sacrifices for others. Clark asks, "Where does an ethic like that come from?" It is, as I say, a refined village ethic, a refined feudal ethic. The emphasis on craftsmanship in Japan is also part of the feudal ethic, something we Anglo-Saxons used to have and which the Germans and the Scandinavians still retain to some extent. One's identity in the feudal society depends on one's workplace, and the quality of the work one does." [6]

In Anglo-Saxon societies, people's very names came from the craft they were pursuing. With a name like Smith, for example, you could go back far enough up the family tree and find a person who made a living as a blacksmith. A Taylor once made clothing for a living. A Miller ground grain, a Brewer produced Ale and so on. I bring this up because as we approach the time the Mayans spoke of, when sustainability will be a needed survival strategy, people who contribute to a culture will be the ones who survive. It is the quest of every individual to discover what you were born to do. This can be the height of living your religion. You can live in the past and with the Present at the same time. Religion is of the past, experienced in the Present. The key is to be able to adapt with the Present by understanding the transitory nature of Eternity is Present and no place else. I propose the speed of Light is equally the speed of Space as the Present! I suggest this idea as a meditation.

The key to Japan's success in the time beyond the Mayan Prediction and Hopi vision will be practicality based on what others in the Japanese tribe need. The key will be to put others before oneself--making products not for the sole purpose of profit, but because someone in the tribe might need to use those products to derive a positive benefit.

---

5 Ibid.
6 Ibid.

> *In twenty years in Japan I have never once been expected to give a tip; I have never once been shortchanged. I have left change in a shop and the shopkeeper has run out, down the street, to give me that change back. Forget valuables in a taxi and the chances are more than even, the taxi driver will make an effort to return the goods. Leave a suitcase on a crowded platform at seven o'clock in the morning, and in the evening that suitcase will still be there. If it is not there, it is because some public-minded individual has delivered it into the lost property office, where a very efficient, courteous gentleman will be registering goods handed in, and trying to get them back to their owners.*
> ~ Gregory Clark[7]

Western cultures as well as the cultures of the Middle East, China, and India are based largely on abstract, rationalistic ideas and ideologies. Unlike the Japanese, these cultures are presently on the downward slide or experiencing tremendous sociopolitical upheavals shaking them down to their very foundations.

Despite the terrible deaths and economic consequences of the Great Eastern Japan Earthquake Disaster, the Japanese tribe is rising to the challenge. However, the Japanese government will lose the respect of the Japanese people if Tokyo Electric Power Company (TEPCO) doesn't reveal the truth about the radiation calamity that has befallen the Japanese public.

★ ★ ★ ★ ★ ★ ★   ★ ★ ★ ★ ★ ★ ★   ★ ★ ★ ★ ★ ★ ★

The limits of old ideas that had their political and exploitative uses during the preceding Age of Pisces will begin to recede as the Age of Light begins its spiritual healing of people's dark ignorance. Religion will begin to flourish beyond the bounds of institutions designed to constrict and control the messages of Jesus and Buddha. Also, we will witness the rebirth of science and technology as they come into their own as tools in the service of enlightenment rather than instruments of exploitation. In the next 150 years, religions return to their origin, where everyone will experience the nature of God in the Present, not from an organization or institution.

Science is, after all, a neutral force, a testing of theories. If a scientific theory doesn't work after being subjected to rigorous testing on the proving ground of scientific method, scientists discard it. This is what will happen during the birth of the Age of Aquarius—many new and untried cultural, political, social, religious and philosophical ideas will be put to the test of practicality. In a word, do they "work"? Do they help humans survive and thrive in uncertain times?

There is no consensus within the Western astrological tradition, but the Age of Aquarius is generally considered to be dawning within the period 1900 to 2500 A.D. Here at the dawning, we are witnessing its disruptive labor pains on a worldwide scale. The Age of Aquarius is dawning as you read this book, and the Age of Light shows the way. The change to come in its wake will deliver the unknown regarding the true direction in which Earth will flow toward destiny during this period of turbulence.

7 Ibid.

The exact date of birth or inception of the Age of Aquarius may be debated. The start of an astrological age is actually mysterious. A moment so profound is a private matter for each individual witness. Nevertheless, there is general agreement among astrologers that the Age of Aquarius is in the very early process of decisively dawning, just as the three Magi-astrologers witnessing the appearance of the Star of Bethlehem agreed on the momentousness of the celestial conjunction above the birthplace of Jesus. So too, Light, TimeSpace and the Present are like the three Magi – leading the world out of the Dark into the Age of Light and transforming Space into the Age of Aquarius, where the Present is recognized as the edge of Eternity.

★ ★ ★ ★ ★ ★ ★ ★ ★ ★ ★ ★ ★ ★ ★ ★ ★ ★

Consider for a moment the influence of Light on human affairs throughout recent history.

Prior to the agrarian era, the activities of hunter-gatherers worldwide were limited by the sun. Humans rose at dawn, pursued prey or foraged and had to cease their activities at sunset. Even today, modern American farmers speak of working from "can see to can't see."

Clearly, the invention of the electric light bulb finally freed humans from the solar cycle of day and night, and forever changed the rhythms of work and social life, igniting the Age of Light. The consequences were vast and far-reaching. For the first time in history, civilization underwent a major shift and expansion of focus, enabling humans to increase the scope and complexity of their projects, even reaching for the Moon and inventing technology capable of splitting the atom and destroying the planet. As the Hopi had foretold, humanity will be presented, along the path of evolution, with two choices: Be in heaven by living the way of love and truth or live in hell by living the way of fear and lies.

When Thomas Edison invented the light bulb, he also helped humankind take one small step away from the rhythms of nature and one giant leap for Prometheus. People have been trying to remember and find their spiritual rhythm ever since.

Until now, people have fixated on discovering and attempting to dissect what they choose to believe to be the fundamental elements of God in the external macroscope of expanding geography, politics and technology. Then, in a seeming paradox, as the Aquarian vibrational shift strengthens, we realize we are, in reality, dissecting and discovering the wondrous Universes within our personal selves. It is not surprising, as the world grows spiritually, we discover the new/old religion of science as a signature of the Age of Light.

On February 11, 2016 scientists at the Laser Interferometer Gravitational-Wave Observatory (known as LIGO) announced they found that about one billion light years ago two black holes revolved around each other and eventually merged, releasing the energy of a billion trillion suns in a fraction of a second. The energy LIGO detected is a ripple of gravitational waves, a space-time distortion traveling at the speed of light. On September 14, 2015 the LIGO team found a flickering light and turned it into a sound wave. It was the echo of a gravitational wave, which gave us sound and confirmed Einstein's prediction that gravitational waves existed. This was a missing piece of Einstein's theory of General Relativity that had not been proven. "It looks like there are going to be more of these black holes out there than we imagined," says David Reitze, the executive director of LIGO, and they recorded the most recent ripple on Dec. 26, 2015.

S. James Gates, Jr., Theoretical Physicist explained to the BBC that for the first time we hear the Universe. He went on to say, "It's like opening the door to a dark room and suddenly turning on the lights, that's where we are." We are hearing the smallest of the small undulations of space and time. Now we have proven space/time can be ripped and pulled and they actually exist. This is going to redefine astronomy and allow us to explore back to the big bang. It's going to be like exploring our ultimate ancestor: the Beginning.

It must follow that new revelations in science will continue to transform the physical world as we know it. Scientific miracles arrive in unimaginable fashion as the Age of Light delivers us from the tunnel vision of history into the infinite finite of the Aquarian awareness living in a peaceful harmony with nature. The shape of power, as it is currently configured in society, changes. Governments will decentralize as a greater sense of self-responsibility among people around the world takes hold.

Lao Tzu, the ancient Chinese sage and author of *The Daodejing* or *Tao Te Ching* ("The Way of Power") referred to the best form of government as being what he called "village government."

Centralized government has come in our time to project power in such distorted and fragmentary fashion that its positive effectiveness is dissipated at the local level. Extreme forms of self-interest lead to corruption. Consider the results produced by centralizing the American agricultural industry. As Mateo Kehler, a cheese maker in the U.S. state of Vermont, put it, "The whole industrial food system is failing. It's hugely successful on one level, and on another you've got salmonella-tainted tomatoes and *E. coli* spinach. When a single *E. coli*-laden hamburger bought at Sam's Club [a Walmart subsidiary], as documented by [*The*] *New York Times*, contains fresh fatty edges from Omaha [Nebraska], lean trimmings from old cows in Texas, frozen trimmings from cattle in Uruguay and heated, centrifuged and ammonia-treated carcass remnants from South Dakota, maybe it's time to feel like a single food should come from a single place and taste like it."[8]

The average food contents of a typical American refrigerator have traveled hundreds of miles from many different directions. Thousands of gallons of irreplaceable fossil fuels are burned so consumers in northern climates can eat fresh tomatoes out of season. This vast waste of energy could be eliminated if First World elites ate foods grown closer to home. For another thing, by dealing directly with farmers who produce the food they consume, First World elites could gain a better idea of the value of farm-grown foods and how those goods help both the economy and individual quality of life. Small farmers remember the direct connection with nature all humans felt and some, especially the Japanese tribe, still feel. Translate localization from the agricultural industry back to government, and the benefits are obvious there, too. Local politicians and officials have more practical knowledge of local problems than bureaucrats in a distant governmental center. Also, the ability to respond becomes much more efficient, as local officials take responsibility for solving local problems.

[8] Rowan Jacobsen, "The Reign of Terror," *Edible Sacramento*, Spring 2011.

The Age of Light will see the Japanese tribe and all people becoming much more involved in their own firsthand experience. Such involvement will become a necessity as the power of centralized metropolitan governments falters with the breakdown of energy generation and distribution of food and wasted transportation costs. People in many parts of Asia are wary of food, especially seafood coming in from Japan potentially contaminated from the effects of radiation from Fukushima.

How will it be possible to begin reducing energy consumption and dependence on nuclear and fossil energy? By learning to live a life less centered on consumption as a measurement of one's identity and personal worth. By learning to live a life centered on the satisfactions of firsthand experience; a self-sustaining life focused on giving back to one's tribe. In politics, the influence of the exploitative centralized government will begin to fade, as individual citizens of local regions learn to take care of their own needs. The most valuable asset we possess is not what we own but our ability to DO!

When each local provincial region takes care of its needs, as much as possible, as the Age of Light dawns, then together the regions survive in times of uncertainty. On an as-needed basis, local regions can provide emergency assistance and coherent, logical distribution of resources to each other. As each region becomes more self-sustaining, political interest in "skimming off the top" of this distribution system will become less attractive. Majorities of individuals in local semi-autonomous regions will become self-responsibly engrossed in ensuring survival through sustainability. Energy saved and focused locally will translate into healthier communities able to meet the challenges of the future.

★ ★ ★ ★ ★ ★ ★   ★ ★ ★ ★ ★ ★ ★   ★ ★ ★ ★ ★ ★ ★

Beginning on a massive scale in the 1960s, many incredible advances in psychology, pharmacology and religious studies have helped humankind understand an intriguing variety of expressions of energy, as well as the hitherto unfamiliar conceptualization of time as space. The decade of the Sixties began with Saturn in Capricorn, which changes the *status quo*. Uranus was in Leo as the decade began, speaking to changing ways and forms of self-expression. Leo uses self-expression as a means of release, and just as the decade ended, Uranus entered Virgo. Neptune was in Scorpio for the decade, and the deepest unconscious qualities of our country were being exposed. The combination of Neptune in Scorpio and Uranus in Leo ushered in the sexual revolution that took place as an expression of our liberating evolution of the Sixties. Sex, drugs and rock 'n' roll became the banner of the Sixties.

Your inner space does not contain space, as it has been conceptualized by Newtonian physics. Within each human soul, I postulate the mechanical externalization of time in the form of clocks does not exist within, nor does it control, the human soul and spirit. The physical body appears from nothing and returns to nothing. TimeSpace is the Present.

Freed of the chains of time, people will begin to experience what self-sufficiency truly means in harmony with the natural rhythms of the planet and the Universe, with Eternity as the palette of the Present.

> *We are stardust*
> *We are golden*
> *And we've got to get ourselves*
> *Back to the garden*
> ~ Joni Mitchell, "Woodstock" 1969

As our cities grow, humankind is learning we have to get back to nature and the garden and abandon the city lifestyle for village cultures that create hives of loosely configured independent yet interwoven communities. The key to attaining harmonious inner-space and peace is to attune ourselves to the best of the natural and civilized worlds, living closer to nature while using the inventions of tomorrow. We need to regain direct contact with nature outside us and our human nature from within us. Various news reports in recent years have spoken to the idea that China could have a billion people living in cities by the year 2025. I think in the future, repression of freedom of speech, along with the massive pollution engulfing the country, will help usher in the beginning of the end of China's ability to compete effectively around the globe. This development, in turn, will affect the global economy and bring on a depression or deep recession, as China's economy is currently the workhorse for the world's cash flow. Reports of the Chinese economy slowdown in August of 2015 demonstrated the influence of China's financial market and its impact in regard to monetary value around the world. Entire countries, like people, can and will choose to live in heaven or hell.

Finances and the concept of money, too, are poised now to go through a revolutionary process. With intelligent choices, we can arrive at a more humane way of distributing services and products. Increased awareness of inner-space and peace will lead to a weakening of the traditional motivations of aggression and greed that have characterized Western business models since the Middle Ages. Ultimately, an inner-directed and cooperative peaceful business model will eliminate the need for war, clearly a self-defeating way for humankind to be on the planet. As Carl Sagan, once said, **"Any organism at war with itself is doomed."** [9]

Other intractable problems long plaguing humankind, including poverty, hunger and environmental degradation, may be solved as individuals in diverse cultures begin to experience inner peace. The concept of money will go through a major transformation like the world has never seen. Once the subjective needs engendered by greed and exploitative aggression diminish, money will come to be used according to more objective values. In and of itself, money is neither good nor bad. It's what you do with money that determines the quality of your service to humankind. After all, money doesn't grow on trees, and yet we have let an illusionary device continue to run our world.

The History of Crisis Repeats

On January 26, 2008 Pluto entered Capricorn for the first time since 1762. In 2008 the world economy suffered the worst financial crisis since the Great Depression, which

---

9 Carl Sagan, quoted in *Prehab, Essentials for Successful Change* by Colin Swift.

is now called the Great Recession. The world, 248 years earlier, was embroiled in a vibrational shift similar in intensity to what we are experiencing today. However, the intensity under the influence of the Age of Pisces was expressed in aggression and violence. The true wisdom of Buddha and Jesus was largely misunderstood. Throughout history, religions and centralized governments have consolidated their exploitative power by changing their teachings, as necessary, to tighten their control over the ignorant masses.

In 1762, Catherine the Great became Empress of Russia. Her reign would extend across the most radical upheavals in European history. Though she styled herself a "friend of the Enlightenment" and corresponded with many leading lights of the emerging new social order, she remained loyal to the established order of royalty and centralized government.

By 1789, the economy of France had been manipulated beyond redemption by the entrenched feudal aristocracy and had plunged toward bankruptcy. Astrologically, the influence of Pluto in Capricorn was also building intensity, even after Pluto had completed its transit of Capricorn in March of 1778. As astrologers know, the influence of a major transit can ripple forward in time and still be felt.

When the French Revolution broke out in 1789, Catherine the Great, like all European royalty, felt threatened. But it was not the storming of the Bastille, street fighting in Paris or the Reign of Terror that caused her anxiety. This horrific violence was, to the minds of most of the crowned heads in Europe, but a symptom of a very threatening shift in the power structure that had sustained the aristocracy for hundreds of years.

The 18th century revolutionary convulsions were, I think, vibrational shifts that could not completely manifest on the earthly plane. Thus, prevailing attitudes concerning power and privilege did not change, only the resources that were exploited. Fueled by riches the Spanish conquistadors stole from the Maya and other Native American civilizations and sent back to the Old World, tremendous economic growth brought unprecedented prosperity to 18th century Europe. A new economic class of merchants, manufacturers, and professionals emerged and resented their lack of access to political power, so they threatened to topple the old order.

The presence of Pluto always has enormous, far-reaching effects. According to astrologer Richard Tarnas, "Pluto is associated with the principle of elemental power, depth and intensity; [it] intensifies whatever it touches, sometimes to overwhelming and catastrophic extremes. [Pluto is associated] with the primordial instincts, libidinal and aggressive, destructive and regenerative, volcanic and cathartic, eliminative, transformative, ever-evolving, with the biological processes of birth, sex and death, the cycle of death and rebirth. [Also, Pluto] signals breakdown, decay and fertilization, violence, purgatorial discharge of pent-up energies, purifying fire, situations of life-and-death extremes, power struggles, all that is titanic, potent and massive." [10]

In France in 1789, potent and massive energies were released. Scarcity of food was a flashpoint. The people were angry, and inflation was out of control. The economy of France appeared doomed.

---

10 Richard Tarnas, *Cosmos and Psyche, Intimations of a New World View*, Plume, 2007.

Chapter 1 Eternity = Present

On July 11, 1789, King Louis XVI dismissed the former banker, Jacques Necker, whom he appointed not long before to represent royal interests at the Estates-General. Attempts to reform the political-economic system of France ended. The anger of the French people rose to a fever pitch. They took matters into their own hands. Unfortunately, Louis XVI did not respond proactively to the shifting currents energizing his people. While his people marched in the streets for bread, Louis continued to divert himself by hunting and practicing his personal hobbies of making locks and doing masonry. The people of France were starving. They wanted real reform and an honest distribution of wealth.

On July 14, 1789 they stormed the Bastille Prison, an oppressive symbol of the French Bourbon monarchy. Within a matter of months, the monarchy was finished after its reign of hundreds of years. Ultimately, Louis XVI and Queen Marie Antoinette were both executed by guillotine.

Unrest and violent shifts in the basis of political power around the planet characterized the late 18th century. The British colonies of North America also, of course, rebelled.

✶ ✶ ✶ ✶ ✶ ✶   ✶ ✶ ✶ ✶ ✶ ✶   ✶ ✶ ✶ ✶ ✶ ✶

Having entered Capricorn in 1762, Pluto then moved back into Sagittarius. Subsequently, at the end of 1762, Pluto went retrograde and re-entered Capricorn, staying there 16 years longer before moving into Aquarius. Pluto always has a disruptive effect, weeding out old, outmoded, no-longer-useful ideas, structures and institutions (such as the French royalty in 1789). Astrologically, Aquarius speaks to Enlightenment on many different levels.

America's Founding Fathers, authors of the U.S. Constitution, were all sons of the Enlightenment. Unlike Catherine the Great, with whom many of them exchanged letters and ideas about enlightened governmental reforms, they did not seem to feel threatened by the approaching vibrational shifts in social structures. The Founding Fathers understood they represented the future and not the past, unlike most other monarchs and rulers of the period.

The U.S. Constitution, emphasizing self-responsibility on the basis of its sister document, the Declaration of Independence, (an example of the pen can be mightier than the sword) is a monument to the beginnings of the planet-wide vibrational shift we are experiencing now that Pluto is revisiting Capricorn, where it will stay until January 2024. According to the Sibly Chart, the United States will experience its first Pluto return in 2021-2023. This will be an auspicious period when the people of America experience for the first time its Pluto return, meaning the planet Pluto will be at the approximate location where it was at the birth of the United States. Abraham Lincoln, at the close of *The Gettysburg Address*, sums up what I think will happen at America's first Pluto return: **"This nation, under God, shall have a new birth of freedom — and ... government of the people, by the people, for the people, shall not perish from the earth."** Not government for the corporations, by the corporations with money to buy more influence for more money. The people will demand change, as well as a government that honors its founding ideals.

In our time, the momentous celestial transit of Pluto across Capricorn has ushered in uprising shifts of tectonic power on the political plane. As with the French Revolution, the shift took the form of a violent surge rather than a trickle down of power. In many ways, acts of desperation resolved into more hopefully aligned social structures.

> *The mass of men lead lives of quiet desperation.*
> ~ Henry David Thoreau, *Walden*

Known as the Arab Spring, revolutions spread like wildfire across North Africa and the Middle East in the beginning of the 21st century. Power relationships between common people and their governments were radically redefined in the interests of equality to level the playing field.

The protests in the Middle East began with a single individual, a humble fruit stand operator in a small town in Tunisia. Petty bureaucrats, representatives of the corrupt central Tunisian government, had randomly harassed a man named Mohamed Bouazizi on a daily basis for months. They demanded he pay them bribes. He refused. They seized his fruit. In desperation, Bouazizi seemingly saw no alternative. He set himself on fire in front of the town's municipal offices. After his death, friends remembered Bouazizi had felt his pride had been damaged. To an honorable Tunisian Arab, that loss of pride was the last straw. Who can say what mysteries swirled in his heart. He may have died in protest, but not in vain.

Word of Bouazizi's martyrdom spread, quickly sparking a national uprising media outlets soon dubbed the Arab Spring or Jasmine Revolution. Thousands of Tunisians gathered in streets across their country. In a few weeks, Tunisian President Zine al-Abidine Ben Ali resigned his office. The Arab Spring spread to Egypt. The strongman there, Hosni Mubarak, was soon gone. Bouazizi's martyrdom then inflamed massive protests in Jordan, Algeria, Yemen, Iran, Bahrain and Syria. As with the people of France in 1789, when the masses awaken and make their grievances known, their message cannot be ignored. Governments, no matter how entrenched, cannot stand in the way when the people's anger boils over into righteous condemnation.

★ ★ ★ ★ ★ ★ ★   ★ ★ ★ ★ ★ ★ ★   ★ ★ ★ ★ ★ ★ ★

Since Pluto began its transit of Capricorn in January 2008, earthquakes, tsunamis, hurricanes, typhoons and floods of biblical proportions have wreaked havoc around the world. More climactic, geological and meteorological events are on the way. Since 1998 the planet experienced the hottest years since records have been kept. Officially, 2015 was the hottest year on record but now 2016 and 2017 are two of the hottest years, demonstrating a disturbing trend.

On March 11, 2011 the planet Uranus entered Aries, the first sign of the Zodiac, and a transit that vastly increased disruption across the planet. Uranus will stay in this fire sign for approximately seven years, an astrological event as catastrophic as Pluto's entry into Capricorn. It is not normal for such dramatic astrological events, or transits, to occur so close in time to each other. But then, these are certainly interesting times we live in.

Of course, the Great Eastern Japan Earthquake Disaster struck on March 11, 2011, measuring 9.0 on the Richter scale and causing massive damage and loss of life. Only four major earthquakes in all of recorded human history have been more intense. The subsequent tsunami surged at speeds of up to 500 miles an hour from the undersea epicenter and added to the devastation far inland. It is estimated 250 miles (400 km) of Japan's northern Honshu coastline dropped by two feet (0.6 meters) according to the U.S. Geological Survey. The earthquake moved Japan's main island of Honshu eastward by 8 feet (2.4 meters). And the Pacific Plate was displaced westward near the epicenter 79 feet (24 meters). The rushing waters short-circuited backup generators at several nuclear reactors, which melted down and spread radioactivity across Japan. Thousands evacuated. The nuclear disaster was the worst since Chernobyl in 1986.

The economic consequences of this unprecedented natural disaster—massive loss of life and crippling financial losses of trillions of yen—surged outward with the potential to permanently disable Japan's economic viability and energy-generating potential. Days after the disaster, the value of the Japanese stock market dropped like a rock. Hundreds of factories closed. Some because of earthquake damage; others could not continue operating without parts supplied by earthquake-damaged factories.

The tragedy occurred while Japan's economic deficit had grown deeper than ever before. Japan's public debt was now $9.7 trillion and deepening. Then-Prime Minister Naoto Kan stated, "[O]ur finances could collapse if trust in national bonds is lost and growing national debt is left alone."[11]

East of Honshu, the Pacific plate that lies along the Japan Trench in the Ring of Fire is, no matter what, going to continue to shift. Future ruptures could cause earthquakes and tsunamis more terrible than the Great Eastern Japan Earthquake Disaster. However, the rebuilding of Japan in the Present time offers great opportunities in disguise as the Age of Light dawns—if the Japanese tribe looks within, that is.

> *The answers are always inside the problem, not outside.*
> ~ Marshall McLuhan, *McLuhanisms*

★ ★ ★ ★ ★ ★ ★   ★ ★ ★ ★ ★ ★ ★   ★ ★ ★ ★ ★ ★ ★

The Great Eastern Japan Earthquake Disaster unleashed astonishing energy. According to a Reuters report, "The magnitude 9.0 quake was so powerful it shifted Japan's coastline 8 feet to the east around its epicenter in the Northeast, the U.S. geological survey said."[12] The consequences of the Arab Spring and the Great Eastern Japan Earthquake Disaster, which occurred so close in time in accordance with celestial events, will continue to reverberate around the globe and unpredictably through our social and economic life. And these events comprise—according to mundane astrology, the Hopi Prophecy and the Mayan Prediction—only the first of many upheavals to come. As we have seen, when Uranus enters Aries, as it did on March 11, 2011, sudden, unexpected shifts ensue. Such shifts occur as the vibration of

---

11 "Japan's Prime Minister Warns That Debt Could Bring a Crisis Like That of Greece," *The New York Times*, June 11, 2010, http://www.nytimes.com/2010/06/12/business/global/12yen.html.
12 Shinichi Saoshiro, "Japan's Quake May Impact Time After Altering Its Space," *Reuters.com*, March 26, 2011.

Mother Earth herself changes pitch and tone. Livingkind will have to adapt to many planetary changes. Members of the Japanese tribe are going to be pioneers of this endeavor. They will serve as role models, living intelligently in harmony with nature and its natural forces.

✶ ✶ ✶ ✶ ✶ ✶ ✶   ✶ ✶ ✶ ✶ ✶ ✶ ✶   ✶ ✶ ✶ ✶ ✶ ✶ ✶

From my point of view, the Age of Light dawned in the early 1900s, accompanied by a radical shift in scientific thinking, the flowering of a new consciousness of light and its properties. Specifically, Albert Einstein, publishing his Theory of Relativity in 1905, revolutionized our knowledge of the Universe and how it works. Einstein theorized the speed of light never changes, but observers performing measurements at various speeds approaching the speed of light will obtain different results depending on how fast those observers were traveling at the time they took their measurements. Evidence proved this theory, which redefined our fundamental concepts of space, time, matter, energy and Gravity.

Einstein sparked inquiry in many directions. What is known as the Copenhagen interpretation was the first general attempt to understand the world of atoms as represented by quantum mechanics. The founding father was Danish physicist Niels Bohr, but Werner Heisenberg, Max Born and other physicists also made significant contributions to the understanding of the atomic world. On the atomic level, the observer materially affects the observed reality, something the practical ancestors of today's Japanese tribe knew instinctively centuries ago as a result of their vital somewhat subconscious link to the forces of nature.

In addition to providing the basis for and expanding our understanding of cosmic processes and the geometry of the Universe itself, Einstein's theory revolutionized religion, philosophy, culture and basic assumptions about reality around the world. Clearly, along with Edison's invention of artificial light, Einstein's Theory of Relativity signaled the dawning of the Age of Light. Because of these fundamental changes in our environment and our understanding of it, humankind has been changed forever.

✶ ✶ ✶ ✶ ✶ ✶ ✶   ✶ ✶ ✶ ✶ ✶ ✶ ✶   ✶ ✶ ✶ ✶ ✶ ✶ ✶

Simultaneous with these advances in the study of light, humankind also began waging wars on a scale never before experienced in all of previous recorded history. Einstein's work on relativity was interrupted by World War I. He was a lifelong pacifist. Disgusted by his native Germany's entry into the war, he called nationalism "the measles of mankind." Later he wrote, "At such a time as this, one realizes what a sorry species of animal one belongs to."[13]

Today, the choices leading in the direction of light or chaos offer opportunities or temptations far beyond what anyone living a hundred years ago could have imagined. Wars now can be fought by remote control, with drone aircraft being operated by people pushing buttons on computers and dropping bombs on targets thousands of miles distant. These days, wars are fought comfortably from underground bunkers. Collateral damage? It's part of the cost of war—unpredictable bloody chaos, accounted for with seemingly reasonable explanations offered to the press in clean, well-lighted news conference rooms.

---

13 "The World Wars and Interwar Period, 1941 – 1945," Timeline of World History, *everyhistory.org/all-history.org/383.html*.

Chapter 1 Eternity = Present

Consider this tragedy reported by *The New York Times* in 2008: "Tensions between American forces and the Afghan government over civilian casualties from coalition airstrikes spiked again on Wednesday with a report by Afghan officials that a missile from a United States aircraft had killed 40 civilians and wounded 28 others at a wedding party in the southern province of Kandahar… A U.S. spokesman said 'if innocent people were killed in this operation, we apologize and express our condolences.'"[14]

A bomb dropped on a target does not think or take responsibility for its actions. Only humans may take responsibility for their actions. On one level, this book is about learning how to do just that.

Today, with the dawning of the Age of Light, it will be possible for all of us, especially people of the Japanese tribe, to evolve as the vibrational shift makes its influence felt. We truly can measure ourselves and our experiences by the growing influence of our awareness. Order or chaos? Light or dark? Now the choice falls to us!

★ ★ ★ ★ ★ ★   ★ ★ ★ ★ ★ ★   ★ ★ ★ ★ ★ ★

Pisces, the twelfth astrological sign in the Zodiac, is leaving our collective human consciousness. As the Age of Pisces ends, the new Age of Light is being ushered in with uncertainty and many false moves, but it is entering our lives nonetheless. After centuries where the voices of centralized power leaders dominated the debate over our economic fate, we now have the choice to listen to the inner voice.

As British Prime Minister David Cameron noted in a 2007 speech, "What builds society, what encourages civility, is people taking responsibility. Putting each other before themselves. Parents understanding that it is their responsibility, not the school's responsibility, to bring their kids up with the right values. Neighbors understand that it is their responsibility, not just the council's responsibility, to look out for their neighbors. Business people understanding that it is their responsibility, not just the government's responsibility, to think about the social and environmental consequences of what they do."[15]

In August 2011, rioting broke out across Great Britain. According to media sources, racial tensions were the apparent cause. Since 2006, British police had stopped and searched 310,000 black and South Asian people. Under anti-terror laws, the police did not need probable cause to do so. The riots broke out after police shot a black civilian who they identified as a known gang leader, and the rioting went on for several days until police deployed more than 16,000 officers in cities across Britain to quell it. After the riots were over, politicians and sociologists discussed other possible causes of it.

Prime Minister Cameron was a conservative Tory. Ed Miliband, the leader of the opposition party, argued that, in the wake of the 310,000 police searches and 16,000 officer deployments, "too many Tories end up sounding like they just want to hammer the

---

14 Abdul Waheed Wafa and John F. Burns, "U.S. Airstrike Reported to Hit Afghan Wedding," November 5, 2008, http://www.nytimes.com/2008/11/06/world/asia/06afghan.html?_r=0.
15 David Cameron, "Civility and Social Progress," Speech given at the Royal Society of Arts in London, April 24, 2007.

powerless."[16] Miliband went on to argue governments have a duty to offer poor people opportunities to get training and education so they can take responsibility for improving their life situations themselves.[17]

Many sociologists say the real problem is British youth have nothing useful or interesting to do to occupy their time. For example, in Tottenham, a poor London district with a population including many blacks and South Asians, the local council was forced by budget cuts ordered by the Tory central government to close eight of its thirteen youth centers at the beginning of July 2011. These youth centers shut down just a few weeks prior to the "senseless" riots.[18]

"The centers had offered courses on everything from beauty treatments to DJing, and services ranging from sexual-health tests to exam revision," said Clifford Scott, a senior lecturer in social psychology at the University of Liverpool. "A lot of those radicalized youth who were on the street Saturday night would have been going to those youth centers. They no longer had anywhere else to go."[19]

In the weeks prior to the riots, Tottenham was just one of many jurisdictions across Great Britain forced to close youth centers and other institutions designed to provide resources people could use to build and reinforce personal accountability. If the minds of the British youths had been engaged in learning skills they thought were interesting enough to eventually make a living from, perhaps they might not have been as susceptible to "acting out" with random violence when Earth's atmosphere was hit by heavy, intense space storms radiating from the sun.

On August 10, 2011 Reuters reported "Earth's magnetic field is still reverberating from a coronal mass ejection (CME) strike on August 5 that sparked one of the strongest geomagnetic storms in years."[20] CMEs are bursts of highly charged particles thrown from the sun into space and at Earth. After observing three large CMEs burst out of the sun, U.S. government scientists had warned solar storms could cause power blackouts. After August 5, observers in England spotted the aurora borealis, or northern lights, caused by charged particles in the Earth's atmosphere. Concerning the worst riots in Britain in decades, the Reuters staff wondered, "[C]ould the cause for all the madness really be the star at the center of our solar system?"[21]

Reuters went on to say, "Some academics have claimed that such geomagnetic storms can affect humans, altering moods and leading people into negative behavior through effects on their biochemistry … A 2003 study by the Federal Reserve Bank of Atlanta found that such storms could affect the stock market, as traders were more likely to make

---

16 Patrick Wintour, "UK Riots: Four Days of Chaos That Reshaped the Political Landscape," The Guardian, August 11, 2011, http://www.theguardian.com/uk/2011/aug/11/uk-riots-cameron-miliband-aftermath.
17 William Lee Adams, "London Riots: Why the Violence Is Spreading Across England," Time.com, August 10, 2011, http://content.time.com/time/world/article/0,8599,2087701,00.html.
18 Ibid.
19 Ibid.
20 "Did Solar Flares Cause the London Riots?" Reuters, August 15, 2011, http://theweek.com/article/index/218318/did-solar-flares-cause-the-london-riots.
21 Ibid.

pessimistic choices. 'Unusually high levels of geomagnetic activity have a negative, statistically and economically significant effect on the following week's stock returns for all U.S. stock market indices,' the authors found in their report. It could, of course, be mere coincidence that this has been a rollercoaster week on the markets, and that Britain was rocked by a wave of ferocious rioting and looting."[22]

The Reuters report concluded by mentioning the solar CME cycle is on an upswing that will peak in 2013. There are likely to be more geomagnetic storms heading Earth's way in the years to come.

> *Although I don't feel that it's at all necessary to tell you how I feel about the principle of individuality, I know that I'm going to have to spend the rest of my life expressing it one way or another, and I think that I'll accomplish more by expressing it on the keys of a typewriter than by letting it express itself in sudden outbursts of frustrated violence*
> ~ Hunter S. Thompson in a letter to a friend, *The Proud Highway*, 1957

★ ★ ★ ★ ★ ★   ★ ★ ★ ★ ★ ★   ★ ★ ★ ★ ★ ★

As members of the Japanese tribe evolve and begin to see and act on the benefits of self-sufficiency and sustainable economics, Mother Earth will continue to deliver the intervention or, literally, communicate from nature. During the Age of Pisces, many events took place, I think, because of the direct, unfiltered influence of humankind's unconsciousness and subconsciousness. There is a difference. An unconscious person is someone who is not in the Present and, thus, is unaware of the consequences of his or her actions. On the other hand, the subconscious, or the Higher Self, can influence or direct an individual here on Earth. I think Present awareness is the best approach for living, and this point of view benefits everyone. If the subconscious becomes conscious awareness, then inspiration flows creating harmony in the Present, which is ephemeral and eternal.

In the symbol of Pisces, the two attached fish are depicted swimming in opposite directions, indicating duality and contradiction. During the Age of Pisces, humankind, especially Europeans, embarked on voyages of exploration in a ruthless, calculated spirit of exploitation.

As control over nature was secured in the Age of Pisces through building sea lanes, dams, canals, cities and so on, myths also flourished. Myths are stories handed down to us. They are essential components of our lives that remind us of our interconnectedness due to our action and relationships with one another and to the mystery of life itself.

At the same time, the advancement of science evoked humankind's desire to move away from the limits of the past in order to embrace an unknown future. The Age of Pisces was an era when organized religion was dominant. However, there were also signs it was starting to decline. Doctrinaire religious thinking will no longer manipulate humankind's ignorance. How appropriate, in the dawning of the Age of Light,

22 Ibid.

people embrace their spiritual consciousness while using the science of today so our descendants may live in the Present with a consciousness that experiences existence at the speed of light.

★ ★ ★ ★ ★ ★ ★   ★ ★ ★ ★ ★ ★ ★   ★ ★ ★ ★ ★ ★ ★

In contrast with the Age of Pisces—when water was seen as a limitless resource that could be exploited without consequences—in the Aquarian Age, clean, fresh water is to become scarcer than any other major resource humans rely on.

John F. Kennedy once said, "Anyone who can solve the problems of water will be worthy of two Nobel prizes – one for peace and one for science." Kennedy's words still ring true today. According to figures from the Organization of Economic Co-operation and Development (OECD), one billion people lack access to clean drinking water today.[23]

The UN Climate Report of 2007 predicted global warming will cause precipitation levels in many developing countries to drop further. The OECD expects demand for water to increase by 50% during the next 30 years, mostly in large developing countries such as China, India, Brazil and Russia.

According to Open Knowledge, "Because water is often not appreciated as a limited resource, it is poorly managed. In a global survey of urban water management conducted for the Third World Centre for Water Management (TWCWM), Western European cities showed surprisingly bad results. The agricultural sector, which uses over 90% of all fresh water consumed, has to be reformed … It takes a liter of water to produce a calorie of food. **This means each of us 'eats' around 3,000 liters of 'virtual' water every day."**[24]

In her 2016 article, "Celebrity Chefs Hope to Press Congress on Food Waste," in *The New York Times*, Jennifer Steinhauer reported that 70 billion pounds of food is wasted annually in the United States. Mind you, this is just one country in the world. PBS reported $218 billion is spent in the United States annually for food never eaten. Mankind doesn't have a choice for saving the planet. We are destined to stop polluting our home and wasting our resources or the polluting and waste will stop us. Life without conflict is the only way to live.

Attitudes and agricultural business practices based on outmoded values have to change. Up until now, a resource, if deemed limitless, would be exploited. That approach must come to an end. Wasteful water usage has to change as people change and consciously evolve due to their awakening. There will come a turning point within, not unlike the experience of 15th and 16th century Portuguese sailor-explorers who finally made the turn around and beyond the Cape of Good Hope at the southern tip of Africa and suddenly saw their way clear on a course all the way to the fabled spices of India! The world is going to turn a corner, and the path will be clear, for intelligent living is the only way.

---

23 Open Knowledge, *knowledge.allianz.com*.
24 Ibid.

Chapter 1 Eternity = Present

Since ancient times, the circle has been widely recognized as the perfect symbol, and the ancients recognized its significance. With the dawning of the Aquarian Age, a spiritual outpouring will begin nurturing humankind. Aquarius, the Water Carrier, is the sign under which the Earth can begin to heal. In most symbols of Aquarius, the Water Carrier is seen pouring out wiggly shapes that resemble water. These shapes also represent the Age of Light, resembling the frequency of light.

It is true humankind comes from the stars. Humanity is an expression of light. The Japanese tribe is destined to manifest the essence of the Age of Light as a way of life and serve as an example to the rest of the Earth's inhabitants. After all, Japan's Sun Sign is Aquarius.

It's written in the stars as well as within: You are right where you are supposed to be— or you would not be here! As my mother once told me, "You are what you are, whether you know it or not." There was a big bang 13.8 billion years ago, and you just happened to appear from nowhere and here you are! I find that to be unbelievable, amazing, and beyond comprehension. We are miracles living as subjective temporal centers of the Universe: liquid light glowing on the edge of Eternity.

At this time, the universal spirit of people —the invisible light of each of our spirits, especially in Japan—is preparing for further illumination. Many people will make the transition and see light and become expressions of that light, while others will diminish and disappear into the darkness, only to find that darkness is but a shadow of light.

For Japan, the Great Eastern Japan Earthquake Disaster was a tragedy marking the arrival of the Dark before the Light. I see this as a time for the Japanese to reexamine their nation's political priorities—specifically its future energy generation and consumption patterns. I think an overhaul of Japanese cultural values is in order in light of the birth of the New Age now taking place. The changes in the Japanese will inspire the world. And perhaps the Japanese have the most healing and growing to do by letting go of the past. Letting go may seem unimaginable for the Japanese, but they can benefit by doing away with patterns of belief that no longer serve them—as we all can. We can especially benefit by letting go of our ignorance, which can illuminate the Light that surrounds us.

"The New Age" is a much-overused term, especially in the marketing realm. Nonetheless, we are now moving into the Fifth World, according to the Hopi Prophecy, or the Fifth Sun as the Mayans saw it. As with any birth, there must be a period of difficulty and struggle to find the foundation upon which to begin creating a clear path for the future. The vibrational change occurring now is affecting our consciousness, such that we are coming into a new socioeconomic order arising from Mother Earth.

Religious leaders who have based their dogmas and teachings on fear, ignorance, control and misguided interpretations of ancient texts have threatened humanity for millennia. But now we are entering a vibrational shift that has the potential to change this "power-over" mentality—in other words, power not shared among equals. The vibrational shift is just that—it does not end the world, nor does it doom humanity. In fact, it will renew humanity with cooperation, not competition. Humankind in this century redirects its negative energy to serving each other, healing our oceans and eliminating the garbage on the planet. This is the beginning for creating an economic world order based on sharing and restoring the health of our planet, as we rediscover the planet as our garden and home.

Humankind has come a long way from worshiping Sun gods, Moon goddesses and golden calves. Bleeding lambs as a sacrifice to gods, crucifying martyrs and sacrificing virgins to an unknown mysterious Universe are thankfully also things of the past. Today some of these practices are still embedded in many cultures around the world.

★ ★

The Astrological eras (like the Age of Pisces or Age of Aquarius, for example) progress in a counterclockwise direction "back to the ancient future." Thus, the wheel of the Zodiac eras moves in the opposite direction from the progress of the monthly signs through the year. Aries is the beginning of spring, the rebirth of the Earth, as the days get longer. It is the first sign of the Zodiac. Immediately preceding Aries, Pisces is the last sign, and Aquarius precedes Pisces.

Christianity tells us Jesus said, "I am the light and the way." During the Age of Pisces, in my opinion, Christ said, "You are the light and the way." The message Christ taught was completely misunderstood, because his followers, predominantly Jewish, could not relate to such an equal acknowledgment with the Creator. It could not have been otherwise at the time.

Even over the many centuries since and through many translations from the original language of Aramaic, the message from the time of Jesus Christ is obvious. In *The Power of Myth*, Joseph Campbell, states, "[N]ow according to the normal way of thinking about the Christian religion, we cannot identify with Jesus, we have to imitate Jesus. To say, 'I and the father are one,' as Jesus said, is blasphemy for us. However, in the Thomas gospel that was dug up in Egypt some forty years ago, Jesus says, 'He who drinks from my mouth will become as I am, and I shall be he.' Now, that is exactly Buddhism. We are all manifestations of Buddha consciousness, or Christ consciousness, only we don't know it. **The word 'Buddha' means 'the one who woke up.' We are all to do that – to wake up to the Christ and Buddha consciousness within us.** This is blasphemy in the normal way of Christian thinking, but it is the very essence of Christian Gnosticism and of the Thomas Gospel."[25] Now, with the coming shift in humankind's consciousness, the teaching of Christ will finally be understood more completely, as well as the teachings of Buddha and all enlightened men and women throughout history since Christ first brought His good news to humankind. Today, their teachings are misunderstood, and the good news has not yet been understood. But it's finally understood in the Age of Light.

To say the Age of Light is the dawning of a new Era of Consciousness is not a cliché. The words now used in marketing slogans have meanings we will be able to understand more completely as the Age blossoms. Choices people make around the world now will

---
25 Joseph Campbell (with Bill Moyers), *The Power of Myth*, June 1986.

determine the future, and life can either destroy itself, or the people of the world can heal and redeem our Paradise that has been lost.

The mystical Mayan calendar-makers and the Hopi Elder-prophets advised us to live in harmony. As we now enter the Fifth Mayan Sun cycle, we are leaving the Fourth Sun cycle. There is agreement among the Maya that, after the Mayan Long Count Calendar would end on December 21, 2012, their ancient calendar-makers weren't sure what events would transpire. The Hopi Elders in their prophecies also were unclear what would happen next. In my astrological analysis, especially relating to events in Japan after 2012, the core of the vibrational shift will unfold with many unexpected facets until the year 2095-97, when Pluto enters Taurus for a major airquake for stable change in America. When the Great Eastern Japan Earthquake Disaster shifted ever so slightly the Earth's axis, I took this to be a powerful physical symbol of the vibrational shift both the Earth and humankind's consciousness are beginning to undergo.

People are destroying the Earth's ecosystem because they have deluded themselves that greed and selfishness are virtues. Each individual human is responsible for the good, the bad and the ignorance that humankind perpetrates. These are not external abstractions ("the Devil makes evil") conceived by organized religion to instill fear and obedience in us here on Earth. The good, the bad and the ignorant are us.

The Age of Light will be, among other things, a conceptual disinfectant, a cleaning and clearing out of the debris of ideas no longer viable. The shift is happening, and we will experience a difficult transition from ignorance to love, forgiveness and understanding, a transition that will be evident as this century comes to a close.

War is an example of an outdated idea. So is intolerance, such as that expressed by religious fundamentalism as terrorism, as we know it is more than mental illness. It also signifies spiritual corruption, as the Dark Ages are not going quiet into that good night. The dawning is awake and starting to thrive.

It is unusual for significant astrological events to occur in such rapid succession— Pluto entered Capricorn in 2008; Uranus entered Aries on March 11, 2011; and on April 5, 2011 Neptune entered Pisces at the height of the Arab Spring revolutions. These rapid-fire transits herald accelerating changes leading toward the Age of Light set to begin, according to the Mayan calendar, on December 21, 2012. And it was a day like any other day, and the shift has indeed taken place.

An important lesson to remember during this time of transition will be to give attention, which is the simplest act of love. The simplest and most beautiful truths are free and, like anything worth having, freely available. It's the material wealth of the world that imprisons humankind. The greatest gifts of all lead us to love each other. Some of the greatest gifts of all are priceless, which money cannot buy. These gifts are love, awareness, and forgiveness.

> *The strongest of all warriors are these two, time and patience.*
> ~ Tolstoy, *War and Peace*

Chapter 2

The Four Directions of Light

The Present Future: United States, China, and Japan

The Ascending Light

I had a vision in which four feathers of light were revealed to me in a configuration like points of a compass or face of a clock. The feathers, or directions, represent wisdom handed down from one generation to the next. I came to realize as we enter the Age of Light, time will become a tool subject to the inner needs of humankind, rather than an external device designed to control daily life. Time will be measured differently according to the relative intensity of people's experience. In the New Age, people will simultaneously recognize and become expressions of the spirit of Gaia, the pagan name for Mother Earth. This is key to understanding the Age of Light.

My soul's purpose has provided a unique life experience that allowed me to write this book. I was born in Tokyo, Japan. In researching and writing this book, I am coming home spiritually to my birthplace. The Japanese have nothing to fear in the future. Fear is manufactured from illusion. I know this, and you will learn this if you haven't already. In fact, the world has nothing to fear about the future, because it does not exist. The way we take care of the future is here and now, the Present. The future is a human-made concept that truly does not exist.

As Franklin Delano Roosevelt said during his first inauguration in 1933, "The only thing we have to fear is fear itself."

Don't be afraid of the gift of life as Nature performs her magical dance. It is the expression of wisdom to recognize Mother Earth as the most immediate power determining the destiny of humanity. We have the opportunity to celebrate the conscious energy exchange between Sun and Earth that is humankind's journey of destiny. Know that the journey is the destiny. We learn about destiny and our ability to manifest integrity with the vibrational shifts within nature's wisdom. Rather than succumbing to the false shadow of our man-made fears, consider being present and aware to experience illumination by giving attention, which is the simplest act of love for all you do.

Mother Earth has delivered the message: In order to transcend time, we are going to have to seek to rediscover our natural authenticity and realign our internal harmony with the Universe. We all die and know death is a great gift, just as life is a great gift. Enjoy each gift as given and then move on to the next gift. We are here to enjoy and learn from experience, which is a never-ending process: You don't go away when you die. You are where you are, there is nowhere else to be with a body or not.

Existence is eternal. If you are here now, you have always been here and you will always be here. Or you could not be here now! As we rationally oriented humans learn to embrace the eternal lessons of love, the world and each individual will embody his or her destiny, which is to, **"be a light unto yourself and the world."**

> *The world is its own magic.*
> ~ Shunryu Suzuki, Japanese Zen priest[26]

The Four Directions of Light are as follows:
1. Each Person is a Spiritual Being of the Alpha and Omega.
2. You are a Mask of God contributing to the Fabric of Creation!
3. Woman and Man are Equal in Different Ways.
4. The Universe is as it is and Thou art That!

The four directions are universal truths for humankind to use as humanity moves into the next pivotal vibration in human history, an existence comprising, as the Mayan calendar-makers prophesied so long ago, "the end of time, but not the end of the world."

Each Person is a Spiritual Being of the Alpha and Omega
You represent the Alpha and the Omega. This direction of light is the first lesson the Age of Light teaches. In Christianity, the first and last letters of the Greek alphabet are used to distinguish the continuous comprehension of God. Alpha and Omega mean simply that God includes all that there is. Livingkind, all that we are, is included.

The circle represents the Alpha and Omega, which is the childlike innocence we all share as human beings. Childlike innocence means being your authentic self, for there is no one else to be. (If you didn't know who you were, who would you be?) We live as a participatory form of Light, and our physical body represents that Light. Through using the tool of observation, we create an awareness enabling an enlightened way of life, which is subjectively universal.

You are the world on the Alpha-Omega continuum. You are the Universe, and you represent the shortest and longest distance to enlightenment, which is You! To wake up

26 Quoted in *Zen Miracles* by Brenda Shoshanna.

from the shadows of fear is to be an instrument of Light, which supports you in serving others. Consciousness travels at the speed of Light. TimeSpace, Gravity, Dark Energy and Dark Matter appear to comprise the fabric of the Universe. In this century, the world's Consciousness delivers a wake-up call as TimeSpace expands and implodes. We are Time-Space and liquid light. Breath is another form of invisible Light, which is Prana, the Sanskrit word for life source.

You Are a Mask of God Contributing to the Fabric of Creation

We want to think about God. God is a thought. God is a name. God is an idea. But its reference is to something that transcends all thinking. The ultimate mystery of being is beyond all categories of thought.
– Joseph Campbell, *The Power of Myth*

You are a capable creator in your own right. In fact, you are the equation Einstein searched for all those years. The Unified Field Theory = YOU! Einstein spent most of his life looking for the answer that could bring everything—life, time, the Universe—together in a simple formula like $E=MC^2$. You are the Unified Field, which will become known in the New Age.

I think God-creation, the unknown you, represents the Unified Field and is expanding at the speed of TimeSpace. As we move into the unknown, human experience is going to transform by means of recognition of what and who we are, and what we represent. Under many organized religious institutions, humankind has decided to define the idea of God as someone or something existing outside the individual human sphere of reality. Accordingly, we, or to be more precise, some of our religious institutions, have created God in our own image. This is the most profound misconception to have occurred in the history of humanity's existence on this planet. Let us take responsibility for the fact we have defined God by way of our ignorance. Now is the time to acknowledge the God we pray to is us, and the God we pray to is IN us. In fact, God has us surrounded and permeates us with what we have defined as God! The choice is ours. There are many masks of God. TimeSpace is a mask; Light is a mask; Spirit is a mask; Gravity is a mask.

In order to survive and thrive during the coming vibrational shifts, the Mayans predicted people must live in the eternal moment of Now as an integral thread woven in and strengthening the fabric of creation. Instead of praying to God, let us take action to help your fellow human beings, another direct representation of this God we know so little about. The God gene may be in our DNA in every cell in our body. This code, keyed to creation and embedded in every cell in your body, gives you the curiosity to explore outside your comfort zone as you constantly change towards awakening.

The Unified Field Theory = I have seen the Eye of God, and it is Us.
~ Clint Cochran, Mystic

Woman and Man are Equal in Different Ways

Feminine and masculine represent the yin and yang energies, both essential interwoven threads in the fabric of the Universe. They are independent and bound in balance and have incredible power for expanding the potential of the individual creative force. In the Aquarian Age, people come to understand they are a person first and their gender is second.

Yet, in many parts of the world if you ask a man how many children he has, he will tell you only how many male children he has fathered. These fathers, out of the ignorance engrained by centuries of culture and tradition, don't mention their female children. In China, the "one-child policy" has severely distorted the natural balance of the population. The Chinese government bureaucrats intruded even into the womb by punishing parents for having "illegal" children.

Yuan Chao-ren from Hunan Province described the behavior of Chinese family-planning bureaucrats: "Before 1997 they usually punished us by tearing down our houses for breaching the one-child policy ... After 2000 they began to confiscate our children."[27]

Local officials would take "illegal" children and pack them off to orphanages where they were put up for adoption. Foreign adoptive parents paid thousands per child. The bureaucrats took a kickback.

The government's one-child policy has contributed to another horrific feature of family life, the practice of aborting female fetuses to ensure the lone child is a son. Other than female fetus abortion and female babies being sent to orphanages in alarming numbers, the ramifications of the one child policy have also contributed to human trafficking from nearby countries such as Cambodia and Vietnam. In fact, The Guardian reported in 2016 that China's gender ratio problems were contributing to human trafficking for brides for its excessive population of male children that were coming of age to marry.[28]

Government interference in the most important and basic human activity, reproduction of the human race, is an abomination, shortsighted and heartless. And, with the spread of birth control, it is arguably unnecessary. Government interference short circuits the energy individuals need to take responsibility for their own actions and futures.

However, the abomination of the one-child policy is like polite tea party chatter compared with the tragedies of women who, by the thousands, are raped and beaten every day around the world. In contrast with the meddling Chinese family-planning bureaucrats, many governments stand back and do little to stop these atrocities or prosecute the perpetrators. These senseless tragedies are replicated in virtually all countries around the world. In fundamentalist countries like Saudi Arabia, women are being punished with lashes and jail time for being raped.[29] This is horrific, evil and beyond comprehension.

How extensive has rape become in our society? So extensive this crime even infects the officials charged with protecting us domestically, such as police officers, and globally, such as persons in the military. According to social critic and political activist Naomi Wolf, "The numbers around the level of sex assault in the military are staggering. There is so much of this going on in the US military that women soldiers' advocacy groups have created a new term for it: military sexual trauma or MST. In 2016, there were 6,172

---

27 "Illegal Children Will Be Confiscated," *The Economist*, July 25, 2011, available at http://www.rascott.com/News%20 pages/Archive%20-%20July%202011.htm.

28 "Weddings From Hell: The Cambodian Brides Trafficked to China." *The Guardian*, 1 February 2016. https://www.theguardian.com/global-development/2016/feb/01/weddings-from-hell-cambodian-brides-trafficked-china

29 Eltahawy, Mona. "Punished for Being Raped." *The New York Times*, 29, November, 2007. http://www.nytimes.com/2007/11/29/opinion/29iht-edeltahawy.1.8528543.html?mcubz=0

cases of sexual assault reported within the military. In 2017, we find 6,082 sexual assault were reported within the military. The Service Women's Action Network notes that rape is always under-reported, and that a military context offers additional hurdles to rape victims: the Department of Defense, they point out, estimates that these numbers are misleading because fewer than 14% of survivors report an assault. The DoD estimates that in 2010 alone, over 19,000 sexual assaults occurred in the military.

"'Prosecution rates for sexual predators are astoundingly low,' DoD officials note. In 2011, "officials received 3,192 sexual assault reports. But only 1,518 of those reports led to referrals for possible disciplinary action, and only 191 military members were convicted at court martial.'"[30]

This is the same U.S. military tasked with defending our country from invasion, terrorism and other harm from enemies outside our borders. We cannot allow our mothers, sisters, and daughters to be treated in this disgraceful way. **Violence against women must end!**

As the Age of Light comes to pass, the atrocity of rape has to stop. Humankind must come to the conscious realization women are the Mothers of us all, the bringers of life and change into the world. Simple logic must lead to the conclusion women are due enormous respect, and yet in industrialized and primitive countries alike, women do not receive anywhere near their due.

All of humanity is born of woman. Women keep on giving and sacrificing. The policy of manipulating the Chinese birth rate has shown a drop precipitously. As reported in *The Independent* in November 2013, "Demographers estimate that the birth rate necessary to keep a population stable is 2.1 children per woman. This drop means the Chinese population is projected to peak in 2017 and to decline thereafter."[31] While it has been projected the continually expanding Chinese economy could have problems in the future due to the one-child policy, in an unexpected reversal of sorts, the Communist Party recently relaxed the policy.[32] In 2014, China finally reversed its one-child-per-family policy, but it is too late for this shift to have much impact on Chinese society in the short term.

In the new Age of Light, women will demand their equal rights, not just to vote or to achieve career advancement, but literally to life. All forms of discrimination are abhorrent, but the worst is directed towards women and the disregard of children in poverty. The consequences of this form of discrimination will have to be recognized and acknowledged by governments as destruction of life and the root of terrorism. Acknowledgment that Woman and Man are naturally and completely different and equal becomes a reality as the Age of Light dawns.

---

30 Naomi Wolf, "A Culture of Coverup: Rape in the Ranks of the US Military," The Guardian, June 14, 2012, http://www.theguardian.com/commentisfree/2012/jun/14/culture-coverup-rape-ranks-us-military.

31 Ben Chu, "Great Leap Forward: China Loosens Notorious One-Child Policy Which Prevented Up to 400M Births to Bankroll Ageing Population," The Independent, November 16, 2013, http://www.independent.co.uk/news/world/asia/great-leap-forward-china-loosens-notorious-onechild-policy-which-prevented-up-to-400m-births-to-bankroll-ageing-population-8943267.html.

32 The one-child policy was never comprehensive, even in the earliest years. It did not cover China's 56 ethnic minority groups, and families in the countryside were allowed to have an extra child if their first-born was a girl.

According to a public opinion poll conducted in Egypt and Pakistan, roughly 75% of Muslim respondents want to make it legal to stone to death any woman who commits adultery.[33] (The poll results did not indicate if any of the poll respondents were women.) Shockingly, there was hardly a mention in the mainstream media concerning this poll. (Case in point: I found this information on the BBC News in the summer of 2013.) Surely, this is an example of the coarsening of emotions and narrowing and darkening of male consciousness. This discriminatory attitude is prevalent in the world on various levels and, when objectively observed, shows how functionally insane much of the world lives. The horrific way women are treated is considered a normal way to live for billions of people who accept patriarchal cultural norms today.

This narrow-hearted and cruel attitude toward women creates precisely the kind of world humankind will have to let go of in order to embrace the dawning Age of Light, when peace and love for everyone as equals will prevail. Women in Asia, the Middle East, Africa, North America, South America and Europe –worldwide—must be recognized for their essential role in the destiny of humankind. Women must play a greater role in governments around the world in order to stop rape-enablers. Women must become a major force within the ruling classes as the Age of Light is lit.

The Universe is as it is and Thou Art That

The study of quantum physics is going to reveal to humanity the kind of stuff of which we are made. The reason I think it would be best for people to stop believing in false and unnatural concepts, such as the superiority of the male gender, is due to the lack of any realistically perceivable context for such a cultural bias. That is, through the static and seemingly overpowering filters of male-dominated media coverage and government bureaucratic harassment, it is difficult to perceive that which cannot be put into words. **The media has become the message, manipulating masses by exaggerating current events out of proportion, which in turn provides a false narrative for what is happening around the world at any given moment. Those who control the message, control those who receive the propaganda.**

Belief is, of course, a powerful and wondrous social technology for creativity. However, when you apply it to your life, you may experience unforeseen consequences. Belief can be destructive when it is induced in the service of goals for which you cannot take responsibility and that do not enhance your sense of self-responsibility (from which true community grows). In the new Age of Light, belief will find its truly useful focus once again, instead of serving the goals of religion, the media, and bureaucrats. A truly useful belief is not to believe but to be a witness to the enormous energy that permeates all things. I have found to redirect and channel that energy in helping each other and especially those in need is a good way to serve creation. Be yourself and honor your ability to do anything. Giving attention is the essence of love. Whatever you do, do it in the Present. The Present contains the Past, which is all there is. Eckhart Tolle reminds us of this in *The Power of Now*.

Through incredible breakthroughs and discoveries, science continues to offer us glimpses into the nature of things and how the Universe works. The delivery of the Mayan Prediction message, from my point of view, is for us to rebirth humankind's conscious-

---

33 "Poll: ~75% of Muslims in Egypt, Pakistan Favor Stoning People for Adultery," Examiner.com, December 6, 2010, http://www.examiner.com/article/poll-75-of-muslims-egypt-pakistan-favor-stoning-people-for-adultery

ness and set it free of false shadows, like fear, ignorance and pretending to know God, which in turn reveals the Age of Light. These four directions of Light I have described can provide a sustainable strategy for the survival of humankind.

You are the eternal energy of the Universe as it is. I think one of the best descriptions relative to the nature of nothing as everything comes from a *Zen Poem*:

> ***You cannot catch hold of it nor can you get rid of it, in not being able to get it you get it, when you speak it's silent, when you are silent it speaks.***

Most people unquestioningly hold many beliefs as true. We base our beliefs upon a reality that is really an illusion. (And it is all temporal—there is no permanence.) Many think they want good government and justice for all; these are nice, safe, abstract concepts in which to believe. Yet, in daily life perhaps what most people really crave deep in their hearts is that things go on as normal and tomorrow is pretty much the same as today. We are afraid of change and, though some believe in better alternatives, we tend to resist creating those alternatives. It is easier to believe than to do. For example, many believe in equality for all, but equality is not being applied in real human terms. Money in most societies overrides ideals like equality. Science is as close to truth as we know it. The new awareness that takes place will mean belief systems cannot dominate as they have in the past. This dawning will light the way out of false realms of belief. Beliefs will give way to science, which becomes the new religion in the future. **Science as Truth!**

Every day begins with a glorious display of sunlight, and each day ends as we enter into darkness. As the sun constantly radiates its wondrous light without stint or compromise, it doesn't acknowledge the dark. It just shines. Light is the source of our consciousness. There is no shadow within Light. Only humankind has false shadows created from belief systems, like fear, which influence, on the most intimate, personal level, the choices we make. The chaos we create is the destiny we have chosen, or the peace we embrace is the destiny we can choose.

When you take responsibility for your own existence, you will be one with the Universe. You are an expression of the spirit and unity of Light, the complexity of existence. As Jon Stewart would say, "And now your moment of Zen." You will be part of it, and it is being part of you. You can't turn your back on it because it is you. You won't be able to say, "I was just following orders" or, "That's not fair." No one will be listening. You will own yourself. To believe will be a quaint notion of the past. I know you may reject this idea if you have a life based on belief. Nonetheless, the Present is the new religion. Be yourself without religion and be yourself without fear. Just be you. There is no one else to be. See existence as it is, not as you believe it to be! Our beliefs don't change the nature of God.

> ***"We are Liquid Light traveling at the speed of TimeSpace balancing on the edge of Eternity"***

The Mayan Prediction speaks to an upgrade of our consciousness. When we activate the portion of our brainpower we are not currently using, we can then proceed to activate the rest of our DNA and, in turn, inherit the destiny that awaits us all: Paradise as Earth.

Chapter 2 The Four Directions of Light

The Universe was here before we arrived, and the Universe will be here after we are gone. Our moment of transition as we now enter the Age of Light will signal we have returned home from whence we came.

All beings are flowers
Blooming
In a blooming Universe.
　　～ Soen Nakagawa Roshi [34]

Thinking at the speed of Space is thought itself. Life appears to move slowly relative to the Present. Most of us experience living near the speed of light, and energy slows down as we approach such an idea of being. Space travels faster than the speed of light, and space provides the space for light to travel through.

For me, Zen is the perfect way of understanding the Universe as it is rather than as we have been led to believe it to be. "In Zen practice, it is said that the best instruction is no instruction, the best encouragement is no encouragement," wrote Brenda Shoshanna in her book Zen Miracles, in which she quotes Soen Nakagawa Roshi.[35]

Rinzai Gigen was the founder of one of the main schools of Zen. He died in A.D. 866; the date of his birth is unknown. Rinzai Zen is dynamic and uncompromising. It was first practiced, according to Shoshanna, in Japan in the 13th century. She also quoted Rinzai Gigen as saying, "When I'm hungry, I eat; when I'm tired, I sleep. Fools laugh at me. But the wise understand."[36]

What are these countries to make of this statement now in the 21st century with the Age of Light dawning? Shoshanna writes in Zen Miracles, "How many… can really eat when we're hungry or sleep when we're tired? How many can really taste the food we are eating, appreciate it, and digest it?"[37]

How many devote their full attention to really tasting and appreciating the food they are eating instead of eating the wrong food, or trying to compensate for feeling lonely or looking for a distraction from being with people it is not a pleasure to be with? Zen is many confusing things, but the core of the Zen practice is simple: It teaches how to totally reclaim your life and mind. Shoshanna writes, "It is anti-authoritarian in the sense that Zen students are taught how to totally reclaim their lives and minds. They become able to take back all the scattered power and energy they have given to thousands of 'authorities' they have found or projected in the outside world. After years of practice, a Zen student is finally able to walk on this earth with his [or her] own two feet, to live the life given to him [or her]. He [or she] is able to laugh when he [or she] laughs, cry when he [or she] cries. He [or she] is wholehearted and without deception."[38]

---

34 Soen Nakagawa, *The Soen Roku: The Sayings and Doings of Master Soen*, Zen Studies Press, 1986.
35 Brenda Shoshanna, *Zen Miracles: Finding Peace in an Insane World*, 2011.
36 Ibid.
37 Ibid.
38 Ibid.

Zen is also a perfect means to provide Japan the direction for leading the way for the rest of the world as we enter the Age of Light. Despite the Eastern Japan Great Earthquake Disaster and fears about the future, Japan is here to stay. Let any doubts be dispelled here and now! The Japanese tribe is going to, in my opinion, rediscover the core essence of Zen (though not, perhaps, in so many words) and, through Zen, self-responsibility and a sustainable lifestyle free of wasteful consumption.

Mother Earth provides a home for every living creature on earth. Joy and suffering are shared by all living things. The life lessons will continue into the Age of Light. After the passing of the Age of Pisces, we will have a great deal to learn about how to live peaceful lives.

Look at any time period in humankind's history, and it is full of violence—war, killing, the forcible exertion of power. As just one example, today slavery is an even bigger business than ever before.[39]

> *What we need to be doing is not just changing who holds power, but changing the way we conceive of power. There is the power we're all familiar with — power over. But there is another kind of power — power from within...We must not be sidetracked by the dramas of power-over, the seduction of addictions, or the thrill of control. We must go deeper.*
> ~ Starhawk (born Miriam Simos), an American writer, social activist and pagan in the Reclaiming tradition

✶ ✶ ✶ ✶ ✶ ✶ ✶   ✶ ✶ ✶ ✶ ✶ ✶ ✶   ✶ ✶ ✶ ✶ ✶ ✶ ✶

In many positive ways, we are moving forward. But before the dawn of the Age of Light, we must effectively let go of what the English poet William Blake called "the mind-forged manacles" and begin living sustainably while taking responsibility for our own existence. We cannot continue to depend on others to sustain us.

Along with the Mayan calendar-makers, Hopi prophets and many other people in the past made predictions concerning this transition period we are entering. All agreed on one central point: from here on, many rules that have heretofore governed human conduct and interaction with the planet will no longer apply.

To investigate our authentic inner selves and function effectively among the wonders of the dawning Age of Light, we will let go of many socially acceptable ideas about our existence. I did not come to this discovery with a faith, a belief, or any preconceived idea about the Mayan Prediction, creation or life itself. As a mystic detective, I am always looking into the mystery of mysteries, which brings us back to the most basic mysteries of all: What is existence? Why are we here? Who are we? I have learned when you let go of the need to solve the mystery of life, then that mystery reveals itself.

Many astrological data and interpretations found along with the Mayan Prediction in surviving Mayan records were similarly recorded by astrologer-priests who flourished in Egypt around the time the first Egyptian hieroglyphics were created. There are many

---

39 See *www.freetheslaves.net*.

similarities between the Mayan and Egyptian views of our solar system as well. For example, they both recognized we would be in direct alignment with the center of the Milky Way in 2012.

The Pleiades

The Pleiades Cluster star system, in the shape of a very small dipper found at 28° 36' in the constellation Taurus, was recognized historically by many cultures, especially in Greece and Africa. In Greek mythology, Pleiades were seven sisters, daughters of the god Atlas who had been turned into stars. Among many cultures that weren't in physical contact with each other, the Pleiades were seen as a mythological portal through which all life on this planet originates. In Africa, the Egyptians recorded that when our solar system would travel in alignment with this star cluster in 2012, a major evolutionary move forward for humanity would be in store.

Astrologers in many cultures shared the opinion humankind's ancestors entered existence on this planet through the portal of the Pleiades. North Americans, Africans, Egyptians and Maya looked to this star cluster as our star-seeding origin. The Pleiades were recognized as a cosmic portal that many prayed to and meditated on for centuries.

In December 2010, astronomers reported they had discovered there are 300 sextillion stars in the universe. This is three times more stars than previously had been thought to exist.[40] For purposes of clarification, 300 sextillion means the number 3 followed by 23 zeros! Will this discovery force astronomers to rethink how galaxies are configured and created? Are we on the brink of discovering scientifically the basic fabric from which we are created?

In current history, we have witnessed many nearly identical concepts manifesting into physical existence at nearly the same time all over the world. Historically, people did not know what was happening in other parts of the world as we do today. However, the pattern of near-simultaneous patterns began to be recognized in the 19th century, when inventors and theorists were discovered to have been working on similar projects at practically the same points in time. For example, while Charles Darwin was assembling evidence to prove his theory of natural selection, others were also exploring this phenomenon.[41] Also, in the fields of photography and motion pictures several inventors actually created working cameras within months of each other.

Prior to the 1800s, most people traveled only a few miles from their birthplaces in their entire lifetimes. Although we hardly give a thought to jumping on a plane and jetting across continents in a matter of hours, it is amazing how widely our horizons have expanded in the last 100 years.

In the United States on May 20, 1926, President Calvin Coolidge signed the Air Commerce Act of 1926 into law. At first glance, issues the law dealt with appear rather mun-

---

40 Memmott, Mark. "'Trillions of Earth's' Could be Orbiting 300 Sextillion Stars". *NPR*, 1 December 2010, http://www.npr.org/sections/thetwo-way/2010/12/01/131730552/-trillions-of-earths-could-be-orbiting-300-sextillion-stars

41 There were theories of evolution before Darwin published On the *Origin of Species*. See "Natural Selection: Charles Darwin and Alfred Russel Wallace" http://evolution.berkeley.edu/evolibrary/article/history_14

dane. The Act was intended to establish and propagate air commerce, as well as arrange for aeronautical research and development. The Act also streamlined the process of obtaining a pilot's license and provided for the establishment of a centralized office charged with issuing airworthiness certificates for aircraft and aircraft components. However, taking a look at the big picture, these seemingly petty bureaucratic arrangements widened humankind's horizons on an unprecedented scale. With a stroke of President Coolidge's pen, the air travel industry was truly getting off the ground.

The implications were enormous and far beyond anything the lawyers and bureaucrats who wrote this law could have imagined—a harbinger of the dawning of the Age of Light. May 20, 1926 was, I dare say, a milestone in humankind's reconceptualization of time—the beginning of the end of time and its measurement and hold on the mind of humankind. We are moving more and more rapidly to the day when people will no longer be subject to time. After the end of time, human interaction will multiply in ways hitherto unknown.

> *Everything that rises must converge.*
> ~ Flannery O'Connor, "Everything That Rises Must Converge"

★ ★ ★ ★ ★ ★ ★   ★ ★ ★ ★ ★ ★ ★   ★ ★ ★ ★ ★ ★ ★

The Mayan astrologer-priests preserved—in the form of their calendar and predictions—the spiritual knowledge that can enable us today to learn how to navigate the end of time. Though they are no longer the advanced civilization they once were, they did put up a heroic fight against the Spanish conquistadores long ago, and their descendants live on today as farmers and villagers in traditional Mayan lands.

The people of the world learn they, too, have a choice to make concerning the direction the future journey of humankind takes. This direction is the combined force of all the choices members of humankind make. Ironic as it seems, each one of us must learn how to break away from the madness and insanity of humanity if our world is to survive. The importance of the individual cannot be underestimated.

> *The individual has always had to struggle to keep from being overwhelmed by the tribe. If you try it, you will be lonely often, and sometimes frightened. Nevertheless, no price is too high to pay for the privilege of owning yourself.*
> ~ Friedrich Nietzsche

Rumi, the great Sufi poet, said, "Out beyond the ideas of right doing and wrong doing, there is a field. I will meet you there." This is the Mystical way, or state of consciousness, that those who accept the Present as a way of life flourish as the Age of Light dawns. This means not choosing to do something but doing without doing, a choice a Zen student would instantly recognize. It is a choice that happens while living in harmony with your doing and being. All that is and all that has been and all that will be are the quantum soup in which we live, and we choose to drown, float, or swim with the prescient ocean of cosmic-energy, which is the essence of creation.

Chapter 2 The Four Directions of Light

Choiceless observation of life is a way to flow with the eternal All, and one's experience becomes stillness, as Meditation, a state of being beyond the ages. The Present incubates all ages.

Quantum field theory – a theory in physics; the interaction of two separate physical systems is attributed to a field that extends from one to the other and is manifested in a particle exchange between the two systems.

> *Quantum leap – an abrupt change, sudden increase or dramatic advance.*
> ~ Merriam-Webster's Collegiate Dictionary, Eleventh Edition

Envision human experience as the unified field of interaction. You are Art and Science, interacting as a participatory stardust living in the Present. For every action there is a reaction, which is why each thought, action and choice affects all that's happening and all that exists. Our human life is unified with the Present energy in the micro and macro, and we are one with this field of dreams. We can choose to wake up or continue to live the nightmare that humankind perpetrates.

During most of his life, Einstein looked at the world as though it were something apart from us, as though we humans were detached observers of this place called space. However, John Archibald Wheeler, a scientist and fellow professor of Einstein's at Princeton University, contradicted the notion of detached observation. Wheeler stated that in actuality we, each of us, are an integral part of the universe. Wheeler even went on to say we are participating with creation itself.[42]

Physicists are the new mythological storytellers who teach us the new lessons gathered from scientific discovery. Their lessons will guide us into our future lives after the end of time. Professor Wheeler also said he recognized everyone is interrelated and, on the smallest subatomic level, quantum physics seems to be the answer to how the exchange happens.

YOU are the participatory expression of the unknown known as You.

The exciting implications of quantum physics in the realm of our senses reflect the reality that we are, simply put, all in this existence together, interacting without barriers. On the microcosmic level, there are no barriers. Realize the only reality is the Present in our daily lives as we enter the Age of Light.

> *In the Universe, there are immeasurable indescribable forces, which those who live "of the source" call intention…and that absolutely everything that exists in the entire cosmos is attached to intent by a connection link.*
> *Sorcerers are not only concerned with understanding and explaining that connecting link. But they are especially concerned with cleansing it of the numbing affects brought about by all of the concerns of living at ordinary levels of consciousness.*
> ~ Carlos Castaneda, Sorcerer

---

[42] Jones, Marina. "John Wheeler's Participatory Universe" *Futurism*, 13 February 2014. https://futurism.com/john-wheelers-participatory-universe/

The first time I heard Indian spiritual master, Jiddu Krishnamurti speak was years ago at the Masonic temple in San Francisco. I found him so refreshing and illuminating I went backstage to meet this extraordinary man.

As I made my way backstage, I felt a real sensation of illumination from his simple brilliance. I knew it was imperative to meet him. As he walked in my direction, he started to stumble gently as if he were extremely tired. I quickly caught his arm and shoulder and broke his fall. When he stood on his own two feet again, he looked directly into my eyes. We were just a foot or so from each other, and, with a slight nod and the closing and opening of his eyes, we looked directly at each other. Not a word was exchanged; I experienced stillness.

> *Communication with others develops differently as we sit in silence. It becomes deep, profound and lasting... Finally, it is easy to realize that our words, actions and false mannerisms, rather than bringing us closer to one another, can serve as walls to keep others away.*
> ~ Brenda Shoshanna, PhD, *Zen Miracles*

Little did I know, meeting Krishnamurti was the beginning of a journey toward a life without time for me. What I had experienced with my father and mother beginning in Japan was what I also experienced with Krishnamurti: time standing still and a glimpse into Eternity, which provided me a deep, clear sense of knowing without knowing.

You are an expression of the Present Eternal now as a temporal flame of the first water, which is Light, and that is I, you, he, she, we — all of us living in the garden of the mystics, as Rumi foretold.

Consider this information about stardust and the human body from Physics Central's website: Since stardust atoms are the heavier elements, the percentage of star mass in our body is much more impressive. Most of the hydrogen in our body floats around in the form of water. The human body is about 60% water, and hydrogen only accounts for 11% of that water mass. Even though water consists of two hydrogen atoms for every oxygen, hydrogen has much less mass. We can conclude that 93% of the mass in our body is stardust. Just think, long ago someone may have wished upon a star that you are made of.[43]

> *We are such stuff as dreams are made on.*
> ~ William Shakespeare, *The Tempest*

The Ascending Light

The 21st century, barely begun, is going to include explosive, difficult and previously unmet challenges for humankind. In response, or synergistically, humankind will evolve in new directions at an accelerating pace never before experienced. Concepts of money, energy and politics will turn in on themselves, cocoon and then blossom in unfamiliar patterns. The internet and social media will rapidly shape events in ways now not entirely imaginable.

---

43 "How Much of the human Body is Made Up of Stardust?" *Physics Central. http://www.physicscentral.com/explore/poster-stardust.cfm*

In this troubling but also potentially humane and enlightened context, the world's economy will evolve according to a paradigm shift or reprioritization of values from quantity to quality. The idea of "more is better" is a false concept that has driven our current age of exploitation. An economy that is both portable and sustainable has to be about embodying the opposite and revolutionary concept of "less is more." [44]

Van der Rohe is also justly famous for his assertion that, "God is in the details" with regard to an honest expression of materials. Along these lines, there is an apocryphal legend about Michelangelo's sculptural method. The Old Master is said to have begun his sculptural process by simply observing a block of granite. Eventually, he would recognize the image he had envisioned within the stone. From there, the sculptor's task was simply to chip away inessential stone until only his art remained.

> *What's the use of a fine house if you haven't got a tolerable planet to put it on?*
> ~ Henry David Thoreau

✶ ✶ ✶ ✶ ✶ ✶ ✶   ✶ ✶ ✶ ✶ ✶ ✶ ✶   ✶ ✶ ✶ ✶ ✶ ✶ ✶

Japan's giant, overbearing, ideologically obsessed neighbor across a short strait of sea to the west is currently on track to grow the biggest economy in the world sometime within the next 12 years. In my estimation, this prioritization of resources by the Chinese elite is a shift in the wrong direction.

The necessity of finding sustainable energy resources will eventually inspire Japan to develop an economic strategy the opposite of the ideologically based approach China has pursued. As we enter the altered space-time realm of the Age of Light, members of the Japanese tribe will discover the true antidote to China's political and economic mistakes in finding their own inner sense of peace and self-responsibility.

> *Only years [after the Great Leap Forward] would I begin to realize how the weak human brain succumbs to crackpot ideologies, and the ease with which unscrupulous leaders can use those ideologies to unseat rivals.*
> ~ Gregory Clark[45]

In 1958, Chinese Communist Chairman Mao Zedong became obsessed with "saving face." He decided to modernize the Chinese economy, skipping over the evolution the original capitalist countries had undergone to achieve their status as great world powers. That evolution had consisted of the slow process of invention and implementation of new technologies. For machinery and capital expenditure, Mao would substitute the one great resource China had at its disposal—the vast population of Chinese people. Manpower, Mao believed, would enable China to take a Great Leap Forward and industrialize its economy in a fraction of the time it had taken European countries and the United States.[46]

---

44 The phrase "less is more" was coined by modernist architect Ludwig Mies van der Rohe in reference to minimalist, unornamented design. By this, he meant that ornamentation such as that which graces Victorian-style buildings can actually distract from a building's function.
45 Gregory Clark, *www.gregoryclark.net*.
46 "Great Leap Forward." *Encyclopædia Britannic*, 20 July 2016, https://www.britannica.com/event/Great-Leap-Forward.

The Great Leap Forward strategy for economic development was symbolized by the small backyard steel furnaces that soon appeared in almost every village and city neighborhood. Tended by virtually every Chinese citizen, the furnaces were intended to enable China to produce its own steel and vastly accelerate the industrialization process. The Great Leap Forward was based on the efforts of the Chinese people pulling together to support many other grassroots-based projects, such as building irrigation systems, industrialized agriculture, and manufacturing.[47]

But "saving face" and the Great Leap Forward cost the lives of more than 20 million Chinese people.[48] This happened because the bureaucracy that managed the Great Leap Forward mandated the ideological purity, with which industrialization projects were executed, trumped the expertise and experience of the people who worked on those projects. Bureaucrats became obsessed with statistics that would show the world China was indeed rapidly becoming industrialized.

In villages and cities across China, leaders placed at the local levels who felt pressure to meet production quotes led to melting of plows and kitchen implements in these backyard steel furnaces. Houses were torn down to provide firewood for the furnaces. But the vast majority of steel produced in the backyard furnaces was of inferior quality. Without quality fuel such as coal, the furnaces could not get hot enough to produce quality steel.[49]

With their farm implements melted down to raise their steel quotas, China's peasants could not produce enough food to keep millions from starving. Even so, Chinese exports of grain increased during the time of the Great Leap Forward (1958-60). The Chinese economy began to break down. In desperation, the Communist government gave the peasants back their own private land and new farm implements. Respect for the peasants' knowledge of how to work their own land was also returned, and government officials' interference in daily farming activities lessened to a manageable degree.[50]

The Great Leap Forward timeframe of 1958-60 was also accompanied by disasters and poor farming techniques that decimated agricultural crops.[51] But as harvests shrank, bureaucratic mania increased. Thus, when humans disengage their thoughts and actions from the harmony of natural processes on the planet, we see how the planet responds.

> *[T]he egalitarian enthusiasm and progress in the early years of the [Chinese] Communist revolution were soon to be ended by a piece of Maoist insanity called the Great Leap Forward. Reliable reports of thousands dying of hunger and even cannibalism began to trickle out to our Hong Kong office. Making sense of it all was not easy.*
> ~ Gregory Clark[52]

---

47 Ibid
48 Ibid
49 Watkins, Thayer. "The Great Leap Forward Period in China, 1958-1960." San Jose State University Department of Economics, *http://www.sjsu.edu/faculty/watkins/greatleap.htm*.
50 "Great Leap Forward." *Encyclopædia Britannica*, 20 July 2016, *https://www.britannica.com/event/Great-Leap-Forward*.
51 Ibid
52 Gregory Clark, *www.gregoryclark.net*.

Chapter 2 The Four Directions of Light

The Japanese tribe is practical and down-to-earth compared with the ideologically obsessed Chinese bureaucrats. Modern Japan and the rest of the world will do well to avoid the mistakes and terrible excesses of the Great Leap. People can have harmony in their lives if they listen to their hearts and take responsibility for their own lives.

> *Your vision will become clear only when you can look into your own heart. Who looks outside, dreams; who looks inside, awakes.*
> ~ Carl Gustav Jung

★ ★ ★ ★ ★ ★   ★ ★ ★ ★ ★ ★   ★ ★ ★ ★ ★ ★

In August 2011, India entered a bilateral trade agreement with Japan. This was India's first such agreement with a developed, industrialized country. Duties and tariffs on 94% of imports from each country were immediately slashed. The two countries also agreed to circumvent China's nearly exclusive monopoly of the world's supply of rare earth minerals.[53]

This is an example of how China's single-minded focus on growth could backfire. When other countries become economically self-sufficient, they gain the ability to escape exploitative economic relationships with China. In the long run, this does not bode well for the Chinese economy because its unrealistic priorities cannot be supported long-term as the Age of Light unfolds.

To Americans, the shift in economic relationships in Asia and around the world is going to be unsettling. In the near future, we are going to witness a race between China and India to surpass the United States as the new economic powerhouse. In addition, Brazil's GDP rate is averaging 0.58% from 1996 through 2017.[54] Brazil will weigh in increasingly on world economic events and policy. Unexpected problems like the Zika virus, including Brazil's political and environmental landscape are erupting. Pollution in Brazil's environment is a major problem for its economy with global warming starting to take its toll on everyone.

I predict Japan changes its priorities during this period to a less exploitative, growth-oriented economic paradigm, one that is more sustainable. This shift occurs by increasing the money supply, which will lower the strong yen and allow Japan to reverse a 20-year economic slump. The global economy is still finding its way and unexpected consequences are difficult to discern.

In light of these emerging economic realities and recent reassessments of the use of nuclear power in the wake of the Great Eastern Japan Earthquake Disaster, Japan will shift to renewable energy production. Also, the Japanese tribe will lower demand for precious resources as its members become more self-responsible and less dependent on external resources for food, energy, consumption and individual spiritual growth.

Japan's indebtedness is going to be a challenging obstacle to achieving the goals of economic independence and sustainability. In August 2011, President Barack Obama

---

53 *http://zeenews.india.com.*
54 "Brazil GDP Growth Rate." *Trading Economics,* https://tradingeconomics.com/brazil/gdp-growth.

signed a bill raising the debt ceiling in response to a real threat the United States might actually default on trillions of dollars of debt.[55] Standard and Poor's lowered the United States' credit rating, and word of the default upset economies around the world.[56] Such ripple effects will become inevitable as economies become ever more intimately connected. By becoming more self-sufficient and focused on sustainability in the future, Japan can avoid being entrapped by economic calamities.

Weighed down by tremendous debt, the U.S. economy is going to struggle to recover for many years to come. In 2017, the United States was in debt to China by $1.15 trillion.[57]

> *God looks after fools, drunkards, and the United States.*
> ~ anonymous

The political U.S. government's inept weakness has major implications for the rest of the world since the international monetary system is tied to the dollar. If America's economic and/or political paralysis continues its current reputation and downward slide, the role of the dollar as the international standard for all other currencies may be assigned to a combination of currencies. As China and India grow, we may see an average valuation of the United States with these two countries' currencies substituted as the new international standard-bearing role.

In an unexpected turnaround, since 2013 the United States has been on the threshold of becoming energy self-reliant. As noted on EnergyandCapital.com, "There's a revolution afoot, and it has nothing to do with Occupiers or Tea Partiers ... It's a new industrial revolution. At stake are billions of dollars of oil and natural gas profits. Millionaires have been made overnight as America skyrocketed to the number one natural gas producer in the world, and reclaimed our place as an international oil giant."[58] This new reality could stem the tide for U.S. indebtedness to countries like Saudi Arabia and China.

With its historic dependence on the United States, Japan should now begin exploring ways to attain economic and energy independence. The way the United States has handled its massive debt to China and other countries should set a negative example for Japanese policymakers, politicians, and citizens. This is the road that should be less traveled as the Age of Light dawns. In 2017, the price of oil in the world market sits at $49.83 USD a barrel, and the impact on the world stage is yet to be seen.[59] One thing is certain, volatility could be a mainstay for some time.

---

55 "What's Happening With the Debt Ceiling Explained." *Mother Jones*, 3 August 2011, http://www.motherjones.com/politics/2011/08/whats-happening-debt-ceiling-explained/

56 Brandimarte, Walter and Daniel Bases. "United States Loses Prized AAA Credit Rating From S&P." *Reuters*, 6 August 2011, https://www.reuters.com/article/us-usa-debt-downgrade/united-states-loses-prized-aaa-credit-rating-from-sp-idUSTRE7746VF20110807.

57 Mullen, Jethro. "China is America's Biggest Creditor Once Again." *CNN Money*, 16 August, 2017, http://money.cnn.com/2017/08/16/investing/china-us-debt-treasuries/index.html.

58 "Petroleum Profits from the New American Oil Boom," *Energy & Capital*, January 6, 2014, http://www.energyand-capital.com/aqx_p/15305?gclid=CN2umbitnLsCFQZffgod1zsAc.

59 "Oil Price Commodity." *Business Insider*, 15 September 2017, http://markets.businessinsider.com/commodities/oil-price?type=wti

Chapter 2 The Four Directions of Light

Many of the problems handicapping the United States stem from the country's lack of political will to make the hard choices needed to restore a sound economy. Such choices involve sacrifice, which goes against the grain of the self-indulgent culture that has developed in America in the wake of decades of unprecedented prosperity and accumulation of material wealth. As a template for U.S. governmental operating procedures, the U.S. Constitution has ceased to function effectively as American governing elites have long abandoned many Constitutional principles. After all, the American Founding Fathers who authored the U.S. Constitution (and the Declaration of Independence) were afraid of centralized power because they themselves were revolutionaries. Greed, the exercise of power for its own sake and selfish political interests, has undermined personal freedoms.

Since the end of the Second World War, the economic and military interests of the United States and Japan have been strongly intertwined to the benefit of both. The pursuit of different inner priorities for the Japanese people, priorities consistent with the American ideals of personal freedom stated in the Declaration of Independence, ideals that address quality of life. For without love, joy, and health, a truly cooperative society cannot be supported.

★ ★ ★ ★ ★ ★   ★ ★ ★ ★ ★ ★   ★ ★ ★ ★ ★ ★

The energy field in Japan has up to now been dominated by aggressive, externally directed conquerors and capitalists, with the result Japan has become a nation largely made up of a nervous, dissatisfied people preoccupied with the impossible task of living up to ideals of perfection while dwelling on past achievements. The past is important, and we must be grateful for the achievements of those who lived before us, but contemplation of and striving to measure up to a past ideal can blind us to engaging with life right in front of our eyes.

Eckhart Tolle talks a great deal about the evolution of inner change in his book A New Earth. His central idea is we can transcend our false roles as captives of time. The Present moment flows, and there is no permanence, ever. Life is a continuance of owing energy, like the river of life itself.[60]

> *Something is true when it resonates with and expresses your innermost Being, when it is in alignment with your Inner Purpose ... Fulfilling your Primary Purpose is laying the foundations for a new reality, a new earth.*
> ~ Eckhart Tolle, *A New Earth*

Tolle created a stir with such comments as: "The certainty is complete. There is no need for confirmation from any external source. The realization of peace is so deep that, even if I met Thee Buddha and The Buddha said, 'You are wrong,' I would say, 'Oh, isn't that interesting, even The Buddha can be wrong.'" [61]

Tolle grew up in Germany after World War II. He played as a child in bombed-out buildings. He has said pain was in the energy field of his country. Since then, he has discovered the key to releasing his pain, which is to recognize his "false self" that did not exist

---

60 Eckhart Tolle, *A New Earth*, New York: Dutton, 2005.
61 "Profile: Eckhart Tolle - Of the Present, Future and Mother," The *Vancouver Sun*, October 16, 2008.

in the "suchness of now." He was depressed and feeling his country's pain, and suddenly he realized this depressed self was not his real self.

As a child growing up in West Germany, I, too, played in bombed-out buildings and pillboxes left in ruins after World War II. These playgrounds did not depress me, however. When I was about eleven, I stood between a burned-out World War II bunker and a Roman pillar just a few hundred yards away. I saw the wonder of the span of more than a thousand years right before me. In the surrounding countryside, my friend Pete Majawski, a painter and spy who had worked for my father in counterintelligence, also took delight. He had learned to paint while imprisoned in a concentration camp using his own hair, mud, and a board. "Let's go hunting for deer without guns," Pete would say.

My parents were very loving and kind. No matter where we were living or traveling, I felt I was the most important person they knew. I was the center of their Universe, and I experienced life in a positive way without fear to interfere with my learning. To me, the way we all criticize and judge each other speaks volumes about the level of fear a person has experienced and embodies at any given moment. Eckhart Tolle took a different route than I did. He decided to transcend the world with its amazing panoply of sensations. A *Vancouver Sun* reporter related this about Tolle: "He had another self that transcended [his disconnectedness to the world around him and ultimately his personal suffering]. He heard an inner voice say, 'Resist nothing,' and he let go." This is not to say Tolle advocated escapism from our Present responsibilities. Rather, true self-realization is, he asserted, "to be who you are, to feel within you the good that has no opposite, the joy of Being that depends on nothing outside yourself." [62] In other words, follow your bliss.

★ ★ ★ ★ ★ ★ ★   ★ ★ ★ ★ ★ ★ ★   ★ ★ ★ ★ ★ ★ ★

Together, members of the Japanese tribe, depending no longer on authorities outside themselves, will find they have the ability to unleash incredible energies. The Great Eastern Japan Earthquake Disaster will affect Japan's fabric in its entirety over the next several decades.

Mayan astrology, in the form of the calendar I previously discussed, expressed in mythological parables that humankind would be coming to the end of the last major astrological cycle. "The first shall be last, and the last shall be first," Jesus said. When a cycle of life ends, it begins, and as it begins, it ends. This concept is also symbolized in the Bible by the first and last letters of the Greek alphabet (Alpha "A" and Omega "Ω").

Such comprehensive terms can lead one to think there must be an infinite number of possible outcomes during the Age of Light. Amid all those thoroughly rationalized expectations, what's left—what is actually going to happen—will come as a complete surprise. Language truly can limit the thinking and imagining process! One thing is sure: We will have to wait, see, be, and listen as the Universe speaks. But will anyone be listening?

---

62 Ibid.

One other thing is certain: the world will not be destroyed during the New Age to come. However, it will not be business as usual; spiritual growth around the world will accelerate, which will change the world as it is. And being aware and Present, we will begin to responsibly heal our environment.

★ ★ ★ ★ ★ ★ ★   ★ ★ ★ ★ ★ ★ ★   ★ ★ ★ ★ ★ ★ ★

The United States, China and Japan are going to continue to be major players in the world economy to come. Their economic interactions will significantly influence sociopolitical events worldwide as the Age of Light unfolds. Based on my astrological calculations, I contend humankind will evolve as a result of meeting these challenges.

One thing I would like to point out: as a result of my astrological analysis of the current circumstances, I see Japan and the rest of the world must deal with the Chinese creation of a new kind of capitalistic economic model based on state control that can threaten, in unforeseen ways, the loosely regulated free-market capitalism of Western economies. The so-called free-market system has, at this point in time, caused the worst damage—known as the Great Recession—to the world economy since the Great Depression. And, there is more uncertainty to come.

In the United States, most of the government regulations put in place after the Great Depression to limit greed and speculation were gutted in the decade or so prior to 2008. Currently, China has an unfair advantage because its government regulates and protects from foreign competitors its capitalist enterprises. A small, elite group is now steering the Chinese economic ship into exploring a new economic relationship with the West, a relationship based on exploitation of Western countries' free-market economies. Because the Chinese economic growth engine has been kept relatively free of foreign competition, many Western countries, especially the United States, have amassed huge debt now held by the Chinese.

In 2015, the US Census Bureau estimated 136.9 million people in China were over the age of 65.[63] This surge in an older Chinese population is going to have a tremendous impact on China's economy and the internal social structure in a way that country has never before seen. Its budget will have to change to accommodate the rising costs of medical care, nursing homes, pensions, and many more unprecedented expenses. As a consequence, China will vastly increase the exploitative power of its economy around the world to compensate.

Another problem facing both China and India is vastly increasing urban populations. A press release by the United Nations states that revision, to be completed in 2014, of World Urbanization Prospects by the UN Population Division of the Department of Economic and Social Affairs projects that by 2050 urbanization will contribute to world population growth by a possible 2.5 billion more.[64] Countries largely contributing to this are India, China, and Nigeria, accounting for 37 percent contribution to this number col-

---

63 Holodny, Elena. "This is a Pretty Worrying Chart for China's Demographic Future." *Business Insider*, 16 May 2016, http://www.businessinsider.com/china-working-age-population-already-shrinking-2016-5

64 "Press Release." *United Nations*, Department of Public Information, 10 July, New York, https://esa.un.org/unpd/wup/Publications/Files/WUP2014-PressRelease.pdf

lectively.⁶⁵ This statistic alone speaks urgently to the increased chance of global tragedies occurring on the scale of the Great Eastern Japan Earthquake Disaster. Nature, with its inherent intelligence and for its own protection, is going to react with violent weather and geological upheavals to counter the devastation the exploitative demands emerging countries and an increasing world population will force upon ever-increasing fragile planetary ecosystems. Water—the availability of and access to this precious resource—will comprise the epicenter of a looming tragedy I can see is on its way. Essentially, water will be the new oil. Right now, many corporations are jockeying to own as many of the water rights as can be bought all over the world.

Along with water, another critical problem people around the world must grapple with will involve freedom of speech. Today it is nearly impossible for any country to try to impose control over free speech. Such suppressive efforts cannot succeed because, like water, human expression is essential to survival. Recently, The *New York Times* reported a, "Chinese woman was sentenced to one year in a labor camp... after she forwarded a satirical microblog message that urged recipients to attack the Japanese Pavilion at the Shanghai World Expo." ⁶⁶

And yet when one blog is shut down or Google access denied, ordinary people will still find a way to express their dreams, hopes, and fears. Spirit is something no one can destroy.

Clearly, the Chinese governing elite (is or are) going to have a difficult time as we move into this new era in which awareness is widened, opened, and accentuated. And, it would be wise for the Japanese and other governments to be firm with China on all political fronts and seek independence whenever possible. This lessening of China's exportable financial power will be due to the growing number of consumers it has to deal with domestically. A major crisis is looming as the Chinese population grows beyond the government's ability to control it as strictly as in the past. China will need an estimated 776 million or more tons of grain by 2030.⁶⁷ The crisis for China is tied to the affluent nature of societies that demand more and create an abundance of waste.

As far as large-scale movement from an exploitative business model to sustainability goes, if a rational response is not forthcoming, major natural disasters are going to await the Chinese public.

Unsustainable expansion of the Chinese economy will, in turn, impact Japan and other nations in ways we don't yet understand. I see natural upheavals, including droughts, out-of-control fires, and more earthquakes on the horizon during the next decade. Such cataclysmic changes await China if it continues on its present exploitative path. Concurrently, the role Japan plays in its evolving relationship with China will be of critical importance in determining the shape of Japan's future.

---

65 Andrew Jacobs, "Chinese Woman Imprisoned for Twitter Message," The *New York Times*, November 18, 2010.
66 Andrew Jacobs, "Chinese Woman Imprisoned for Twitter Message," The *New York Times*, November 18, 2010.
67 Long, Guoqiang. "Will China Liberlize Its Grain Trade?" *Brookings Institution*, 1 November 1999, https://www.brookings.edu/research/will-china-liberalize-its-grain-trade/

Chapter 2 The Four Directions of Light

Scientists and policymakers in the United States, China, and Japan, the world's leading economic powers and producers of carbon-dioxide emissions, become aware of and concerned about finding solutions to the problems global warming (climate change) is bringing to the world's ecosystem now. In 2010, a temperature of 129° Fahrenheit (53.7° Celsius) broke records in a Pakistani town. That is the fourth-highest temperature ever recorded in that area. More generally, meteorological data collected around the world indicates 2010 was one of the hottest years since recordkeeping began 139 years ago.[68] In 2016, the world has seen records broken, as NASA confirms the warmest surface temperatures and Arctic sea ice melt.[69]

Japan, too, will suffer hotter weather. It will be wise for Japan to prepare for this eventuality by making sound, rational decisions regarding energy generation and consumption. If, despite the Fukushima Daiichi nuclear disaster, Japan continues to build nuclear plants, the government must somehow convince the people of Japan that what happened in 2011 will never happen again. Yet even persuasive rhetoric cannot solve the problem of living on the Ring of Fire, home to earthquakes and volcanoes of the Pacific where the tectonic plates are constantly shifting with undoubtedly more earthquakes on the horizon. Japan currently has few other options for generating its own energy domestically. In a classic instance of misguided short-term thinking, lobbyists promoted nuclear power as capable of lowering Japan's carbon footprint compared with dirtier sources such as coal. These public-relations manipulators failed to mention the consequences of an out-of-control nuclear accident, after which an unimaginable number of Japanese people could perish. Building nuclear plants on geological fault lines that have already spawned earthquakes is not adaptive, in the Darwinian sense, to the Age of Light to come.

New means of energy generation must and will be discovered as Japan evolves along the Aquarian path to become a Light unto the whole world. Here, the choice between the darkness of a nuclear winter and the blessings of the Age of Light could not be clearer. Japan has the opportunity to become an example of how the rest of the world can live in harmony with love, compassion and forgiveness as a way of life. Japan has the opportunity to return to its Zen-ability to live in harmony with nature. Perhaps, Japan solves it energy problem by creating a technology able to access the ring of fire with its infinite source of energy that Japan straddles.

---

68 Vidal, John and Declan Walsh. "Temperatures Reach record High in Pakistan." *The Guardian*, 1 June 2010, https://www.theguardian.com/world/2010/jun/01/pakistan-record-temperatures-heatwave

69 "2016 Climate Trends Continue to Break Records." *NASA*, 19 July 2016, https://www.nasa.gov/feature/goddard/2016/climate-trends-continue-to-break-records

The problem then is: Is it possible for a mind that has been so conditioned – brought up in innumerable sects, religions, and all the superstitions, fears - to break away from itself and thereby bring about a new mind? The old mind is essentially the mind that is bound by authority. I am not using the word authority in the legalistic sense; but by that word I mean authority as tradition, authority as knowledge, authority as experience, authority as the means of finding security and remaining that security, outwardly or inwardly, because, after all, that is what the mind is always seeking – a place where it can be secure, undisturbed. Such authority may be the self-imposed authority of an idea or the so-called religious idea of God, which has no reality to a religious person. An idea is not a fact, it is a fiction. God is a fiction; you may believe in it, but still it is a fiction. But to find God you must completely destroy the fiction, because the old mind is the mind that is frightened, is ambitious, is fearful of death, of living, and of relationship; and it is always consciously or unconsciously, seeking a permanency, security.

~ Krishnamurti, J. Krishnamurti, The Book of Life

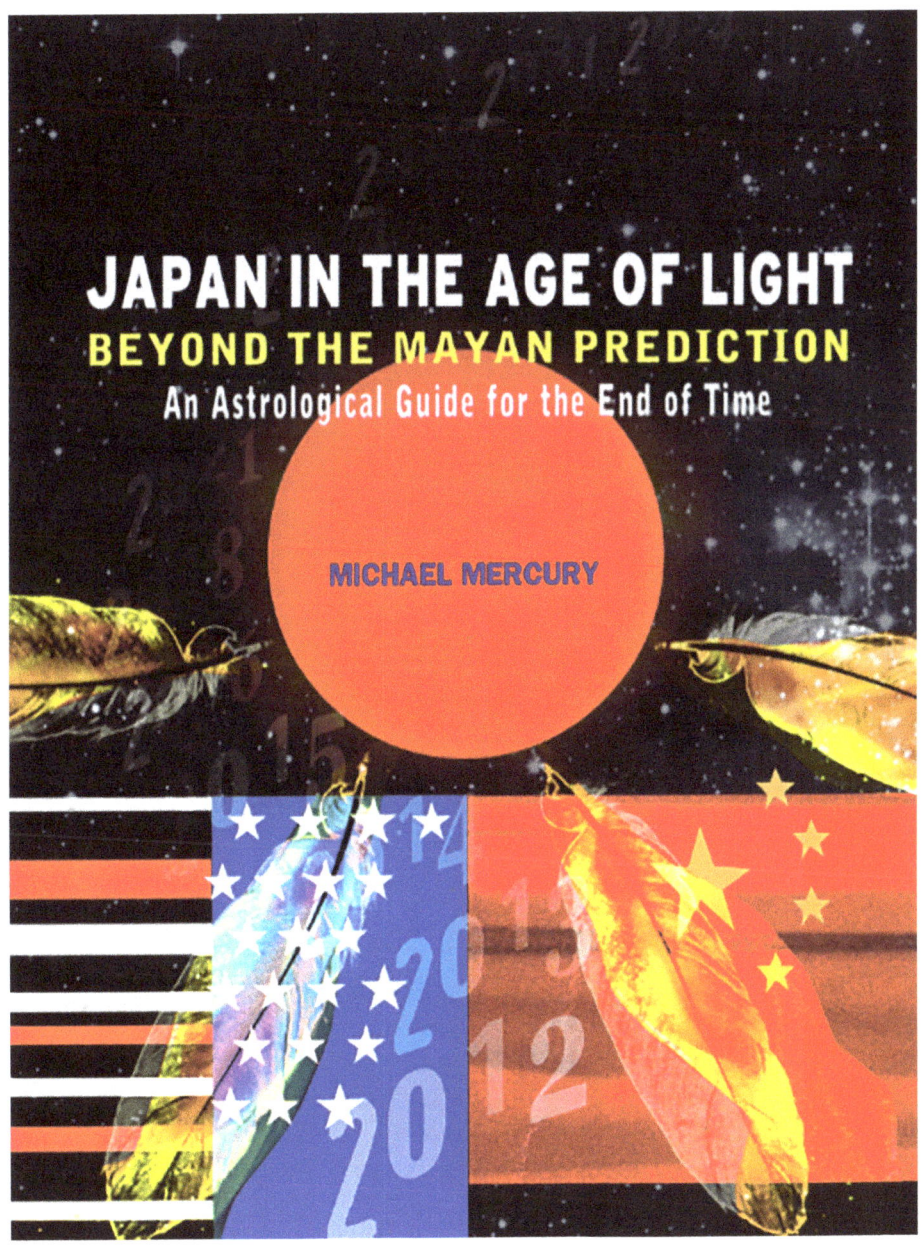

Chapter 3

Awareness

Heaven or Hell?

The I Ching: Universal Wisdom for the Age of Light

Change, Constantly Arriving

As Above, So Below

Heaven or Hell?

We created the concept of God every time we gaze into the mystery of our existence on Earth, living between heaven and hell, the macro and the micro, a mirror reflection of an imploding and exploding Universe. In John Lennon's words:

> Imagine there's no heaven,
> it's easy if you try, no hell below us,
> above us only sky,
> imagine all the people living for today.

Living for today is living in the Present. We are participants in life as expressions of the unknown, and we can save the planet if we learn to let go of our ignorance. As stewards of the planet, we are destroying our very existence through a life based on consumerism. Mother Earth has no choice but to eliminate our hellion approach. It's not too late to change our ways.

Any livingkind is a singular temporal experience of the center of the Universe, from that point of view, any point anywhere!

I propose the idea of mathematics (algebra, geometry, calculus, and logic) is another form of consciousness. Mathematics and physics are languages which can explain the Universe, and it will be recognized as a form of consciousness as a language for the Present. The Present is evidence of God!

Humanity has always included visionaries and saints who declare humankind, as a whole, wants peace. Most humans say they agree with this idea, but people have been killing each other for tens of thousands of years and for many incredibly stupid reasons, reasons predicated primarily on fear. When are we going to stop killing one another? When are we going to stop the insults, injury, and rape of our women and men and children?

★ ★ ★ ★ ★ ★   ★ ★ ★ ★ ★ ★   ★ ★ ★ ★ ★ ★

As human beings put aside their savagery and begin to awake as the first spark of liquid stardust lifts the veil for the Age of Light, together you and I will be born again. We will learn from the past and live in the Present as we view the future and past as Present. We're examining how we are going to influence the world, something the Mayans predicted centuries ago. We can, therefore, also considered inevitable relationships of the United States, China, and Japan according to factors related to the Mayan Prediction.

China's continuing rhetoric against Japan concerning disputed islands in the South China Sea could be a step toward Hell on Earth if war were to break out between these two nations. As reported recently in The Atlantic, "[A]s China becomes more powerful militarily, its capabilities and interests will necessarily shift, and countries like the United States and Japan will have to adjust. Rather than being a discrete event that can be resolved through negotiation and diplomacy, the current trends suggest the Sino-Japanese crisis over the Senkaku-Diaoyu Islands will merely be the prelude to larger conflicts down the road."[70] I examine these kinds of complex issues between Japan and China more thoroughly later in the book.

We are entering the throes of the end of time itself. After Japan overcomes the trials and tests of its national character, including the Great Eastern Japan Earthquake Disaster and the pending crisis with China, the Japanese tribe will be the first people on the planet to live as examples of the peaceful and nurturing Culture of Light. The Japanese government and people will acknowledge and demonstrate real remorse for the horrific and evil acts perpetrated during World War II.

As they venture into the Age of Light, the Japanese tribe will represent ways to live beyond time. Consider the fact Japan is the only country in the world to have experienced a catastrophe on the scale of the Great Eastern Japan Earthquake Disaster with not one case of looting reported anywhere in its geographic territory. In most any other country so afflicted, thievery would have been out of control. Also consider as a facet of Japan's uniqueness, the country experiences less than 1 murder per 100,000 people. This makes

---

[70] Matt Schiavenza, "How a Tiny Island Chain Explains the China-Japan Dispute," The Atlantic, December 4, 2013, http://www.theatlantic.com/china/archive/2013/12/how-a-tiny-island-chain-explains-the-china-japan-dispute/281995/.

it one the lowest crime rate countries in the world! If we compare Japan's number to the United States, it jumps to 4.8 per 100,000.[71]

These statistics help illuminate Japan's role as a beacon to the world. As Japan evolves toward the Light, its people will build on this solid foundation and work on the areas in its character and culture that can and should be strengthened. By mid-century, I see the Japanese making a significant change in their innate character, transforming into a family of conscious individuals who live lives of service; forgiveness as the essence of love. Strength is not abandoned with love and awareness; on the contrary, there is no more powerful force than Love. This may be true, and yet we may want to be open to finding out there may be more going on with love than we think or understand! This maxim may seem naïve, but beware those who have forgotten they, too, were once children.

The Japanese people have demonstrated grace under pressure, discipline, self-sacrifice and concern for others in responding to the Great Eastern Japan Earthquake Disaster. No other country in the world could have recovered as compassionately and efficiently from such terrible devastation. There have been significant mistakes made by the government and private industry that led to the disaster at Fukushima Daiichi nuclear plant. And yet in their recovery, the people of Japan are teaching the world about courage and discipline and how to avoid useless panic in a crisis. Such lessons are critical, especially since it could take more than 40 to 60 years for the Japanese to totally recover from the 2011 earthquake due to delays and problems along the way.

Because of the organization of Japanese society and the values associated with that society, the Japanese people have the potential to play an important role in either healing the planet or participating in its destruction. As with individuals, so it goes with tribes and nations: We make choices every day that influence the direction life will take. Living in this era of transition, the Japanese tribe and the rest of the world have spiritual work to do to help balance the planet's energies with appreciation and love. Japan can lead the world in taking advantage of the opportunity the Mayans and Hopi foretold by becoming responsible stewards of the earth. Working to preserve clean water, we as a planet will extract millions of tons of plastic and garbage from the oceans.

★ ★ ★ ★ ★ ★ ★   ★ ★ ★ ★ ★ ★ ★   ★ ★ ★ ★ ★ ★ ★

Historian and anthropologist, Carlos Barrios, intensively investigated present-day Mayan culture, as well as historic and mythological Mayan culture. The website sacredroad.org, a platform for Saq' Be', Organization for Mayan and Indigenous Spiritual Studies, writes of him, "after studying with traditional elders for 25 years since the age of 19, he...[became] a Mayan Ajq'ij, a ceremonial priest and spiritual guide [of the] Eagle Clan."[72] Based on his experience and knowledge, Barrios pointed out occurrences on December 21, 2012 would comprise an important pivotal moment along humanity's evolutionary path for each individual.[73] As we enter the new era, the paradigm of "living locally" truly will simultaneously equate to "living globally."

---

71 Engel, Pamela. "How Japan's Murder Rate Got to Be So Incredibly Low." *Business Insider*, 11 April 2014.
72 Barrios, Carlos. "Steep Uphill Climb to 2012." *Sacredroad.org*, 22 August 2003. See: McFadden, Steven. "Messages From the Mayan Milieu" copyright 2002.

We can no longer live as we have in the past. But to live an awakened life, a new paradigm is needed.

Those who become conscious will soon see how essential it will be to rearrange economic and spiritual priorities and take care of the planet first. Otherwise, we will lose this precious gift called life. There is much work to be done. Really, though, all that is necessary is for each individual to allow awakening to take place and be open to participating in creating a healthy, happy planet, which will occur through acceptance of the reality that humans, and only humans, can make the difference. We have created evil on earth, and we can change the harmful lifestyles destroying the planet.

Through their 2012 Prediction, the Mayans offered to teach us how to change our ways. It is now time to live by the practical ideals exemplified by Christ when he ordained, "Love thy neighbor as thyself." Such a simple, harmonious directive has been so very difficult for human beings to put into action. But we must try to love our planet as ourselves if Earth and humanity are to survive. The first step is to love ourselves. Only then can we truly give and receive from others and heal planet Earth.

Life as we know it is the greatest gift. But nothing is permanent, and our lives too shall pass. How long will living kind remain on this Earth? When people understand the nature and powerful effects of belief, they will stop believing and start seeing life as it is, not as they wish it to be. They will love life the way one can. Don't get me wrong—belief is one of the most powerful means humankind has within its consciousness. However, it seems people don't turn to belief to save the world and themselves; instead, they have too often used belief to enslave, demean, and destroy each other and nature.

I respect and admire those who strive to live according to any belief system, no matter how that system is organized. Instead of abstract concepts of belief, cooperate with each other and let us rejuvenate the Earth; it's a robust and effective way of expressing the essence of God.

Just because you believe something, it does not follow that something is absolutely true. If you can think of something specifically to believe in, then that belief is more than likely not true. It has been said that, "life is beyond comprehension,"[73] which is all the more reason to see creation for what it is! I know the world would be better off instead of believing; just love. Instead of worshiping God and serving our ignorance; serve your fellow human and the planet. I think if your concept of God exists, then serving your fellow human would please God rather than worshiping what can't be understood.

> *"All happiness or unhappiness solely depends upon the quality of the object to which we are attached by Love."*
> ~ Baruch Spinoza

---

[73] Friedrich Dürrenmatt is largely quoted as saying "Human life is beyond comprehension."
www.MichaelMercury.com

When Rabbi Herbert Goldstein of the International Synagogue in New York sent Einstein a cablegram bluntly asking, "Do you believe in God?" Einstein replied, "I believe in Spinoza's God who reveals Himself in the orderly harmony of what exists, not in a God who concerns himself with the fates and actions of human beings."[74] In the Age of Light, humanity will mature by way of our evolving consciousness and let go of destructive beliefs (all of them—religious, political, and financial—no exceptions). These beliefs are killing and enslaving people in the name of a transcendent, detached God. Here is one of the lessons preserved for centuries in the Mayan Prediction for our use today: Pay attention and embrace the universe for what it actually is. Years ago during a dark place in my life, a line from an untitled poem I found in a barn attic helped me peer from my darkness and see love from a new position: "To give attention is the simplest act of love."

Jesus Christ and the Buddha are still showing us their love and leading the way for all of us as we enter an Illuminating Age. Let's give attention to each other and Mother Earth and all her creatures.

★ ★

> *No more self-defeating device could be discovered than the one society has developed in dealing with the criminal. It proclaims his career in such loud and dramatic forms that both he and the community accept the judgment as a fixed description. He becomes conscious of himself as a criminal, and the community expects him to live up to his reputation, and will not credit him if he does not live up to it.*
> ~ Frank Tannenbaum[75]

Might not the media be considered a metaphoric magnetic field being twisted by upheavals from below, from the collective consciousness of the community? Clearly, the expectations the community has of criminals tear at the fabric of society, making these expectations a dark obstacle to the coming of the Light.

Spectator/voyeur and criminal/terrorist—perhaps it is time to consciously shift the paradigm from passivity and vicariously living through others (criminals, celebrities, for example) to taking charge of our own survival and destinies. Humankind has to grow up and lovingly take charge, or we will go the way of the dinosaur. We shall adapt to what we have created or we shall perish. Children who grow up with anti-social behavior demonstrate our tribe or society has failed that child and/or person. It is the parents of today who are responsible for the parents of the future.

Everyone is interconnected. Many cultures in ancient times were destroyed by horrific upheavals. We are now entering a period in history in which we and the exploitative culture we created are in the unique position of actually being able to destroy life-supporting ecosystems. I predict people around the planet are going to experience a direct change in their perceptions in the coming years, which is why it is so important for us to

---

74 As quoted and discussed in Victor J. Stenger, *Has Science Found God? The Latest Results in the Search for Purpose in the Universe*, Prometheus Books, 2003.
75 Frank Tannenbaum, Crime and the Community, Columbia University Press, 1963.

learn to live the most mentally proactive and physically healthy, sustainable lifestyle we possibly can.

Since March 11, 2011, the Japanese have been pioneers in these areas. As shown by the resilience and adaptability of their culture to the horrific events of the Great Eastern Japan Earthquake Disaster, they are acting as role models for people around the planet as change in our world accelerates. The Japanese are beginning a major psychological and cultural overhaul in regard to their perceptions about their government, which they have traditionally accepted without question. Now the Japanese tribe is beginning to ask questions about the past, present, and future as they are awakened.

✶ ✶ ✶ ✶ ✶ ✶ ✶   ✶ ✶ ✶ ✶ ✶ ✶ ✶   ✶ ✶ ✶ ✶ ✶ ✶ ✶

The I Ching: Universal Wisdom for the Age of Light

The *I Ching*, or *Book of Changes*, is one of the most important practical presentations of wisdom humans have ever gleaned from the processes of nature and revealed to humankind through the ages. The authorship of the *I Ching* is commonly attributed to Fu Hsi, a legendary Chinese Emperor who flourished in the third millennium B.C. Later, Emperor Wen, founder of the Chou Dynasty (1150-249 B.C.), wrote essays on the meanings of the 64 hexagrams. Over the following millennia, it is believed Confucius and many others subsequently contributed to the *I Ching*. Information contained in this work has been earnestly gleaned from observations of nature and revealed to humankind throughout the ages.

While the age of the *I Ching* is debatable, its practical application is not. People persist in consulting the *I Ching* because they have for centuries found its information to be universally relevant and useful.

The *I Ching* reveals the cosmos from a highly spiritual and contemplative point of reference. This unique work is premised upon a relationship between its content and various aspects of the consciousness of the people who consult it. The content consists of sixty-four chapters, each of which is devoted to commentary on visual configurations called "Hexagrams." These hexagrams include broken lines and whole lines, also known as "Moving" and "Non-Moving" lines. The combination of lines within an individual hexagram indicates change. The individual seeking wisdom consults the hexagrams in various ways by throwing yarrow sticks and picking up the stalks or, more commonly, tossing coins. In this way, as author R. L. Wing explains, the ritual of stopping time is used like the shutter of a camera, "in order to capture a picture of the moment and examine in detail its meaning."[76] Wing further notes this ritual of stopping time (or "change") with a particular question in mind is, "a way of aligning your Self and your circumstances within the background of all that is unfolding in the Universe and...in the process, discovering this intricate and perplexing world to be something that you have intimately understood all along."[77]

✶ ✶ ✶ ✶ ✶ ✶ ✶   ✶ ✶ ✶ ✶ ✶ ✶ ✶   ✶ ✶ ✶ ✶ ✶ ✶ ✶

---

76 R.L. Wing, *The I Ching Workbook*, Doubleday and Company, 1978 [hereinafter: *Wing, I Ching Workbook*].
77 Ibid.

As I prepared my astrological analysis and interpretation for the United States, China, and Japan, I began to wonder what this ancient text would reveal for the December 21, 2012 period and beyond. I asked the *I Ching's* advice regarding the Mayan Predication for 2012 and how that prediction relates to forces shaping our world as we encounter **"the end of time, not the end of the world."**

My thinking was shaped by R. L. Wing's wonderful *I Ching Workbook* and by another work, *The I Ching, The Book of Changes*.[78] I have worked for more than forty years with various English translations of the *I Ching*. Here is what the *I Ching* imparted to me regarding the period of the Mayan Prediction for the year 2012 and beyond:

Hexagram 46, Advancement (pushing upward) without any moving lines. (Sheng)

"The upper trigram K'UN, responsiveness, forms a receptive atmosphere for the fruition of SUN, small, steady efforts, below. Without changing lines, ADVANCEMENT *will occur only with a diligent and long-term approach toward the object of your inquiry. You cannot expect to make a giant leap toward your objective through a single sweeping gesture. Instead, through modest, industrious efforts, you must build a substantial base upon which you may then reach your aim."*[79] In Hexagram 46 (referred to as SHENG), R. L. Wing's translation, I found this phrase: "As it so appropriately states in the Bible about times like these, 'The lines are fallen unto me in pleasant places, yea I have a goodly heritage.'"[80]

I think Hexagram 46, named Advancement (pushing upward), is significant because, although it literally speaks to personal power and how persistence can overcome adversity, it also encompasses the esteem and respect the world holds for Japan. "[T]hrough modest, industrious efforts, you must build a substantial base upon which you may then reach your aim."[81]

This portion of Hexagram 46 speaks to the recovery efforts underway to repair the damage caused by the Great Eastern Japan Earthquake Disaster. From clearing debris to rebuilding bridges to containing radiation emitted by the Fukushima reactor meltdowns, each step back to normal builds "a substantial base." The result will not be grand new monuments but instead an energy-sustainable tribe leading the way. Yes, Japan is by no means perfect nor will it ever be. Much is learned for the rest of the world by the way the Japanese adapt to surviving their own darkness, that brings the Age of Light.

Japan can become a practical role model for people seeking sustainable survival strategies with its handling of one of the greatest catastrophes of modern times. Not since World

---

78 *The I Ching, The Book of Changes*, Wilhelm/Baynes, Princeton University Press, 1967.
79 Wing, *I Ching Workbook Hexagram 46*, citod at noto 87.
80 Ibid.
81 Ibid.

War II has Japan been placed in such a vulnerable and precarious position. Japan learns humility, which comes at a great price, and the reward is priceless. The Japanese people have experienced more death and destruction from nuclear bombs, and now a nuclear power plant accident.

Hexagram 46 speaks to the coming success—which becomes tremendous in scope—of the Japanese people in overcoming disasters. As Japan moves forward into the Age of Light, her people should vigilantly avoid slipping into muddled thinking or losing sight of the ultimate objective, which is to sustainably survive and thrive.

As with war, so it is with recovery efforts and regaining national footing in the midst of massively changing circumstances. All the more reason for Japan to "*through modest, industrious efforts … build a substantial base.*" Flexibility and cooperation in applying these efforts and keeping an open mind as to specific objectives to meet in surviving as a nation will be key. In the Age of Light, each individual Japanese citizen will look within and take responsibility. No longer can individuals rely on authority figures to do all their thinking for them. This responsibility applies to all of us.

Instead of worrying or stressing *about* your life, consider being joyful, loving, kind and blissful *in* your life. In biblical terms, we could say this catastrophe couldn't have come to a better people at a better time to teach humankind the best lessons, through example, of being human. **The females of the world must (and will) stand up and take their rightful place in equal power for guiding the world forward.** Only with all the voices of female and male and all the wisdom currently lying dormant tapped into may the genius of the world be effectively applied to healing and sustaining the land. Although it may be difficult to discern in the midst of overwhelming evidence seemingly to the contrary, everything will happen in our best interests to aid our development and growth as the Age of Light dawns.

✦ ✦ ✦ ✦ ✦ ✦ ✦   ✦ ✦ ✦ ✦ ✦ ✦ ✦   ✦ ✦ ✦ ✦ ✦ ✦ ✦

It is, is it not, extraordinary we are here…breathing, living as conscious forms of creation and alive, blessed with all the amazing opportunities we've been given to learn and experience. It did not surprise me the world received a positive response to the question I posed to the *I Ching*: What is your wisdom for the world concerning 2012 and the Mayan Prediction?

Hexagram 46 speaks to working on and through each individual. That, I think, will come to be centered on the will of humankind. Every one of us on this planet has the opportunity to express love or ignorance—the choice is ours to make. You know what has to be done. And, as many interpretations of the *I Ching* have borne out over the centuries, good luck is created, both in achieving the immediate good and in sustaining the long-lasting strength of character and the will to seek a better world. As my mother used to say to me, "God helps those who help themselves."

As the efforts toward recovery continue, we will perceive unexpected synchronicity between the routine details of life and the changing but positive shifts in the political and economic recovery of the world. All things are interrelated. The world is one organism spinning in space, living its moment in the Sun. Lighted by the Sun, we, as spiritual beings, are deeply involved in the peculiar human condition. As we develop and follow strategies for individual and planetary survival, we are trying to understand that which we cannot even conceive fully in its true scope and configuration. The human condition is a contradiction, which is the essence of the evolutionary energy moving forward, seeking resolution.

Humankind is constantly complaining, criticizing, and judging life. Yet, nobody really wants to die. Death, the ending of strife, is the great healer. Yet, how ironic humankind often fears love and death, the greatest healing energies on the planet.

All nations discover the spiritual journey so as to forgive their family tribal members for the past evil they inflicted on themselves and in the world over centuries. Let it be stated all countries have to answer for their pasts. I am not here to point fingers at the evils that have been done in the name of righteousness. To live in the Present is to be in a state of forgiveness, which is a life of non-judgment.

We have a future world made up of people who are going to be performing a great deal of soul searching as we create a new and better world based on love, truth, forgiveness, and humility. In the midst of these efforts, some individuals will wish for assistance, perhaps on a deep and personal level. People have wonderful imaginations, capable of conjuring the most outlandish and yet plausible scenarios, like aliens coming in to save the world. However, most of the wishful thinking about such ideas as alien assistance in our time of need is based on fear, low self-esteem, and the media playing on people's fears. Encouraging speculation that aliens could care enough about us to help us is just another way for unscrupulous people to make money.

For my part, I leave room for all kinds of possibilities. Once an idea is proven to be true, then I have no problem accepting that idea. In the meantime, I don't waste time and energy on speculation. Life becomes more infinite in depth and scope when you are open to the limitlessness of the unknown, which is far beyond our limited imaginations and belief systems. I think our capacity for thinking is great, but that capacity is also limited! If we can accept our ignorance as a place to start, then ignorance turns into humility. This enables us to let go of ourselves so we can become beings who are always in the moment, regretting nothing. If the Kingdom of Heaven exists, it is now and nowhere else! I learned when we stop judging everyone and everything and accept life the way it is, then heaven reveals itself.

I know what is at this moment and nothing more! And by meditating in the Present as an act of living, being and doing, one's awareness becomes...

Change, Constantly Arriving

> *If you want security, embrace change.*
> ~ William Lilly, Elizabethan-era Christian Astrologer

So many factors are affecting the environment. Beginning March 11, 2011 the earth started to react with extreme weather, and it continues to this day. Yes, the planet *reacts because it is alive.* It is not simply a blank slate to be acted upon, conventions of exploitative philosophical and business models to the contrary.

As we do unto the earth, so we do unto ourselves.

As you read this book in the midst of going about your daily routines, the coral reefs around the world are dying, which affects tens of thousands of species of fish, mammals, bees, frogs, along with entire ecosystems. This death of the coral reefs, which anchor thousands of micro-ecosystems, signals the beginning of the end of a way of life based on exploitation. Will we change our current survival strategy based on eradication of other species, or do we find it within ourselves to participate in, rather than destroy, our ecosystems?

It's just a matter of when: We survive or go the way of the dinosaur.

We may want to consider changing our perspectives and value systems, so we can preserve whatever pristine environments remain and restore much of what we have almost destroyed. If governments want to spur the economies of the world, an essential starting point would be investment in cleaning up the water, land and air. The profit in these endeavors may not build up bank accounts quite as quickly as in extracting resources from the planet, but these endeavors will nonetheless build up the ecosystems sustaining the planet and allow it and us to survive.

Such actions can be the saving grace that allows humankind to live with dignity in a world sustained for a healthier future for generations to come. To evolve past exploitative lifestyles and survive, we must discover the ultimate energy source, which is love, and seek it out in nature. Nature will provide the energy we seek. The vibrational shift that is occurring is preparing the way for us to use the Sun's energy, an endlessly replenished energy that can sustain the world in the Age of Light.

I observe life as a scientist aware of the nature of relativity, and I live like an artist, Present and spontaneous! I discovered this way of life through a lifetime of deep awareness of the cosmic and natural forces that, in many interesting and unexpected ways, influence and shape everyday reality. Energy forces are a transparent Present, as a reflective experience, imploding and exploding in infinite levels, directions and dimensions traveling from where it came, traveling at the speed of Space, the only frontier.

There is a Cosmic Ocean of Light which permeates all livingkind, and nothing or any species is going to change creation. We are creation, a brief candle of Light speeding, flowing in the stillness.

As Above, So Below

I think the first indication of the Age of Light was Einstein's revelation of the Theory of Relativity. I took note the seeding—perhaps the conception and first sign—of the Age of Light.

Unfortunately, along with that seeding and the receding of the Age of Pisces, there is going to be a great deal of violence in the world, as is the case with all births and endings. Economic turmoil is also an inevitable part of the changing of the Ages. The environment is clearly going to be the major priority for several generations to come. Natural disasters will be commonplace like never before: extreme weather, earthquakes, tsunamis, floods, landslides, volcanoes, droughts, wildfires and typhoons of unprecedented magnitude.

Sudden and powerful expressions of nature are going to occur as a form of cleaning up the mess we have created with our garbage, the byproducts of an exploitative business model. Global climate change has arrived—which speaks to the delicate health of the atmosphere and its vulnerability to sunspot radiation. Changes in how humankind interacts with the planet and its ecosystems will become necessary if we are to survive.

There is always resistance to change in political circles and among business communities. However, in my research I have many times been pleasantly surprised to discover instances when, after humankind creates a terrible crisis, individual characters rise to the occasion—out of the blue, as it were—and express a timely genius to solve the problems the mass of humanity has created.

Astrologically speaking, transits signify change. In April 2010, the planet began to experience the early stages of a rare and transformative transit, Uranus Square Pluto. Even though there was 7° to 8° of separation in April 2010, the early stages of this unique square grew closer to its exact 90° on June 8, 2012. Even a separation of 8° was starting to influence the planet.

The 2010 BP oil spill in the Gulf of Mexico pumped crude oil for eighty-seven days. It turned out to be the largest oil spill in the United States.[82] This disaster speaks to the unusual square between Uranus and Pluto, which was expressed on Earth. Pluto represents the dying of the old world in which oil has been a main source of energy. At the same time, Uranus, especially in Aries, representing scientific discoveries, ushers in a new dynamic whereby energy can be used for the betterment of humankind without such side effects as pollution.

On April 20, 2010, Uranus was at 28° Pisces, Neptune was at 28° Aquarius, Jupiter was at 21° Pisces, Mars was at 8° Leo, Pluto was at 5° retrograde and Saturn was at 29° retro- grade. (Refer to chart on the next page). Around May 28, 2010, Pluto in Capricorn Square to Uranus in Aries spoke to the idea of significant change in the status quo by means of peaceful protest or violence and revolution. The end of the Gaddafi regime in Libya is another example of "out with the old and in with the flowering." As we have seen with the Arab Spring, Uranus awakens the world and brings forth an urge to take risks, while Pluto speaks to the difficulties of transformation by way of revolution, which brings death, destruction and displacement of tens of millions of people from their homes.

---

[82] "Gulf Oil Spill." *Smithsonian Ocean Portal.* ocean.si.edu/gulf-oil-spill

Chapter 3 Awareness

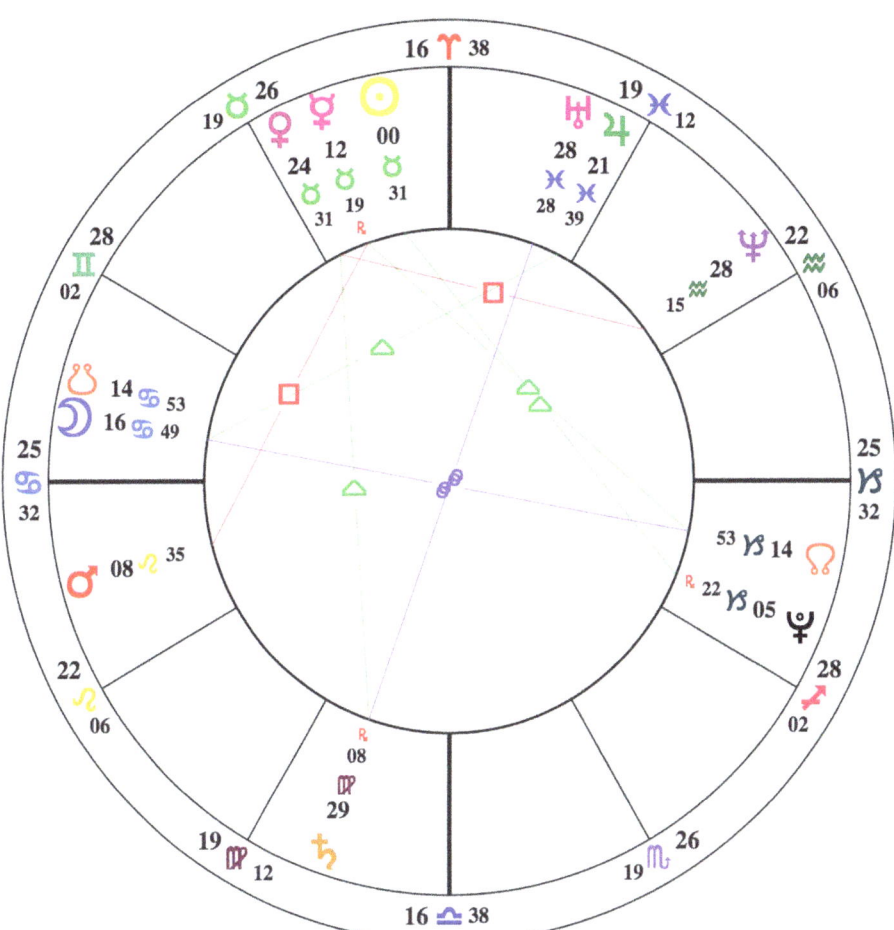

Uranus in Aries was square to Pluto in Capricorn when the Great Eastern Japan Earthquake Disaster wreaked havoc in that country. As an astrologer, I use a wider degree span between the outer planets when it comes to major aspects in regards to their effect on our planet. As Richard Tarnas stated in his extraordinary book *Cosmos and Psyche*, "[A]lignments of the ongoing Uranus-Pluto cycle coincided with comparable historical periods of epochal revolutionary upheaval, social liberation, and radical cultural change in each century...."[83]

83 Tarnas, Richard. *Cosmos and Psyche*. Viking Penguin, 2006.

On March 12, 2011 at 9:53 a.m. (Japan Standard Time), Uranus entered Aries, and Saturn was at 15° Libra. I contend when a large planet moves from one astrological sign to another, there is always a major shift somewhere on the Earth—what I call "an 'air-quake.'" In this case, this major shift took place in Japan, and according to NASA, this shift affected the world axis by shortening the length of the day by about 1.8 microseconds.[84]

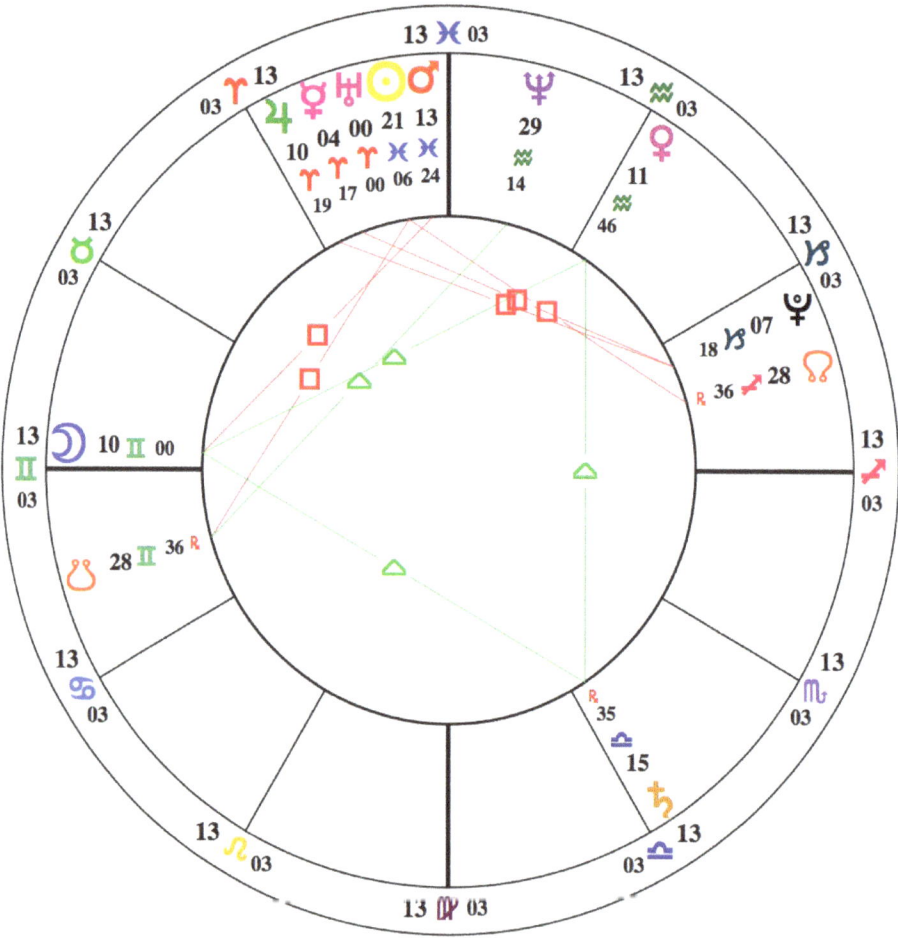

84 Buis, Alan. "Japan Quake May Have Shortened Earth Days, Moved Axis." *NASA*, www.nasa.gov/topics/earth/features/japanquake/earth20110314.html

Chapter 3 Awareness

I will present a chart and discuss the relationship among the United States, China, and Japan later in the book. For now, I will just point out Pluto entering Capricorn speaks to a new perceptive, practical people being in positions of power, recognizing the need for change to take place and making choices that lead to a shift in circumstances promoting the Age of Light. **Pluto represents the potential for the dawning of a political era that will demand new approaches and real change.**

Powerful changes in the United States, China, and Japan will parallel a cosmic shift occurring during the early stages of the seeding of the Age of Light. This Uranus and Pluto dynamic is similar to the release of energy in so many directions that we experienced in the 1960s, which brought about many revolutionary changes. During that tumultuous decade, people felt the electrifying air of change in their lives.

The United States and China may be the largest economies in the world, but Japan demonstrates in the years to come how to live in harmony with nature. The 2011 earthquake in Japan was the beginning of the reawakening of the Japanese tribe.

We are going to sense a change equally as electrifying, a change that will awaken people all over the world during the next eight years. In January 2024, Pluto will enter Aquarius. Another 'air-quake' is manifest in 2020-2024. This is the first time the United States will experience its first Pluto return dating to the founding of the nation in 1776. I go further into this later in the book. Astrologically, it appears it will be an intense time for change with some lulls. Similar extremes will be felt simultaneously in widely separated cultures and countries concerning every aspect known to humankind.

A number of changing conditions are going to record weather as it is currently known in locales around the planet. Global warming, simply put, stems from carbon dioxide emissions into the atmosphere. An energy crisis stemming from the "peak oil" phenomenon is going to affect everyone. International terrorism, like an outbreak of disease, is going to continue to create chaotic overlapping waves of destruction. Crime and violence can increase as the Age of Pisces wanes. Perhaps a better name for self-destructive perpetrators of terrorism would be "mentally ill people," as those who use violence to attempt to solve problems are out of balance with the natural world. As the Age of Light dawns, new ways are found to counteract such behaviors, so people will not continue to contribute to the tumultuous negative changes taking place in nature and the human world. Eliminating poverty, ignorance, and providing healthcare, and education for everyone on the planet is a good place to start.

As I watch the astrological portents unfold, I must warn that extremists' acts will have profound ramifications. When strong astrological positions of larger planets are set off by a planet like Mars in Aries, the effects can be quite dynamic. Furthermore, in September 2015, Chile experienced natural disasters including colossal earthquakes.[85] A series of full SuperMoons from August 29 to October of 2015 is an example of how SuperMoons can bring forth major earthquakes. is in turn could spur volcanic eruptions on an epic scale.

---

85 "Central Chile Earthquake and Tsunami, September 16, 2015." *NOAA, www.ngdc.noaa.gov/hazard/16sep2015.html*

Going back to 2010, Pluto in Capricorn had been square to Uranus in Aries off and on and had demonstrated that unsettling clashes of ordinary people with authority (as we have seen in the Arab Spring) will also erupt as immigrants from poor regions flood into affluent countries. As we have witnessed in Europe due to the Syrian crisis in 2015, civil unrest, revolutions, and outbreaks of violence resulted in a tragic waste of human life and material resources. In the fall of 2013, an exact square between Pluto and Uranus occurred, and we witnessed the U.S. Congress shut down the government and needlessly manufacture distrust between the American people and those they had elected to serve.

In many instances, technology ends up creating more problems than it can solve due to the ignorance, greed, and chaos that result from shortsighted applications. We can avoid such problems if we make the right choices. It takes patience and determination to seek a new world as beneficial to all humanity as need be. We must be on the lookout for signs of the narrowing isolation of men and women as they struggle to awaken after centuries of ignorance. Politicians divide and conquer to gain personal power, but such a modus operandi will be the way of the past as harmony, cooperation, and unity lead the way to a better America and a better life on our beautiful planet.

★ ★

A right-angle square (90°) between Uranus and Pluto is rare. Whenever it appears, a new era for the world is ushered in. I have researched many historic instances of the Uranus-Pluto square. Every time it occurs, there has also been a major transition in the human sphere. The last time we witnessed this celestial occurrence was in the autumn of 1929 when the Great Depression began.

This transit is short but always powerful. It often highlights some type of impending problem with the world economy. This transit, in my estimation, will serve to remind the world's leaders we are going to have to shift from oil as our primary energy resource to more sustainable fuels. When the tipping point of "peak oil" is reached in this century or the next—and it's just a question of when—the slope on the other side will be steep, as oil reserves are exhausted and new oil fields become more difficult to access. We will solve this dilemma by choosing to fight over dwindling energy resources by changing our lifestyle to conserve and, thereby, lessen the pressure on those resources. It is imperative to develop sustainable resources or the consequences will be catastrophic. Unfortunately, the melting Arctic has Russia, China, and the United States exploring for what is estimated to be 13% of the world's untapped oil reserves.[86] Will there be an oil spill in the Arctic? Yes, and it is just a question of when.

The next crucial results of the choices we're making now will be felt by January 2072 and February 15-March 1, 2073, when Pluto in Aries at 5° will be an exact square to Uranus in Pluto at 5°. Trading planets and trading signs, it signifies the complete cycle of our current choices. We are destroying various ecosystems and inflict-

---

86 Mcalister, Terry. "The New Cold War." *The Guardian*, 16 June 2015,
   www.theguardian.com/environment/ng-interactive/2015/jun/16/drilling-oil-gas-arctic-alaska

ing great change concerning the planet if we do not change the way we are currently living by the end of this century, if not sooner. Our choices now affect the ancient-Present now.

✶ ✶ ✶ ✶ ✶ ✶ ✶   ✶ ✶ ✶ ✶ ✶ ✶ ✶   ✶ ✶ ✶ ✶ ✶ ✶ ✶

From April to July 5 of 2010, Uranus Square Pluto approached to within 3° of each other, continuing disruptive and transformational effects that will continue to unfold until 2019. The challenging and resurrecting nature of a Uranus-Pluto square approached within 1° in 2011. It became a square and continued through most of 2012 and into 2013. In 2014, December transiting Uranus-Pluto was exact with Pluto poised to enter the Second House, and transiting Mars conjunct Pluto in the U.S. Sibly chart in the Second House dealing with national wealth. I see this Pluto transit sustaining long-term financial problems for the United States for many years to come. I expand on this topic later in the book.

During this period of human existence on the planet, everyone will find it necessary to some degree to examine their internal self-image. This process is going to continue for a lifetime and many years to come as people around the world undergo the most significant tonal transformation in recorded history.

✶ ✶ ✶ ✶ ✶ ✶ ✶   ✶ ✶ ✶ ✶ ✶ ✶ ✶   ✶ ✶ ✶ ✶ ✶ ✶ ✶

Pluto rules that which has been buried underground and overlooked. The value of Uranus is to awaken and bring to light what Pluto has hidden. The Sign of Pisces, which Uranus has been transiting, rules both the ocean and oil. Uranus Square to Pluto was associated with the Katrina Disaster in the Southern United States. Eventually, Uranus Square Pluto could well change the oil-based energy generation/consumption model. We can and will have another oil or energy crisis far worse than the BP spill that devastated ecosystems in the Gulf of Mexico. It is just a question of when.

As China grows into a superpower, its population is, surely as tomorrow's sunrise, going to need greater energy with levels of consumption like the world has never seen. Could China's insatiable demands for energy be the impetus for an energy crisis the likes of which the world has never known?

No matter the criteria by which it ultimately is defined, we, the inhabitants of planet Earth, are soon going to find ourselves poised on the brink of the most important transitional moment humanity has ever had to face.

> *Life is a series of natural changes. Don't resist them. That only creates sorrow. Let reality be reality. Let things flow naturally forward in whatever way they like.*
> ~ Lao Tzu

The Uranus Square to Pluto became more aligned and culminated in 2012. Behind the *status quo* curtain of power, a race among world leaders took place to ensure energy would be available for the future. As mentioned, this transit last occurred in the early 1930s. Back then, that timeframe culminated with Otto Hahn, and Fritz Strassmann discovering nuclear fission in 1938.[87] That event changed the world forever.

The oil spill in U.S. territorial waters, along with an oil spill in China during the summer of 2010 (a well-kept secret), began a similar, potentially destructive transitional time period. We can expect more environmental disasters associated with oil in the near future. This reality speaks to the imperative need on the part of humanity and the Japanese people in particular (the only people ever to have suffered an atomic attack) for awareness that a new direction of energy production and consumption will be found.

In the summer of 2011, *The New York Times* reported a new direction for energy generation may indeed be on Japan's political horizon: "In a nation plagued by weak political leadership, it has fallen to the local governor of an obscure southern prefecture to make a crucial decision that could help determine the future of nuclear power in Japan after the Fukushima Daiichi accident. The governor, Yasushi Furukawa of Saga Prefecture, must decide in coming days whether to support a request by Prime Minister Naoto Kan to restart two reactors at a local nuclear power plant."[88]

The article goes on to say if Furukawa decided not to restart the reactors, other governors might follow, and every nuclear reactor could end up being shut down within months. This is precisely the type of change on a practical, local level that needs to take place in order for Japan to light the path for the rest of the world toward a more sustainable use of energy.

> *I feel a great responsibility has been suddenly placed upon me.*
> ~ Yassushi Furukawa[89]

Responsibility is what the coming Age of Light is going to be all about! It's about individuals stepping up where the central government and other institutions prove incapable of taking the action necessary to lessen the dangers to humanity and the planet.

"Prime Minister Kan is running away from a decision that the national government should be making," The *New York Times* quoted Governor Furukawa as saying. Meanwhile, Japan's tiny anti-nuclear movement gained credibility after the Fukushima Daiichi accident. A full 82% of people polled by the *Tokyo Shimbun* said they wanted to get rid of nuclear reactors. "Many people support us from the shadows, but they are afraid of being disliked as radicals," one anti-nuclear activist told *The New York Times*.[90]

---

87 "Otto Hahn." *Atomic Heritage Foundation*, www.atomicheritage.org/profile/otto-hahn
88 Fackler, Martin. "A Governor's Power to Shape the Future of a Nuclear Japan." *The New York Times*, July 2, 2011, www.nytimes.com/2011/07/03/world/asia/03japan.html.
89 Ibid.
90 Ibid.

And yet I am aware of the ability of Japanese individuals to search their hearts, overcome their fears and take responsibility for helping to bring about the dawning of a sane sustainable energy future as the Age of Light is ushered in. Japan can lead the way as the world's peoples struggle to find a new way of dealing with energy. It may not happen right away, but sometime in this century the nations of the world are going to have to change, because the Earth and the people of the world are going to demand change.

Though perhaps not in Japan, revolution in many countries is going to violently accelerate this process of change as we move closer to 2024. On January 21, 2024, Pluto enters Aquarius, and a new vibrational wave is ushered in. A rational process of change is possible, so long as the people make it possible.

With the combination of horrific weather patterns and the pollution of the water and Earth, humankind is faced with a new dilemma as the Age of Light dawns. Ignorance and inertia on a grand scale have led humanity to become the energy-wasting consumers we are. Humankind's actions are responsible for sending the world into a crisis mode of eco-destruction. From 2012 through 2029, there is a shift of Universal Consciousness many consider to be cosmic by nature. However, my observation is Consciousness is a biological expression of the brain and nervous system. I see the vibration of the Universe is changing and in turn it affects our biological goo, which shifts our Consciousness.

Existence exists from where we have to go, which is where we come from, which is where we are, somewhere to arrive, the Present. This is part of the next transition for the human experience. Japan has the opportunity to be Paradise on Earth, heaven as a way of life, an opportunity that manifests in small, subtle ways in Japanese daily life as part of many positive possibilities for Japan's future.

Determining the future of nuclear energy in Japan is going to have a huge effect not only on Japan but also on the world's economy. As Governor Furukawa told *The New York Times*, "It is easy to see the business groups who favor restarting the nuclear reactors, but the public unease that opposes it is shapeless."[91]

While politicians agonize over Japan's energy future and the Japanese people make their feelings known, the consensus must be found to create energy solutions that keep the manufacturing sector of the Japanese economy growing. The people of Japan, in my estimation, intuitively understand this peaceful and sustainable way of life. Each year Japan travels closer to manifesting a sustainable, harmonious daily lifestyle as the century reveals itself.

The people of Japan, the culture of Japan and the nation of Japan will be as they have been, and what they will be is what they are doing right now. Japan is the potential to be the New-Old Shangri-La of the Age of Light. As the world transitions from the Age of Pisces to the Age of Aquarius, Japan becomes a reluctant leader analogous to, if you pardon the whimsical image, Rudolph the Red-Nosed Reindeer shining through darkness to unite with the Age of Light.

---

91 Ibid.

From an astrological point of view, I see this period Japan is entering as a tremendous opportunity for a genuine breakthrough when it comes to the way in which energy is perceived and generated. In 2050, Pluto will ascend to the crown of the national chart of Japan. In this defining moment, Japan will be recognized as a country truly constituted of an enlightened culture and people—a new shining city on the hill. The rest of the world's people will be amazed at its revealed example of self-responsibility, light, warmth, and wisdom.

> *"Apart from consciousness,"* answered the Buddha, *"no absolute truths exist. False reasoning declares one view to be true and another view wrong. It is delight in their dearly held opinions that makes them assert that anyone who disagrees is bound to come to a bad end. But no true seeker becomes embroiled in all this. Pass by peacefully and go a stainless way, free from theories, lusts and dogmas."*
> ~ Majjhima Nikaya[92]

By demonstrating a caring consciousness with awareness and truth, the Japanese people will demonstrate that forgiveness, as love, is a sustainable way of living in harmony with nature. This sustainable way of life will reflect the evolution of the Japanese people as they lead humankind out of darkness by their example.

> *"TimeSpace is the Present as Creation."*
> ~ Clint Cochran, Mystic

---

[92] *The Buddha Speaks: A Book of Guidance From the Buddhist Scriptures*, edited by Anne Bancroft, Shambhala, 2000.

Chapter 3 Awareness

As Within, So Without

Chapter 4

The Age of Light

The Dawning of the Age of Aquarius

Quetzalcoatl, a Messenger from Eternity

Wake Up!

The Dawning of the Age of Aquarius

In the New Age, the individual is the key. You are Light, traveling as biological-spirit-infused-goo body, creating time as a vehicle for living Eternity with each breath. Of course, the individual has always been the key. The planet is evolving to a frequency that provides people the opportunity to experience the entirety of reality as wholeality in harmony with the universe. The Aquarian figure pouring waves from a vessel can be seen as waves of light pouring out like water—as if bringing forth ancient Present wisdom from the fabric of creation. "As above, so below. As within, so without." With the ardent zeal for advances in technology around the world, especially with the arrival of light and light in the last century, it is fitting the 20th century became known as the Space Age. Now the Dawning of the Age of Light is leading us into the Aquarian Age of Peace.

Since I'm using the word consciousness, let's look at the definition so we can agree with what we're talking about.

Simple Definition of Consciousness[93]
- the condition of being conscious
- the normal state of being awake and able to understand what is happening around you
- a person's mind and thoughts
- knowledge that is shared by a group of people

---

[93] *http://www.merriam-webster.com/dictionary/consciousness*

I think Consciousness is evidence Light is the essence of the life we create, and it is derived from the brain and heart; we are liquid stardust. We experience Light from within, corresponding with light as our external experience of light. I think our Consciousness is like the rubbing of two pieces of light together, not unlike sticks rubbing together to create fire. In this case, we are rubbing two elements of light that create Consciousness. Experiencing external light and internal Light is Consciousness, and our biological goo bodies represent the medium in which we manifest.

You are a traveling time machine speeding to stillness in Eternity. You truly are a composite of energy, the sum total of your experiences, memories and thoughts. Let us hypothesize everything in the Universe is traveling at the speed of Space and Light. You are the center of your Universe and experience. It is you, and you are it, and it is altogether your experience and the choices you, and you alone, make. You are one with an interrelatedness to the universe. A favorite thought of mine is this, "why buy anything when you can be everything? It's a lot cheaper." My yoga practice provides awareness about how we live. The Age of Light demands a new evolving consciousness that experiences God in all things and all people. As Buckminster Fuller once said, "God, to me, is a verb."

Mother Earth is awake, and the planet is starting to speak up. Our planet will teach us about humility.

Einstein's assertion that light is traveling at a constant speed will be expanded upon. We discover that light can and does change its speed when it is necessary concerning its purpose of being/doing. At present, we are limited by the instruments that detect and examine our understanding of Dark Energy and Dark Matter, which I think are examples of some form of unknown light. The study and exploration of Dark Energy and Dark Matter is the next frontier.

It was Lao-Tzu who said, "How can I become still? By flowing with the stream."

What we already know about creation is far more wondrous than any institutionalized belief or religion. Human beings are evolving, acquiring the ability to take a mature natural approach to their place in the cosmic scheme of things as we live out the true unfolding meaning of being human! Hence, the idea of being enlightened is going to be understood as the only authentic way of living. In my opinion, to be enlightened means to have conscious Present awareness, which means to be unencumbered with the past or ideologies. I don't know the source of this. I remember hearing about the following exchange. When asked what he received from meditation, the Buddha replied, "Nothing. It is what you lose and let go of that is of value." The Buddha also once said, "When you end your suffering, then you are awake."

I am not a Buddhist, a Christian, a Hindu, or a Muslim, and I don't follow the Jewish religion. I do not follow any particular religion, dogma, or philosophy. Ever since I was a child, I have been a mystic who has loved learning about the mystery of God, creation, and the gift of life. I accept I don't know, which is why life for me is both amazing and beyond comprehension. What will be will be, and until I know, I am content not to know. Death reveals the next phase of our awareness. My thinking is any belief system cannot change the nature of God. I don't believe in anything. I can't afford it, because it takes away my sense of awe and wonder! I live in the Present. This is where I experience the mystery and awesome experience of creation.

★ ★ ★ ★ ★ ★ ★   ★ ★ ★ ★ ★ ★ ★   ★ ★ ★ ★ ★ ★ ★

As we enter the Age of Light and become increasingly Present in the Present, we must become the best listeners we can be. We must listen to the rhythms of our hearts and the energies that power crowds and cultures. Rather than constantly projecting our messages, we must learn to listen as well as the Morse code experts did. Be present by listening from within, and dance with nature as you live and express your music as your spiritual experience.

Humankind has experienced instantaneous communications technology (as we know it) for only the last century and a half. The ramifications of these new technological instruments (so easily taken for granted) are, by far, the most important and radical shift in consciousness humankind has ever experienced in recorded history. All kinds of media are "extensions of the senses," as media prophet Marshall McLuhan described them and their effects.

When we acknowledge the need to listen to as well as send messages, we begin to understand how much we don't know about what creation embodies! This new awareness will give us a new perspective on ego as a false sense of self. Then we can begin to listen to and understand the secrets of the Universe that have heretofore eluded humankind because ego has gotten in the way and kept many of us in the dark. To let go of our ego, which is the false self, we discover our authentic selves—by not having a sense of self at all. Relationships, actions, and intent define us, as change is the now of the universe. We are as elusive as our dreams, and individuals who discover their authentic selves receive a priceless gift.

> *This is the truth, the whole truth and nothing but the truth: As below, so above; and as above, so below. With this knowledge alone you may work miracles. And since all things exist in and emanate from THE ONE Who is the Ultimate Cause, so all things are born after their kind from this ONE. The Sun is the father, the Moon the mother; the wind carried it in his belly. Earth is its nurse and its guardian. It is the Father of all things, the Eternal Will is contained in it. Here, on Earth, its strength, its power remain one and undivided. Earth must be separated from fire, the subtle from the dense, gently, with unremitting care. It arises from the Earth and descends from heaven; it gathers to itself the strength of things above and things below. By means of this one thing all the glory of the world shall be yours and all obscurity flee from you. It is power, strong with the strength of all power, for it will penetrate all mysteries and dispel all ignorance.*
> ~ Hermes Trismegistus

What is the idea of the One? Yoga, yoke, unity is the idea of the One! The eternal questions and answers are a part of the wonderment of being alive. Throughout history, humankind keeps insisting the world is traveling toward a major Armageddon. I don't accept this sort of doomsday prophesy preached from the valley of ignorance, as they imply humankind is incapable of shaping its own future. Healing energy is on its way from the Light that permeates us.

In fact, humankind is responsible for many grand illusions. The world has always wanted to be saved from itself, light triumphing over darkness. Now we are moving into a period when the people of the world can be the world's saviors by taking responsibility for their actions.

Spiritually ill people perpetrate terrorism. It seems humankind is deaf and dumb when it comes to the deaths of innocent children by the tens of thousands every day around the world. These children become abstractions without any seeming relevance to our daily lives. We read about them in the newspaper or on the internet, shake our heads, and move on, feeling a little sadder and perhaps a little more powerless. Poverty on all levels is the root of evil. It is estimated 80 percent of the world lives on less than ten dollars a day.[94] And yet, worldwide, the rate of poverty has declined by 74.1 percent in the last 25 years (1990-2015).[95]

Think of all the senseless death due to poverty and illness around the world, and let us compare this to the several trillions of dollars the American government has spent on going after a small number of terrorists. Now *this* is true ignorance and evil in action. Eliminating poverty and ignorance is the best way to combat terrorism.

As the Age of Light dawns, poverty and ignorance (belief systems) are two elements that are one in the same. Money seems to be a most compelling illusion producing these unjust and cruel limitations on the complete fulfillment of life for billions of people. Money is used as a new form of slavery, and governments utilize money to control the masses. On a daily basis around the world, children are sold into slavery and prostitution.[96] Slavery is perpetrated in the world today at an alarming rate. To further this understanding, UNICEF has estimated 246 million children are in bonded labor, 1.2 million are trafficked, 1 million are sexually exploited, and 300,000 are child soldier.[97]

The sheer number of people on the Earth in the 21st century bears out this fact. The truth is, there is more slavery today than ever before in the history of humankind. Various news outlets have reported an estimated 47 million people around the world are enslaved.[98]

Of course, it is not only children who are enslaved. In fact, the slave-masters themselves are also enslaved to values and a way of thinking that prevent them from looking into their hearts and taking responsibility for their actions. As Jesus said, "Love thy neighbor as thyself."

---

94 Shah, Anup. "Poverty Facts and Stats." *Global Issues*, 7 January 2013, www.globalissues.org/article/26/poverty-facts-and-stats

95 Qiu, Linda. "Did We Really Reduce Extreme Poverty by Half in 30 Years?" *Politifact*, 23 March 2016, www.politifact.com/global-news/statements/2016/mar/23/gayle-smith/did-we-really-reduce-extreme-poverty-half-30-years/

96 "Facts on Children," *UNICEF*, 2007, updated 1 January 2011, www.unicef.org/dump/9482.html.

97 Ibid.

98 Villanueva Siasoco, Ricco. "Modern Slavery: Human Bondage in Africa, Asia and the Dominican Republic." *InfoPlease*, 18 April 2001, www.infoplease.com/spot/slavery1.html#ixzz2sK3gVRzJ.

Money *per se* is not the problem. The problem that holds people back in the Age of Light is the way money is used to control and exploit others. Such uses of money arise from unexamined hearts. As Socrates said, "The unexamined life is not worth living."

Banks were allowed to perpetrate junk investments, and, as we have seen in the United States since the Great Crash of 2008, the taxpayers must bail out those banks because they are deemed "too big to fail." Such bailouts expose the pretense that government is separate from corporations and not unduly influenced by them. During the first week of 2014, U.S. Senate Majority Leader Harry Reid stated on Face the Nation that in the last 30 years, 13% of the nation's wealth has gone to the top one percent of Americans.[99] Additionally, it was widely reported throughout early 2014 the top 85 billionaires in the world have as much wealth as three and a half billion of the poorest people combined.[100] This reverse Robin Hood type of capitalism will bring the social and economic revolution I see beginning in the early 2020s, triggered by the Pluto return in regard to the Sibly chart of the United States. The Occupy Wall Street movement that began in September 2011 was just the tip of the iceberg.

It's the people in government who preempt truth due to the old adage that power corrupts. But that does not mean government is keeping us chained to our self-defeating ways in a master/slave relationship. No, it's the people in the government who are the problem, and "we, the people" are the problem. And, we can be the solution. We have strayed far from the Founding Fathers' intentions. Money has taken the place of ideals in the U.S. government. The United States has become a plutocracy.

We can endlessly analyze our lives and remain detached from the consequences of our actions, or we can step back and with awareness observe the forces at work, relating and connecting all the dots. Then we can use this knowledge as a tool, as we seek to influence and participate in the inner workings of our country. For the most part, the Founding Fathers were enlightened men who lived beyond the limitations of religion while also respecting the beliefs of the masses.

The Universe is its own living entity. Though we lose perspective sometimes, we need to acknowledge the Universe is alive. The Earth and humankind are examples of this amazing miracle called existence. The Mayan Prediction speaks to the evolution of the Spirit of livingkind. As we are moving into the new century of possibilities, it will clearly be helpful to remember our lives are an example of our awareness.

✶ ✶ ✶ ✶ ✶ ✶ ✶   ✶ ✶ ✶ ✶ ✶ ✶ ✶   ✶ ✶ ✶ ✶ ✶ ✶ ✶

Quetzalcoatl, Messenger of Eternity

Mesoamerican civilizations, Toltec cultures and especially the Mayans all spoke to our Present age as the end of a great cycle that would last 5,200 years. The completion of this cycle coincides with the fabled return to Earth of Quetzalcoatl, a deity known to cultures across Mesoamerica.

---

99 *Face the Nation* with Bob Schieffer, CBS News, January 2014.
100 Shin, Laura. "The 85 Richest People in the World Have as Much Wealth as the 35 Billion Poorest". *Forbes*, 23 January 2014, www.forbes.com/sites/laurashin/2014/01/23/the-85-richest-people-in-the-world-have-as-much-wealth-as-the-3-5-billion-poorest/#1f41521a1753

Chapter 4 The Age of Light

Quetzalcoatl, the "Sovereign Plumed Serpent," appears on sculptures and artifacts created by all of these cultures as a combination of a serpent and a bird that represents the union of matter and Spirit.

The message common to humankind is peace, love and simple kindness to those who are in need. There is but one message: Love is all.

My intuition tells me Quetzalcoatl is also equivalent to the Blue Star Spirit the Hopi Prophets stated would be returning to Mother Earth. Mythologist Joseph Campbell was amazed at how different global cultures unknown to one another created similar, if not identical, myths or figures that represent the mystery of our existence. Creation is love!

> **Quetzalcoatl is the god who hands down civilizations, reveals time and discerns the movement of the stars and human destiny.**
> ~ Enrique Florescano, *The Myth of Quetzalcoatl*[101]

After I received my M.F.A. in theatre from the University of California, Davis, I lived in Tehran, Iran, where I worked as a theater studies instructor at Damavand College, an international college for young women. I also taught English to Iranian soldiers for Bell Helicopter on an Iranian airbase. In one of my meditation sessions in Tehran in 1974, I experienced and saw an exploding five-pointed blue star. When it appeared, it was all I could see, and it was all that existed for an eternal moment as I began to faint and my body started to fall to the ground in slow motion. I was overwhelmed by this vision, and I woke up and broke my fall just as I was about to hit the floor. I didn't know what I was witnessing at the time, but the sight amazed me, and I was instantly in a state of awe! I was mesmerized by this unknown, mysterious energy I had experienced. I have come to understand at this point in my life that what I witnessed in that moment was the end of time but not the end of the world. In fact, this is when my magical tour of observation began. Astrology has become my yoga in the garden of the mystics.

While living in Iran, I met many Sufis of the old ways and the Present. I witnessed and experienced mystical moments on walks, and while meditating by the Caspian Sea, I discovered new dimensions as a stranger on a strange planet. I saw we are living on the edge of Eternity as living liquid Light, and we are the source of that Light. Soon after my blue star experience into the mystic, I traveled to the Caspian Sea and southern Iran to Ahvaz, and, yes, I was truly a stranger in a strange land. Yet, I felt at home. I loved the year I lived in Iran. It was one of the most wondrous years I have spent in my life. The people were wonderful, kind, warm, and very friendly.

> *Now conscience wakes to spare the slumbered, wakes the bitter memory of what he was, what is and what must be.*
> ~ John Milton, *Paradise Lost*

When the Age of Light dawns before the Age of Aquarius, Light will open a door to infinite possibilities, for this is the end of time, not the end of the world. A beautiful, mysterious, loving expression will liberate humankind in the twinkling of an eye. With the

---
101 Florescano, Enrique. *The Myth of Quetzalcoatl*, Johns Hopkins University, 2002.

coming of Quetzalcoatl, the past will unfold right before your eyes. Thereafter, the world will never be the same. For the past is always in the Present, it does not go away. As Marcus Aurelius wrote in *The Meditations of Marcus Aurelius*, "The Universe loves nothing so much as to change the things which are and to make new things like them." The past, the future is eternally Present.

✦ ✦ ✦ ✦ ✦ ✦   ✦ ✦ ✦ ✦ ✦ ✦   ✦ ✦ ✦ ✦ ✦ ✦

When the Mayans predicted Quetzalcoatl was going to arrive at the end of the world and the end of time, they may not, I sense, have seen the level of evolution humanity was going to have reached. They didn't see the world now in existence with all the technology and space travel.

There are no absolutes determining the shape of the future. We have had freedom of choice regarding how to live, but very few have chosen to act without fear. Buddha and Jesus Christ are two examples of those who, over the centuries, lived without fear while living in the Present, in the eternal now. It is interesting to note Buddha was the son of a king who became a commoner, and Jesus was the son of a carpenter and pronounced the King of Mankind. The Age of Light delivers the middle ground for all humankind.

Meditation as a way of life takes responsibility for everything you think, do and say. A quiet mind has access to infinite possibilities, but if the mind is constantly thinking, worrying, and cannot stop thinking, then it is isolated and powerless in the banquet of life. Give attention to your actions and thoughts. Flow with the nature of nothing, which is perfection itself! As Fritjof Capra, author of The Tao of Physics wrote, "When the Zen master Po-chang was asked about seeking for the Buddha nature, which is considered conscious awareness, or Enlightenment, he answered, 'It's much like riding an ox in search of the ox.'"[102]

There's an old Polynesian saying that makes me think of Japan and the rest of the world: We are standing on a whale fishing for minnows.

When the Japanese tribe forgives themselves for being human and for not being perfect, then the awakening will begin. The less you think, the more you do. If you want to stop suffering, stop suffering right now by letting go of judgment and desire.

TimeSpace, the museum of the Present

Wake Up!

When, you may ask, will Quetzalcoatl return? Quetzalcoatl will return when the Earth is ready to embrace the Age of Light. Quetzalcoatl is an idea a concept for a major vibrational shift, and the moment this happens is yet to be determined. Our choices for exploitation or cooperation concerning our way of life will set the moment for the shift.

---

[102] Capra, Fritjof. *The Tao of Physics*, Shambhala, 2010.

Chapter 4 The Age of Light

Humankind has been preparing for this coming shift of consciousness for a long time. The problem is we all fall short of perfection, in part because as human beings we hold illusory, abstract ideals of perfection. We define perfection with language that is defining a concept that humans don't understand or know. We acknowledge we are not perfect, yet we decide the definition for perfect! Instead, let's observe the Present as the only example of perfection. Not as we believe perfection to be, however, but what is creation without language? Language only points to what it's attempting to describe and does not understand. Morality and ethics are not necessary when everyone is living in a harmonic awareness that provides love, respect and cooperation as our way of life. The sublime is simple.

On January 26, 2008, Pluto entered Capricorn for the first time in almost 248 years. A major shift in the American political landscape took place at that time. Paralleling this development, Japan's political landscape was about to enter into an historic change of a magnitude that had not been seen in the last 50 years—the Shakaitou party took power and created a new government.

Due to a brief retrograde change in course, Pluto left Capricorn for a bit on June 14, 2008. The little planet reentered Capricorn on November 27, 2008, and it remains in Capricorn until March 23, 2023. The reentry of Pluto marked the beginning of the rise of U.S. President Barack Obama, who won a commanding victory over then Senator Hillary Rodham Clinton in the South Carolina primary at the time.

On February 20, 2022, Pluto is at the exact degree and minute of the Sibly Natal chart, which I have chosen for the United States of America. This is the first time the United States experiences its first Pluto return. Pluto represents revolution, change, death and birth. After the destruction comes the reconstruction. Pluto in Capricorn briefly enters Aquarius in March 2023, and Pluto becomes retrograde in May 2023. Pluto reenters Capricorn on June 11, 2023 until going direct in October 2023. Pluto enters Aquarius on November 20, 2024 and remains in Aquarius until March 9, 2043. This period of Pluto going back and forth from Capricorn to Aquarius signals what I call an 'air-quake.' This is a period of major change around the world, especially in the United States, where an explosion of cultural dimension occurs before 2028. China experiences a cultural revolutionary shift as well by the end of this decade.

Back in 2008, behind the curtains concealing political maneuvering around the world, the second-worst crisis ever to hit the global economy began (the first being the Great Depression of the 1930s). The implosion of major banks in the United States led the collapse, and the world economies followed suit like busted hands in a poker game. Yet, we learned from the first depression that by printing money, you create a faster recovery and prevent a lot of suffering. The reason is simple: money does not exist; it is an illusion. We are very funny creatures.

With Pluto being true to its nature when we find it in Capricorn, it becomes inevitable governments must evolve to address the needs of the public or face revolution that will reshape the structure of the *status quo*!

★ ★ ★ ★ ★ ★ ★   ★ ★ ★ ★ ★ ★ ★   ★ ★ ★ ★ ★ ★ ★

In May 2015, Neptune transited the crown of the Meiji chart of Japan. This Neptune transit showed to be a period of disillusionment for the Japanese people. This transit coincided with Prime Minister Abe's government reinterpreting the constitution with a resolution ending the ban on the deployment of Japan's military. The Diet put together a group of bills that allow Japan's self-defense forces to act if the United States or neighboring countries come under attack.[103] The public outcry against this was unprecedented and has raised fears on the Korean Peninsula and in China that Prime Minister Abe wants to re-militarize Japan.[104] As China rises in power and the power centers of the world economy shift, the Japanese people could become depressed, as familiar relationships and expectations seem less satisfactory than before. With patience, the Japanese people can resist the temptation to use old strategies and tactics to project them too aggressively into rapidly evolving events. It is better for them to hold back and see how the world comes around to the idea it will learn by example from Japan as the Age of Light dawns. It is in keeping with the tradition of Eternity to see a former aggressive military Japan become the nation of peace for the world.

> *The destiny of the Mayan world is related to the destiny of the whole world ... The greatest wisdom is in simplicity ... love, respect, tolerance, sharing, gratitude, forgiveness. It's not complex or elaborate. The real knowledge is free. It's encoded in your DNA. All you need is within you. Great teachers have always pointed to [the simplest solution:] find your heart, and you will find your way.*
> ~ Carlos Barrios *Kam Wuj: El Libro del Destino*[105]

The Maya appreciated and respected there were other spiritual systems and sources of illumination. My friend Robert Zoller, an extraordinary world-class astrologer and author of *The Arabic Parts in Astrology: A Lost Key to Prediction* and many other books, often said to me, "The old ways are the best ways." Soon, everything the nation of Japan does will be in preparation for the Age of Light. The Japanese will draw anew upon the wisdom of their ancestors.

Japan has to reinvent itself for the Present and figure out how to make the old ways useful, especially when it comes to the generation and use of energy. Synthesizing the past ways with new technology could become an example to the world from the enlightened culture evolving in Japan. The rest of the world—one country, tribe, clan, village and person at a time—will evolve.

The Japanese, it must be said, can be and have been at times in the past, very prejudiced toward other races and cultures. All countries and cultures have participated in regrettable acts. Besides eliciting negative responses, prejudice works against the Japanese people. Japan's former colonial mindset must be addressed. Perceiving the world through

---

103 Ford, Matt. "Japan Curtails Its Pacifist Stance." *The Atlantic*, 19 September 2015, *www.theatlantic.com/international/archive/2015/09/japan-pacifism-article-nine/406318/*
104 Ibid.
105 Barrios, Carlos. *Kam Wuj: El Libro del Destino*, Sudamericana, 2000

a filter of cultural superiority should and will eventually no longer be associated with Japan. We all have lessons to learn about overcoming limitations in life, and Japan is no different.

Throughout this evolutionary process, it would be helpful for you to accept the idea time is not linear. Space and gravity are the base of the pyramid, and the Light in your eye is the apex representing time in Eternity as the Present.

The world economic structure is already undergoing a revolutionary metamorphosis such as never before seen in recorded history. Moving forward, it would be best if the Japanese government put up less resistance to their fears, as the Japanese tribe becomes conscious of and acquires its unique position. The Japanese people experience a kinship and cohesiveness not seen elsewhere in modern societies. I think these intriguing social phenomena are rooted in an ancient connection with the natural surroundings of the islands of Japan. As the Japanese tribe begins the process of reevaluating their nation's economic structure, their age-old memories and values will come to the fore.

The Senkaku Islands incident in the early 21st century is a potential instrument for teaching the government of Japan to find a new way to move forward through peaceful means. In the past, the Japanese tendency was to wage war to get what they wanted. Prior to World War II, the Japanese attempted to colonize Asia. Today, Japan's economic opportunities with China are huge, but if both countries maintain the tensions between them, they can destroy the opportunities at their doorsteps. I assert that a financial settlement between Japan and China resolves the Senkaku dilemma. Of course, any settlement between these two countries does not preclude problems elsewhere in the future.

★ ★ ★ ★ ★ ★   ★ ★ ★ ★ ★ ★   ★ ★ ★ ★ ★ ★

At this point in history, we have come to a point of no return in regards to the degradation of the Earth and each other. The Age of Light is the last attempt for us to choose to live in harmony with Earth or be the debris of which we are becoming. As long as monies and economies are the focus of cultures, then the Age of Light is not inherited by man, rather by what remains, which rebirths the Earth. You are the Light, which is the New Age, or you return to the absence of Light.

During the past few years, there have been ample discussions in the media about the 21st century being China's century. Only time will tell if the media pundits are right. Regardless, I do agree this is the century for China to either win or lose. Japan can also be a big winner in conjunction with the emergence of China. In spite of the long-established tension between these two ancient neighbors, the economic bonds the Chinese and Japanese create can financially benefit Japan like never before. If Japan focuses on self-sustainability and environmental cleanup, this can be one of the successful approaches for Japan to influence the Chinese government and the world.

Innovative Japanese technology to clean water and air pollution can and will be important for China and the world. Air pollution from China travels east to Japan, which has been dealing with the extremely harmful particulate matter that travels to its shores.

This can be an area of mutual interest for China and Japan: Two great nations can together discover a solution for their environmental problems by creating a way to bridge the gap between them. In early 2014, it was reported on CNN that Beijing, China, had air pollution 25 times above the level considered healthy. Further, air pollution from China was detected as far away as California in 2014, which shows the growing global problem pollution is creating.

Experience in how to dispense with nuclear soil and water from the Fukushima Daiichi nuclear plant offers many lessons for all of us to learn. The best procedure is to stop using nuclear energy, but humankind has not yet learned that lesson. China is destroying the quality of its citizens' lives with airborne pollution, and Japan can be a good model for China when it comes to cleaning up the environment.

I think the 21st century is going to be both the doing and undoing of China due to the fact no central government can control a billion and a half people. Such control has never happened before, and it is not going to happen by an apparent fearful Communist government. If China wants to survive, it may want to take a page out of the North American playbook and consider creating states or provinces, regions that surrender certain rights and privileges on a federal level but exercise their politics with broad discretion on the local level. Perhaps by adopting and adapting Western ways in this manner, the Chinese can neutralize the forces seeking the breakup of the centralized Chinese state and avoid the fate that overtook another centralized giant, the former Soviet Union.

China's ancient past provides the answer to their potential problems. Lao Tzu, the Daodejing or Tao Te Ching ("The Way of Power"), reminds China the best form of government is "village government." Tribes taking care of their own. In this respect, all tribes of China can become harmonious with one another. Japan is a good example of this and continues to demonstrate this in the Age of Light. It is the true, essential nature of most humans to wish to avoid being ruled and exploited. Human nature is filled with contradictions, which I think is integral to our evolution. However, I think we all wish to live in harmony with nature and to emulate creation as the parent of us all. In the coming New Age of Light, humans who usually fall prey to the temptations of power reveal their true nature. China can learn to stop controlling people and find a framework that allows them to flourish with nature and express their true selves for China to truly benefit.

The problems we experience while adjusting to the New Age of Light are not going to be fully resolved. Humankind has embarked on this evolutionary process toward a destiny yet to be seen or experienced. Still, the Mayan Prediction is reminding the world, so humankind has a basis for choosing the path toward a higher spiritual nature over financial or political paths. We now live in a world context structured around winning and losing. The Mayan Prediction teaches us the vibrational shift is ushering in the Age of Light, which is providing a new way to harmonize with the Present by way of service and cooperation with all of life.

The dualistic paradigms that have shaped the past, pitting the Haves against the Have-Nots and Winners against Losers, are disappearing now. But before this happens, the opposite will occur. The rich will get richer, and the poor will get poorer. It is this kind of capitalism that creates terrorist activities and revolutions. Mother Nature is taking charge of what needs to happen to bring the world to its destiny, which is the Age of Light. Japan is going to play a significant role in this dramatic transformation into a world in which sustainability replaces exploitation. The Unites States and China have their role to play in this regard as well.

Nature is demonstrating to us the telltale signs the world is being forced to change its ways. New births are never easy, and the wisdom and insight I've gained from my astrological studies and observant awareness, in particular, tells me this birthing process will be difficult. But the result is going to be worth it—a celebration of health for the planet and humankind because there is only one destination for us all: love, life, and death are one in the same. Another Holy Trinity, if you will.

Buddhists have a saying: "Enlightenment is not having any preferences."

Meanwhile, we are dealing with the practical consequences of the instability and uncertainty revolutions bring. When Pluto entered Capricorn in 2008, all competent astrologers knew, based on the past, this significant transit was going to bring revolutions capable of toppling governments worldwide. Like the recurring transit of Pluto entering Capricorn, history is also about cycles. History has supported this astrological interpretation time after time.

★ ★ ★ ★ ★ ★   ★ ★ ★ ★ ★ ★   ★ ★ ★ ★ ★ ★

One out of every six people in the world goes hungry every day. Food and water go hand in hand; they are the roots of many of the conditions humankind now faces and it gets worse. In this century, we are going to witness the greatest hunger the world has ever experienced. Hunger brings revolutions, and the government of China is very worried about how secure their hold is on their people. Will desperate, hungry people still support the Chinese government?

Look how quickly the Great Leap Forward was abandoned in the face of the millions of deaths that occurred within a matter of 18 months after it began. The Chinese people, when provoked, are a force to be reckoned with. Mass rejection of political agendas can happen in any nation, as we have seen recently with the Arab Spring and will soon witness in many other regions around the world. I think the Chinese government will continue to stir up old wounds with Japan to distract the people of China from their internal problems.

As much as the Chinese government attempts to censor news and information concerning world events, it is only a matter of time before this approach backfires and brings great change and revolution to China. The United States, with its deepening financial and political problems, is going to experience some of the greatest changes it has ever seen. In terms of sheer economic power and reach, China will match and eventually overtake the United States economically. I do see a cultural revolution coming to the United States and China in the years to come before 2029.

Japan has the opportunity to lead the world by example towards peace. Such leadership will occur as more and more individuals of the Japanese tribe become aware of how to express peace and forgiveness in a positive, constructive manner. The etymological root of the word "forgiveness" comes from the Greek and signifies "starting again, as if the infraction had never happened."

The Maya, Inca and many Native American tribes have lived lives of culturally mandated brutality. Now the pendulum is swinging toward a time of peace and the Age of Light, the prelude to the Age of Aquarius. To give attention is the simplest act of love.

✶ ✶ ✶ ✶ ✶ ✶ ✶   ✶ ✶ ✶ ✶ ✶ ✶ ✶   ✶ ✶ ✶ ✶ ✶ ✶ ✶

I want to make something very clear: I do not "believe in" astrology. Astrology works much of the time, but there are no guarantees in the mystery of life. That's why we wake up in the morning and let the mystery of creation reveal itself before our eyes. I intend here to merely give insights into possibilities for what the world, and particularly the Japanese people, will experience. The Great Eastern Japan Earthquake Disaster will be remembered as the moment when the Mayan vibrational shift began and the consciousness of Japan and the world was awakened. The greatest threat to Japan is Japan itself. The three great lessons for the world are forgiveness, humility, and peace.

By understanding and following the emerging lessons of this New Age of Light, women take their rightful place alongside men to help run and heal the Earth. Elitist and prejudiced points of view towards other races and nations become diminished to historic lows. The responsibilities of financial stability are examined, redefined, and approached with a cooperative hand to those in need of the basics for a better planet in mind. Ultimately, the generation and use of renewable energy will be the most demanding and important task Japan, the United States, and China (with the rest of the world) need to incorporate if we are to reverse the adverse effects being created towards climate change.

> *Life without intelligence and compassion is a life that has no meaning. Live a life with no conflict. There is great beauty in this. Beauty is not a perception; it is a way of living.*
> ~ Jedda Krishnamurti, *Tradition and Revolution*

Chapter 5

United States, China, and Japan

Astrological Synastry Analysis

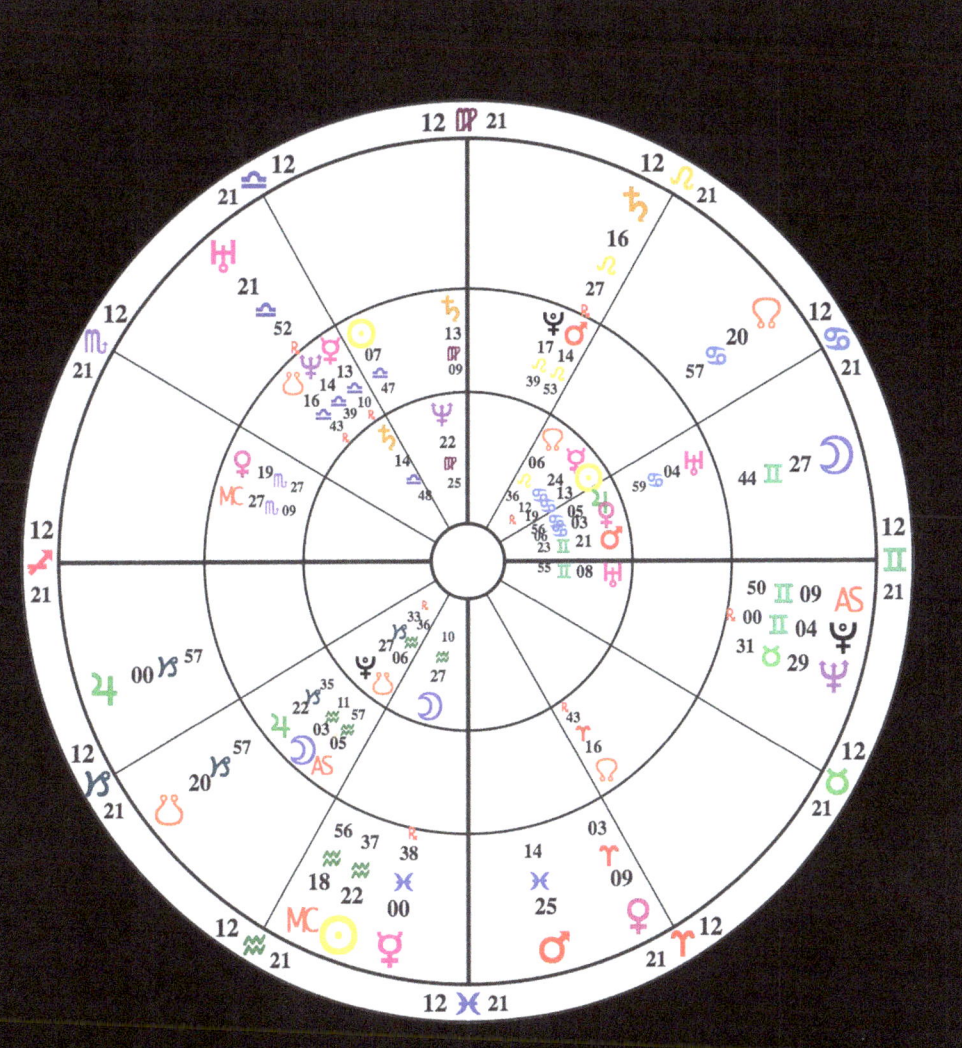

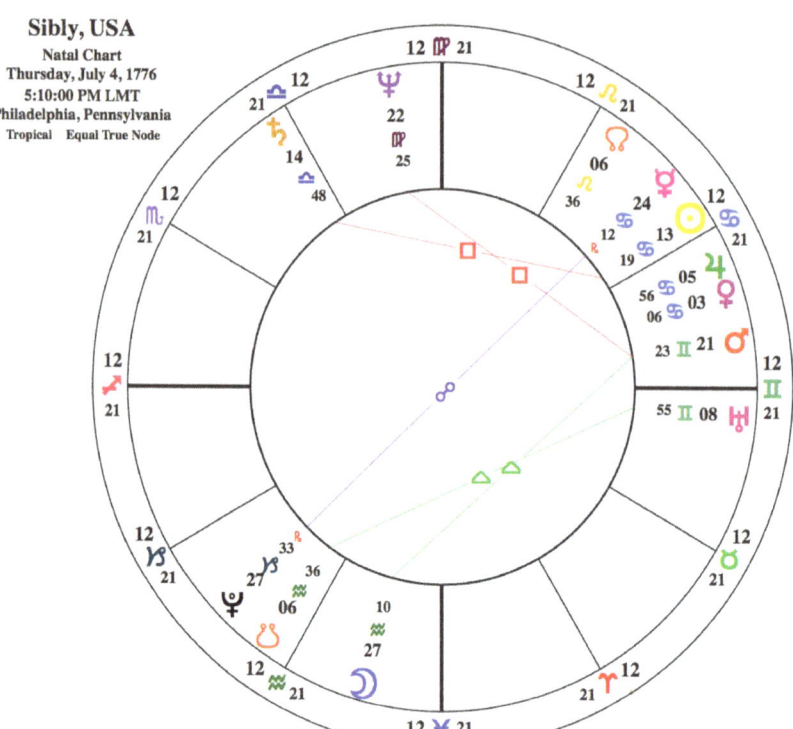

> *"One of the lessons I've been learning in connection with astrology is the importance of humility, the importance of subordinating the individual will to this higher will."*
> ~ Robert Zoller, Author, astrologer, mystic

hen it comes to determining the founding date of an entity (such as a nation, region, or city), the mundane astrologer is faced with many possibilities. To understand the astrologer's dilemma, let's go o topic for just a moment and consider the role history plays as it intertwines with astrology by means of the founding of the United States.

Most astrologers agree the Declaration of Independence was signed on July 4, 1776. However, the exact time of the signing is open to debate. Part of the problem is several dozen people signed the document throughout that day. (In both Natal and mundane astrology, time of day is as crucial as the day itself.) History books include varying accounts of when the final signature was affixed.

The astrology analysis I conduct in this chapter will be based on what is known as the Sibly chart. British astrologer Ebenezer Sibly published the horoscope shown below in 1787. (Incidentally, Sibly was a Freemason, as were American Founding Fathers George Washington, Benjamin Franklin, and John Hancock—all signatories and instrumental framers of the Declaration of Independence).

Chapter 5 United States, China, and Japan

According to the Sibly chart, the signing took place at 5:10 pm on July 4, 1776 in Philadelphia, Pennsylvania. In 1992, mundane astrologer Nicholas Campion won the Marc Edmund Jones Award for his innovative, comprehensive and meticulous research in compiling *The Book of World Horoscopes*. In *The Book of World Horoscopes*, Campion explains the circumstances under which Sibly chose these particular astrological coordinates: "Sibly's American horoscope may not be a national horoscope in the modern sense, set for a precisely timed event, but it is entirely consistent with medieval tradition and the chart is, therefore, presented here not as a horoscope for the Declaration of Independence, but as a horoscope which signifies the Declaration of Independence." [106]

The distinction between "for" and "which signifies" is vital: Quite simply, Sibly devised his horoscope in support of *the idea* of the Declaration of Independence, not for the document itself.

There has long been a great deal of debate over which astrological chart is the most accurate one for the United States. Many opinions as to the configuration of the most precise chart have surfaced over the years. I use the Sibly chart because it includes transits that accurately associate with particular incidents, such as the 9/11 attacks in the United States. Moreover, the Sibly mundane astrology chart intuitively speaks to me.

Before we look into the unknown, let us take a moment to examine the past. As Buddha said, **"What you are is what you have done, and what you will be is what you do now!"**

Transiting Jupiter entered the Sibly Eighth House of death and public mortality on September 16, 2001, just five days after 9/11. The United States has undergone massive transformations ever since. On August 23, 2013 Jupiter was positioned at the exact same astrological site in which it was found in the immediate aftermath of the 9/11 attacks. By the end of summer 2013, U.S. spying activities hit the headlines (again). U.S. security contractor Edward Snowden had revealed National Security Agency violations of public privacy, and Russia ended up providing temporary asylum to Snowden. This has triggered another momentous transformation in the way business is conducted in the halls of government, especially as the world continues to learn a great deal about the inner workings and widespread repercussions of the U.S. spying apparatus. A cultural vibrational shift of transformation starts to occur sometime before the presidential election of 2016 and on through to 2025.

The Sibly chart indicates an energy shift of as-yet-indefinite import beyond the duplicate Jupiter position. Jupiter is beneficial by nature and adds an expansive quality to the astrological House it transits. Here, the Eighth House with Jupiter influence highlights the courts, law, and trade agreements. The transit of Jupiter in the Sibly chart started to make itself felt on August 23, 2013. The idea of personal privacy is fundamental to the American way of life. As with September 11, 2001, the placement once again of Jupiter in the Sibly chart indicates a conscious shift to the United States. In April 2014, the Sibly chart shows Uranus transiting the Fifth House until May 31, 2021, which will mark the beginning of a financially volatile and unpredictable period in the United States. Uranus by nature, brings sudden extreme change to the House it is transiting. Also, the focus is on revolutions, anarchy, innovations, technology, and earthquakes. Uranus in Taurus transiting the Sixth House speaks

---

106 Nicolas Campion, *The Book of World Horoscopes*, The Wessex Astrologer Limited, 2004.

to naval accidents, even explosions on vessels, and Uranus square Saturn in Aquarius in the Third House. Uranus in the Sixth House speaks to the welfare and health of the nation that may be under attack or suffer. These aspects can stir up discontent with employees, teachers, and writers. There's also an emphasis on accidents concerning railways, even explosions, with Saturn in the Third House square to Uranus in the Sixth House.

In April 2014, a cardinal grand cross occurred involving Mars, Jupiter, Uranus, and Pluto, which all attained their maximum position of opposition at 13°. It is interesting to note at this time the U.S. Supreme Court struck down the limits of campaign finance[107]—another major setback for democracy in America. There were several earthquakes around the world, along with an avalanche on Mt. Everest that killed a 12 sherpas,[108] and a South Korean ferry sank, killing 304 of its passengers.[109] All of life is connected.

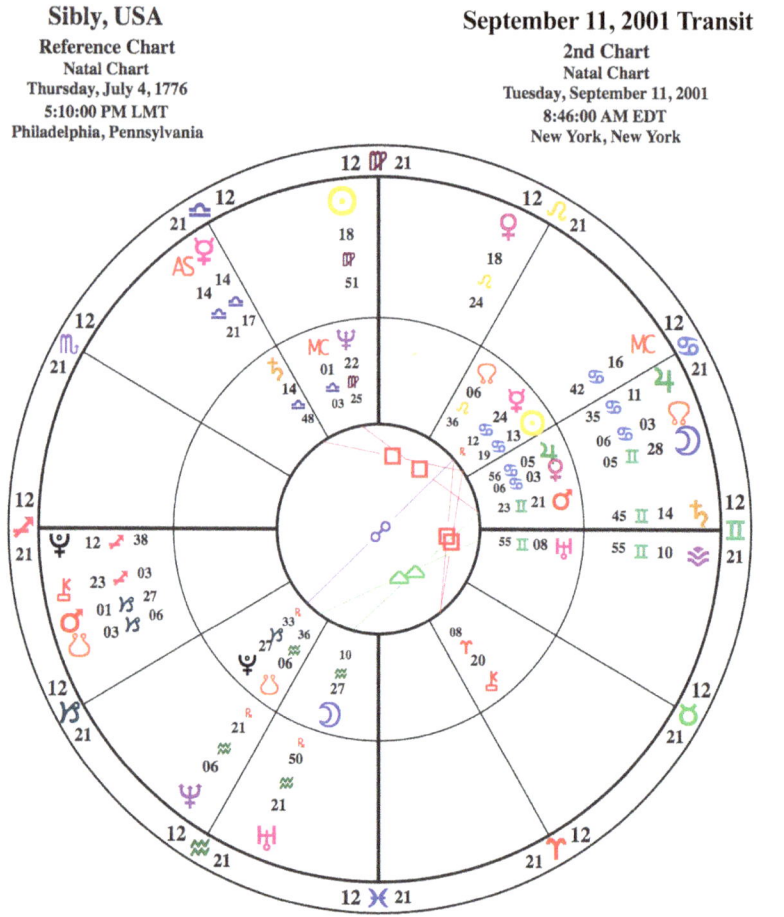

107 Liptak, Adam. "Supreme Court Strikes Down Overall Donation Cap." *The New York Times*, 2 April 2014, www.nytimes.com/2014/04/03/us/politics/supreme-court-ruling-on-campaign-contributions.html?_r=0
108 Payne, Ed and Manesh Shrestha. "Avalanche Kills 12 In Single Deadliest Accident on Everest." *CNN*, 20 April 2014, www.cnn.com/2014/04/18/world/asia/nepal-everest-avalanche/index.html
109 Peters, Daniel. "The Classroom Frozen in Time: eerie pictures of student desks untouched since they drowned in South Korean ferry disaster two years ago." *Daily Mail*, 24 May 2016, www.dailymail.co.uk/news/article-3605976/Eerie-pictures-untouched-classroom-belonging-students-teachers-killed-Sewol-ferry-disaster-South-Korea.html

Chapter 5 United States, China, and Japan

April 21, 2014 was the fifth of seven exact squares between Uranus and Pluto, a period of revolution and terrorism, which remained in effect through 2015. Beginning in 2016, Saturn entered below the horizon of the Sibly Chart First House of national image, national characteristics, and psychology of the masses. Saturn spends approximate 14-year cycle diving into the depths of the Sibly Chart, where Saturn stirs into the deep psyche of the country, it's a time of significant breakthroughs and instability. During this time of change, the more we resist, the more difficult those changes become. Learn to let go and flow with what is taken from you and given to you. The United States has embarked upon an in-depth internal cultural journey of revolutionary awakening.

It took America to have its first black President of the United States to own up that racism is alive and still residing in America. It never went away, and it's been waiting to rear its ugly head. For me, we're not as divided by racism as it appears. The media has a tendency to exaggerate acts of violence, for after all, it does relate to ratings and money. I went to Riverside Military Academy in Gainesville, Georgia, and racism was very apparent almost anywhere you traveled in the South. Let us be grateful those days are gone.

What are we, the people of the United States, going to do about racism? This is an important and defining moment for the United States to come together as a responsible people who have to resolve the destructive nature of racism. America is going to publicly debate the true nature of the Constitution of the United States. Justice, freedom, and equality in the Constitution is based on laws not designed for serving the wealthy and/or white people's interest so they can skirt the law at the expense of the poor and the rest of the nation. Justice, freedom, and equality for everyone!

In 2016, the United States elected Donald J. Trump. In his Natal chart, Mars and Pluto in Leo reside in his Twelfth House which speaks to the role he plays as the steward of a cultural revolution, evident by 2020 to 2025. Revolutions are messy, and this period is not unprecedented. The closer the United States arrives to its first Pluto return, the more people of America resemble the 1960s when the public expressed its frustration with government. Not unlike July 1776, America has a similar general sense of dissatisfaction. Yet, a glacial of light brings forth optimism, awakening the American culture throughout this century. With Japan leading us into the Age of Light, along with the United States and China, it brings a new understanding to the world for the need to be a healthy garden.

If Donald J. Trump is still President of the United States in March-May of 2020, then he steps down to a private life. Health issues or a pending impeachment may be the reason. Either way, he is gone. Robert Mueller, considered one of the most respected lawyers in America and Director of the Federal Bureau of Investigation from 2001 - 2013, is conducting an investigation into the 2016 presidential election. The results of this investigation will play a significant part in the President's departure from office.

Beginning in mid-April 2019, President Trump has transiting Saturn in Capricorn 20° and transiting Pluto in Capricorn at 23°, conjunct in his Fifth House, which includes Real Estate and opposite his Natal Saturn in Cancer at 23° and Venus in Cancer at 25°. The South Node is conjunct Saturn and Pluto, which exposes the results of past karma. Also, transiting Jupiter in Sagittarius at 24° is opposite to his Natal Sun in Gemini, opposite his

Natal Uranus with Sagittarius conjunct Trump's Natal Moon at 21° Sagittarius. At this time he feels remarkably suppressed, and in my meditation, I have seen images of President Trump early in the morning, sitting bedside with his hands in his face, crying that he is not beloved. He never understood you receive what you give. He can't help himself from himself, and he knows this, and that is where the tragedy lies. He is our tragic Shakespearean President, and he represents what needs to be repaired in America and the Age of Light demands no less. The excellent news vibration is beginning to shed its light on the ugly, ignorant and seamy side of the past dark ages. The current thinking and exploitation of our living kind and all living nature have to come to an end! There is a cultural purge manifesting, and this new vibrational light is eliminating our functional insanity as we arrive at the dawn of a new Age. President Trump is impeached in 2019, or by spring of 2020.

On March 30, 2020, President Donald J. Trump has Saturn and Mars in Aquarius 00° crossing into his Sixth House of health and work. His transiting Jupiter and Pluto are in Capricorn 24° and opposite his Natal Venus 25°. In his Natal chart Saturn resides in

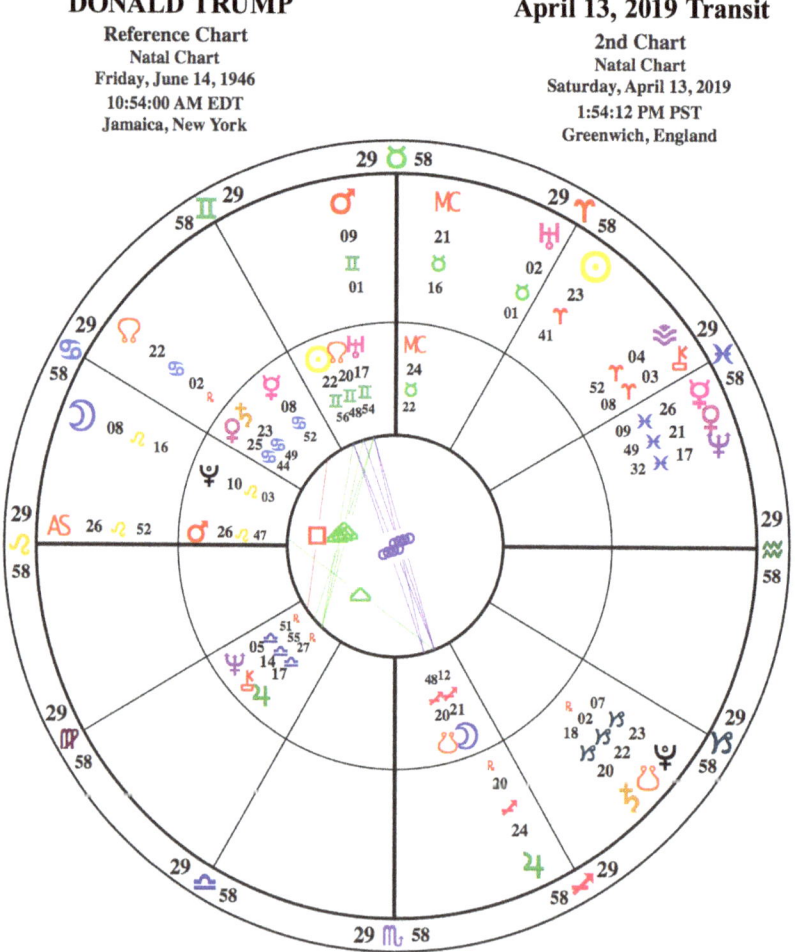

Chapter 5 United States, China, and Japan

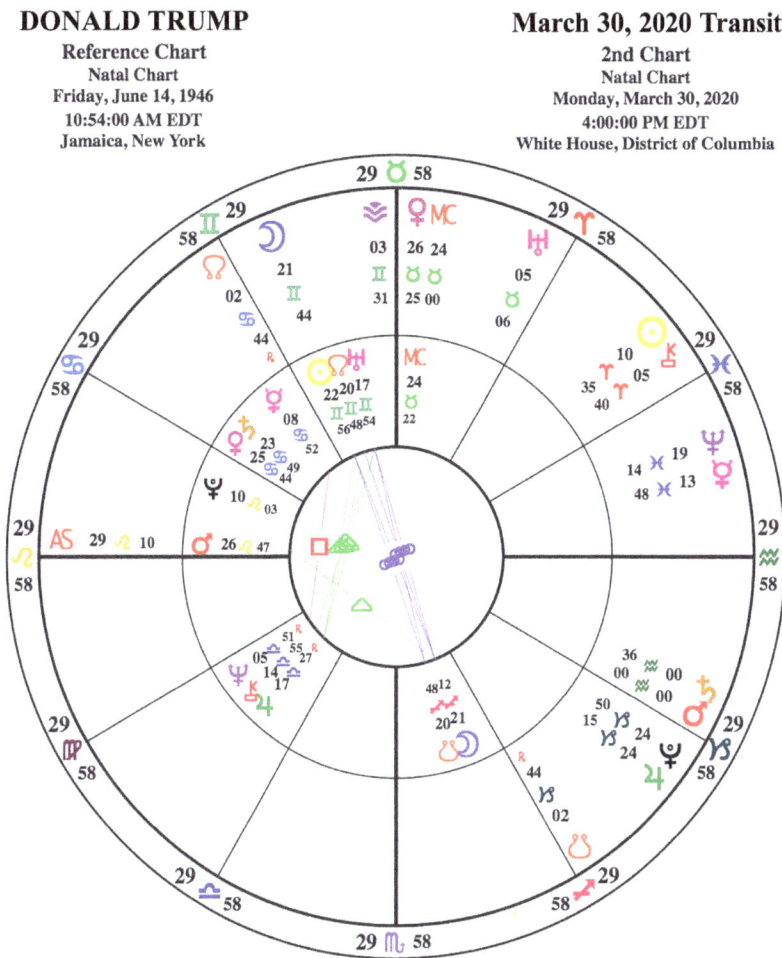

Cancer 23° in his Eleventh House of Friendship and transiting Uranus in Taurus 5° in the Ninth House of foreigners, universities, religious organizations, legal systems, and unruly events. Also, a square that becomes significant as July delivers Uranus in Taurus with an exact square to his Natal Pluto 10° on July 4, 2020. The sudden unexpected nature of Uranus is what changes President Trump's lifestyle. Divorce is on the way after he leaves the Presidency, which complicates his life and simplifies it. A significant change of life is coming to President Donald J. Trump.

Uranus is sudden and can bring abrupt revolution, and this is a major important correction for the country. A group of investors back President Trump, who creates a 24-hour news network called "Trump News" to keep his political gestalt and message relevant.

★ ★ ★ ★ ★ ★ ★   ★ ★ ★ ★ ★ ★ ★   ★ ★ ★ ★ ★ ★ ★

Investors abhor uncertainty in the financial markets, such as the growing (and now largest) debt in United States' history. The volatile swing of the Chinese stock market in 2015 was due to the government's attempt to control (that which cannot be controlled) the rate at which the GDP was declining. Is it wise for China to have a consumer economy equal on the scale of the United States' lifestyle? I think not, if the people of Earth are to survive. You have heard the phrase *time is money*—well, the end of time actually being about the end of money, as we have come to know and use it. United States is entering the end of time but not the end of the United States. This shift will take many decades, but we are now starting on the path to a new way of living in regards to money and what it represents. Certainly, we are moving to a world where we can use smartphones to make payments. In time, hard currency will be a thing of the past. Humanity is on the verge of reconsidering the purpose and power of money, and we create or find a new way of exchanging services for value and worth. Money will become an exchange for services. In this way we discover and create a brave new world where we all serve each other rather than exploiting each other.

In the Sibly chart, transiting Pluto in Capricorn on December 8, 2014 entered the Second House of national wealth. The Pluto transit coincides with hard economic times for the United States, rivaling the severity of the Great Depression of the 1930s. The U.S. government does whatever it can to keep the monetary earthquake to a minimum by adopting drastic policies. The Federal Reserve is at the frontline to stem the tide by loosening up the money supply. However, this time the problem is more closely tied to the broken infrastructure of capitalism.

I noticed in the 2015 Sibly chart of the United States, Pluto in Capricorn is transiting the Second House. Transiting Pluto is in the Second House. The Second House is linked to currency and its circulation, revenue, and activities related to money, banks, stock exchange, money markets, and trade. This would be the perfect condition to expect the unexpected with unintended consequences concerning the American economy and financial institutions around the world. England leaving the European Union is an example of unintended and unexpected consequences.

During 2014, Uranus in Aries at 12° entered the Fifth House. The Fifth House is associated with entertainment, real estate, finance, social media and the overall general economy; all of which influences culture and politics. The placement of Uranus in the Fifth House emphasizes real estate and financial (stock market) speculation activity, ultimately having an impact on the state of the global economy. As a result, with Pluto in Capricorn the American economy will be restructuring its foundation until 2030.

> *"Give me control of a nation's money and I care not who makes its laws."*
> ~ Mayer Amshel Rothschild

> *"Give me control of the nation's media and I will tell them what to think and what to accept."*
> ~ Unknown

The Mayan and Hopi Indians foretold of the extreme weather patterns from drought to flood and wild fires. This foretelling is a direct correlation to the human condition for what Pluto in Capricorn represents through 2023. Pluto is a Cardinal Earth sign representing different fields of significance, such as mining, deforestation, pollution, fracking, geology, governments, and earthquakes. Depth of intensity (and representing the underworld), destructive and regenerative energy are at play. Pluto represents the process of birth and death relating to the act of dismantling a prevailing status quo. Of course, key factors in the daily news include the state of politics and the economy, epidemics and pandemics, wars, fascism and plutocracies, oligarchies, and a whole lot of malarkey.

Japan as the leading example for Asia and the world when it comes to cultural flowering of a unique conscious awareness. The tribe of Japan has the capability to subsume conflicting factions in a close supportive community oriented toward common goals. In contrast, the United States, while still the leader of the Western World, is at the same time a country deeply divided. Following Japan's example, the United States is going to evolve over a long period in terms of its reawakening due to its size and the divisions within its people. Through times both challenging and inspirational, I do see Japan as a pillar of Light guiding the people of the world into the era beyond December 21, 2012. The Japanese people are starting to wake up and will lead the way. I see the United States with its vast capabilities can bask in that Light if not also assist in its own illumination.

In the beginning there is Darkness, and then there is Light. The United States and Japan are experiencing their darkest days since World War II, and the Light leading out of this darkness is a blessing destined to arrive. It may take longer than anyone would want, but creation will determine the content of what is yet to be and when!

Inertia often gets in the way of finding real solutions in politics, especially when moneyed interests block positive change. The American people ultimately find their way through the current political morass, as well as find solutions to the problems politicians and bureaucrats create. In life, recurring themes, transpositions, repetitions, and unexpected developments often converge to define a form that becomes apparent only after it has already occurred. American ideals have been corrupted, and our body politic is attempting to pretend it is not like the rest of the corrupt world.

Japan is recognized by the world as an example of how all nations on Earth should aspire to be in their finest, altruistic, and harmonious moments when it comes to their tribal communion. This is not to say Japan is free from corruption within its own government or corporations. The Japanese have demonstrated stoicism and courage in the way they have recovered from the Great Eastern Japan Earthquake disaster. At the same time, greater numbers of Japanese people than ever before have publicly stated their profound distrust of their government. This distrust is key as the people of Japan go forth beyond the Mayan threshold. Around the world, governments have become the problem, and in many nations they can no longer provide the solution. How governments respond determine their very survival.

The transit of Pluto across the United States' Second House of national wealth is the most significant and the first Pluto return America has experienced, which is an astrological occurrence associated with the slow restructuring of the U.S. economy. It signals economic recovery and restructuring efforts in the United States will be slow, which in turn affects the Japanese economy in the coming decade. It is going to be exceedingly difficult for countries worldwide to exercise their independent economic markets. As long as there is a global economy, all countries flourish together or languish together. Think about it: The U.S. government has spent trillions of dollars on waging wars that have destroyed lives, all supposedly on behalf of the American public. President Trump's reckless blasting of random posts through social media conduits (i.e. Twitter) along with his arrogant manner is bringing the United States down from it's currently perceived position of power and prestige. With a $20-trillion deficit (and deepening), the United States is gradually going to rescind its "manifest destiny," the "exceptionalist" mythology that justified the conquest of the North American continent and eventually the attitude that, as the sole superpower, the United States was almost exclusively responsible for managing the world's affairs. Instead, as the Age of Light unfolds, globalization requires mutual cooperation if humanity is to survive and thrive. The people of the world have arrived at the edge of an unknown, and U.S. exceptionalism fades away. Or does President Trump with America First and a nationalism agenda take their place?

When Japan suffered its financial collapse at the beginning of the 1990s, the Meiji chart featured transiting Neptune in Capricorn and transiting Saturn in Capricorn. Both planets were moving through the Eighth House, and Neptune rules senior citizens, landowners, farmers, and land in general. Saturn highlights the nation's business sense, and it governs the stock exchanges. Transiting Uranus was in Capricorn in the Seventh House of business relationships and relations with other countries, and transiting Pluto in Scorpio was in the Sixth House of the working class, employment, and unemployment. All of these astrological configurations set the stage for the collapse.

In 1991, Japan suffered a major economic downturn. For various reasons, the "bubble" economy it had created, collapsed. Japan has struggled to recover from this debacle ever since, as seen in its numerous economic recoveries and downturns until in 2005 economists projected a 2.2 percent growth for the country's economy.[110]

Japan has a major challenge ahead, but these are the kinds of difficulties that can bring forth the best of a nation. A positive attitude change towards immigration and an appreciation for the services immigrants render would benefit the Japanese tribe. After all, these individuals would almost certainly take jobs the Japanese currently do not want to fill.

Japan doesn't have to prove anything to anyone. The Japanese have demonstrated their remarkable capacity for hard work, most recently during the recent Great Eastern Japan Earthquake Disaster recovery efforts. Now that the Age of Light is underway, Japan's best approach is to put its financial house in order by eliminating its national debt.

A development of innovative kinds of businesses in Japan would be helpful in the recovery efforts, which has the nuclear industry figuring how to proceed. Earthquakes around the world continue to remind the public of the power of nature and our tenuous existence on the planet.

While earthquakes are not going to stop happening, Japan can choose which technologies to develop for future generations. I think nuclear energy in Japan will be abandoned as a commercial industry because the Japanese culture no longer supports its use. And this lack of support is due to the exposure of the truth concerning the depth of contamination that has and is still occurring at the Fukushima Daiichi nuclear plant facility. Germany and Switzerland have already made the commitment to eliminate

---

110 Fackler, Martin. "Take It From Japan: Bubbles Hurt." *The New York Times*, 25 December 2005, www.nytimes.com/2005/12/25/business/yourmoney/take-it-from-japan-bubbles-hurt.html?_r=0

their nuclear plants in the next several decades. While indications are the United States continues to develop its nuclear plants, this policy could change if new disasters strike.

Of course, it will take the Japanese energy industry many decades to make the transition to renewable energy. Meanwhile, Japan has to keep its nuclear industry on an operational footing in order to meet the energy demands of Japanese industries. The transition will be a slow one. It is commonly reported on NHK news network in Japan it could take up to 40 years to clean up the radioactive radiation. Really though, it is likely to take 60 years—assuming the cleanup is ever completed. This region is destined to have more earthquakes prolonging the cleanup. In the Age of Light, we will learn the damage at Fukushima is far worse than we have been led to know.

In the modern era, it has been a cultural truism, even a cliché that work is of the utmost importance in Japan. As the Age of Light unfolds, astrology speaks to Japan's work ethic, which is a tradition that is going to be challenged in Japan. Work as the prime directive in life is going to be reevaluated in light of its cultural and spiritual costs.

> *The trouble with a cheap, specialized education is that you never stop paying for it.*
> ~ Marshall McLuhan

In November 2011, BBC News World Service reported increasing numbers of young people are leaving Tokyo for a life in the country, returning to farming as a way of life not unlike that of their grandparents.[111] It seems perceptions about big city life are changing. These Japanese young people are wary of the long work days demanded of their parents and of the uncertainty of employment. This trend will continue as the winds of change clear the consciousness of the tribe of Japan.

Let's turn our attention to the United States for a moment. The United States ranked 16th among developed countries in the number of college graduates, as of 2011.[112] The United States and Japan have large national debts worldwide. These statistics indicate a slide in the quality of life in the United States that accelerates in the future, but Japan finds a way to finesse their quality of life despite their national debt.

According to the United Nations Educational, Scientific and Cultural Organization (UNESCO), Japan ranks number one among nations in the world in mathematical literacy and second in scientific literacy.

Japan is considered to have developed one of the most competitive educational systems in the world. The test scores of Japanese students in science, mathematics, and reading greatly surpass those of U.S. students.[113]

---

111 Buerk, Roland. "Japan's Youth Turn to Rural Areas Seeking a Slower Life," *BBC News*, 28 November 2011, www.bbc.co.uk/news/business-15850243.

112 de Vise, Daniel. "U.S. Falls in Global Ranking of Young Adults Who Finish College." *The Washington Post*, 13 September 2011, www.washingtonpost.com/local/education/us-falls-in-global-ranking-of-young-adults-who-finish-college/2011/08/22/gIQAAsU3OK_story.html?utm_term=.c3923db3661b

113 Desilver, Drew. "U.S. Students' Academic Achievement Still Lags That of Their Peers In Many Other Countries." *Pew Research Center*, 15 February 2017, www.pewresearch.org/fact-tank/2017/02/15/u-s-students-internationally-math-science/

However, the key for a well-adjusted and healthy life is to find balance between leisure time and study time. As the Mayan Prediction comes to pass, education is going to take on a new direction and focus more on how to be human. It'll no longer just be a means of getting a job. A balanced life is an enlightened life.

The work ethic in Japan embraces the highest standards in the world in terms of quality workmanship and self-sacrifice. Essentially, maintenance of the standard arises from the competitive nature of the modern industrial Japanese state expressed not only in the schools but also in terms of expectations about how business should be done.

Due to the lack of consistent high-quality education and the outsourcing of jobs overseas, the quality of life in the United States has suffered. U.S. companies justify outsourcing practices because those practices enable them to lower the prices of their products. However, as unemployment grows, it seems many consumers will find even the prices of cheap products to be out of their reach.

However, the United States still remains a top competitive economy. Leading companies in the most advanced industries still tend to locate their headquarters on U.S. territory. The United States hosts the largest capital markets, and it has control of its currency—the reserve or standard currency honored around the world. The United States exports everything from aircraft to entertainment to healthcare products around the world. The basic demographics are healthy in the United States compared with those of Japan. The United States will be the only First World country to increase its population in the next 30 years, meaning in the future it is necessary for countries like Japan to support a growing aging population.

The population of Japan, in turn, is declining, which creates a strain on the country's economic growth due to a shortage of workers. As noted on the World Population Review website, "Some reports claim Japan's total population could fall by as much as 30% to around 87 million by 2060 and the reasons, quite simply, point to a disparity in the birth and death rates."[114] This population decrease is a major issue Japan must address. Moreover, as the site also indicates, "Japan is currently the world's oldest country, and it's set to get even older. In 50 years, it's estimated by the government 40% of Japan's population will be over 65...5 decades ago, there were 12 workers for every retiree, [but] there will be an equal 1:1 ratio in 50 years."[115]

The United States has its problems, too. For example, in the last 15 years it has increased 40% of its jobs in the nonproductive healthcare industry and government sector.[116] The United States returns to manufacturing to get its economic prowess back on track. One of the alarming statistics in this vein is found in California, where the state government spends twice as much on prisons than on education. Whether the United States returns to manufacturing or continues to rely on a First World environmental capitalist society remains to be seen. Any attempts to bring manufacturing back to United States can increase competition with countries like Mexico, where many

---

114 *World Population Review*, Japan Population 2014, www.worldpopulationreview.com/countries/japan-population/.
115 Ibid.
116 Pothokoukis, James. "Was Nearly 40% of 'Private Sector' Job Growth in December Subsidized by Government?" *AEIdeas*, 4 January 2013, www.aei-ideas.org/2013/01/nearly-40-of-private-sector-job-growth-in-december-was-subsidized-by-government/.

Japanese carmakers are starting to relocate their factories to save money on tariff import costs.

According to NPR crime and punishment correspondent Laura Sullivan, the incarceration of one inmate costs, on average, approximately $60 per day.[117] According to a June 2010 article published by *The Economist*, yearly spending on a single inmate ranges from $18,000 in Mississippi to approximately $50,000 in California. In comparison, $50,000 is roughly seven times the annual amount spent on education per pupil."[118]

The dialogue in the United States for ideas is politics. Politics means money, which represents control and influence by big business and individuals concerning the monetary system, the paper tiger.

Pluto representing regeneration, the concept of metamorphosis, espionage, organized crime and secrets entered Capricorn in 2008. Since then, we have witnessed the removal of many heads of state, especially in the Middle East in the wake of the Arab Spring. More countries are going to be rocked by revolutions until around the year of 2025 when Pluto enters Aquarius setting up an 'air-quake.' If China has another cultural revolution, it would be at this time. If it doesn't have a revolution, then it won't experience a major change until 2047-2049. Concerning the Natal transit chart of China in February of 2048, Pluto in Pisces transits from 5° to 6° and enters the Second House of national wealth, money markets and financial institutions. In opposition to Pluto and Pisces, Uranus in Virgo at 9° is preparing to enter in the Eighth House of financial relationships with other nations, foreign investments and interest rates. This is a significant lineup for a revolution brought on by this 'air-quake'.

As you look around the world, the critical problem for the average citizen relates to government mismanagement. Russia has a so-called democracy that is, in fact, a plutocracy—a small wealthy elite running the country. The world recently witnessed a sham Russian election, resulting in tens of thousands of Russian citizens taking to the streets and demonstrating against falsified election results.

If world governments plan to return to productive growing economies that serve the people, then here are some important ingredients for success developed in Europe during the 16th century: competition, modern science, rule of law and private property rights, modern medicine, work ethics, and a consumer society. These basic tenets have propelled nations throughout history.[119]

There comes a time when an empire like the United States spends more money on paying down the interest on debt than on national security. All empires have experienced similar situations, and the United States is now losing its preeminent position in the world. However, the United States can climb back to a strong position if the government can become functional once again.

---

117 Sullivan, Laura. "Bail Burden Keeps U.S. Jails Stuffed with Inmates," *NPR News*, 21 January 2010, www.npr.org/2010/01/21/122725771/Bail-Burden-Keeps-U-S-Jails-Stuffed-With-Inmates.
118 "Too Many Laws, Too Many Prisoners," *The Economist*, July 22, 2010, http://www.economist.com/node/16636027.
119 http://legalschnauzer.blogspot.com/2011/03/rule-of-law-seems-to-be-on-life-support.html.

History tends to repeat itself. The decline of the U.S. empire could take 30 years or less. Assuming this decline occurs, a new world order could emerge, and at this juncture China could be the next dominating world empire. Empires come and go, and we are now standing on a precipitous ledge.

While the United States has the world's most powerful military, it no longer has the high level of respect it once had. The current path taken by the United States is typical of past empires that have lost their dominance in the world because of corruption and mismanagement of resources. A good example for dereliction of duty by Congress is the lack of updating the infrastructure of the United States, which exists at a second world level.

The future at this point may be with countries like Brazil, Russia, India, and China (collectively known as BRIC).[120] These countries are going to have a significant influence on the world economy as the Mayan era develops. The BRIC nations are in a position to move from Third World status to First World status. Admittedly, BRIC has a long way to go, but they can learn not to repeat others' mistakes. Russia has recently become a wild card. It's not clear what, where, or when Russia makes its true intentions known in respect to its role in the world. The growth and strength of Brazil's economy for the future has come into question due to political and social unrest stirring in the country for some time. Political unrest and pollution continue to plague the country in the foreseeable future and can derail the promise that Brazil has been working towards.

In 2011, BRIC represented an 18.9% share of the global economy, as pundit Fareed Zakaria reported on CNN's *Global Public Square* program. By 2022, BRIC will represent 25% of the world economy. Japan can take advantage of this opportunity through persistent and imaginative marketing of high-quality products.[121]

Financial growth in Japan has rebounded briefly as the Mayan Prediction unfolds. In September 2013, however, the Japanese economy slowed down and in turn led to a brief upward trend. Japanese Prime Minister Abe attempted to push his conservative agenda on the Japanese people, increasing inflation. As this decade wears on, the BRIC countries will become profitable export markets for Japan, but Japan's overall economic growth will remain stifled as economies around the world decline.

For example, as of 2011, India has experienced an economic slowdown due to the fundamental problems that all governments are facing: corrupt financial practices that are, to a varying degree, left unregulated and uncontrolled. Unexpected crises, such as those experienced in Ukraine, can and do dramatically change the financial stability of countries around the globe. Russia and the EU will be affected by the instability in Ukraine, which, in turn, can affect the world economy.

Beginning on December 21, 2012, the United States experiences a decade of struggle—challenges arise from within its boundaries with the financial arena as the main focus. After this decade—on May 31, 2021, to be precise—the Sibly Chart shows Uranus

---

[120] Jim O'Neill, a British economist employed with investment bank Goldman Sachs, coined the term *BRIC* in early 2000.
[121] Chellaney, Brahma. "The Cracks in the BRICS." *CNN World*, 26 March 2012, reported by Fareed Zakaria on Global Public Square, http://globalpublicsquare.blogs.cnn.com/2012/03/26/the-cracks-in-the-brics/

transits into the Sixth House of health and the working class, and epidemics are associated. Uranus's influence brings uncertainty. In the United States, Uranus delivers political tension between radicals and moderates. Although the concept of individualism is held as an ideal in the conservative wing, those in control do not like rank-and-file members disagreeing with them. Most political parties expect people to toe the party line.

In addition, from 2012 to 2022 Uranus reveals scientific discoveries that in time profoundly change the world. I suspect the hydrogen collider in Switzerland has something to do with this profound change. Also, LIGO's expanded discoveries of gravitational waves rippling from colliding black holes will be significant for understanding the Universe. Mysteries revealed by science and genetic editing in the next several decades are going to completely change the way we view and live in the Universe.

Radiation leaks and the damage resulting from the Great Eastern Japan Earthquake Disaster have perhaps irreparably harmed the Japanese nation. The long-term ramifications are yet to be understood. To date, little has been said about the damage to the ocean off the coast of the Fukushima Daiichi nuclear plant. It will take a decade before the verdict is in.

Great stoicism and discipline with which the Japanese tribe responded to this disaster were epitomized by the workers at the nuclear plant. The firefighters who risked their lives represented the strength and selflessness of the Japanese people. They prevented a complete meltdown by bringing in seawater to cool down the reactors. Workers still enter the contaminated site on a daily basis to perform essential cleanup.

In November 2011, it was reported the first reactor almost had a complete meltdown to bedrock. The consequent impact on the water supply, land and food in Japan would have been a catastrophe beyond comprehension and recovery. At that time, the Japanese government was damaging its own credibility by assuring the public the situation was under control. Now the government has to work hard to regain the public's trust. It has been reported repeatedly on NHK it can take 40 years to bring the Fukushima Daiichi nuclear plant to a complete shutdown. With frequent revelations of more radiation leaks into the soil and possibly into the ocean, the reality is it may take 60 years or more before the Fukushima Daiichi nuclear plant is completely shutdown.[122]

The fear of radiation is becoming pervasive, and many Japanese citizens have understandably become concerned about possible contamination of their food supply. Some now feel they must obtain food from other countries to ensure their safety. It is imperative the government step in and reassure the Japanese public about the safety of the national food supply. Now is the time for the Japanese government to overcome political infighting and deal with these life-threatening problems quickly and efficiently. Doing so is the only way to regain the public's confidence.

On February 2, 2014, the United States entered a period of financial woe, which transpired in part due to Pluto in Capricorn transiting into the Second House of national wealth, money markets, banks and other financial institutions. The U.S. government had

---

[122] ENENEWS, "Now 40 Years to 'Decommission' Fukushima Reactors, Says Gov't Timetable Revealed by NHK — Pushed Back 10 Years," December 15, 2011, http://enenews.com/now-40-years-to-decommission-fukushima-reactors-says-govt-timetable-revealed-by-nhk-video.

to raise the debt limit to pay its bills by the end of February 2014, as the U.S. debt topped $17 trillion and is still climbing. Any declining economic prowess of power for the United States has negative consequences for the Japanese. Then to the surprise of most, on February 10, 2014, the U.S. Congress finally passed legislation to raise the debt limit until the following year without any pork barrel attachments.

In the 21st century, China comes into its own as a world power. I cannot foresee specifics yet as to whether China is a world power for good or ill. However, its aggressive stance during the Senkaku Islands incident with the Japanese Coast Guard does not bode well. Yet, historically China does not attack other countries or look to acquire territory other than around its immediate borders. Unfortunately, the takeover of Tibet and the creation of new islands out of depths of the South China Sea for military outposts are not good omens.

There are limits to the impact politics may have on the financial crisis confronting Japan since the Great Eastern Japan Earthquake Disaster. The disaster exacerbated Japan's long-term prospects, which had been in steady decline for many years. In fact, there have been no trends toward consistent strengthening of the yen since the mid-80s (when Japanese growth was robust). Many factors have contributed to this decline, factors far too numerous to elaborate for the purposes of this book. It is worth mentioning, however, that Japanese private citizens and corporations hold more than 95% of the national debt, according to Bank of Japan. This high percentage contrasts sharply with countries like the United States and Greece that make it standard practice to issue bonds to foreigners. Said another way, the government of Japan is less subject than many other countries to foreign demands and influence. Even though Japan has its largest debt in its history and a debt crisis seems to be pending, the Japanese people have had to reassess and rebuild their morale in the wake of the 3/11 earthquake. A debt crisis will occur if and when foreign markets determine the interest rates on Japanese government bonds. Japan's addiction to credit was fueled in large part by the government's ability to borrow from Japanese corporations and the Japanese people. Now that same dynamic may protect the country from an unforgiving market at a critical time in history when it needs financial protection. Thus, I do not foresee undue foreign influence in Japan's future.

Serious economic problems are confronting many countries around the world as this book goes to press, including the ongoing debt crisis on the verge of imploding from 2014 - 2021. Europe could more than likely devalue the Euro, which could send the world in the direction of an economic recession. In 2015 the flood of over a million Syrian and Middle Eastern refugees into Europe adds to the financial uncertainty abounding from 2015 through 2020. The financial troubles afflicting Greece, Spain, and Italy are bringing these economies to the verge of bankruptcy. Portugal is no longer under EU imposed austerity. They adopted anti-austerity Keynesian economic policies after the socialists took office in 2015. The budget deficit is now the lowest it's been in over 40 years. The Greeks may never come out of their quagmire if they keep following the Troika policies. France has its own financial concerns threatening its viability as an economic power due, in large measure, to its generous, entitlement-based pensions.

Meanwhile, although Germany has mandated austerity for Eurozone countries, it's starting to encounter manufacturing slowdowns as demand lessens in response to uncertainties, such as using the same old economic tools foretold by the Mayan astrologer-priests so many centuries ago. With reduced economic clout, Germany may be a less-formidable opponent in upcoming negotiations with France, Greece, Italy and Spain (countries with weak economies) over austerity enforcement. With its huge debt and massive political instability, it is unclear if Ukraine joins the EU or drifts back into the waiting arms of Russia. As of March 2017, the jury is still out. Make no mistake, events in this region can and will have a major impact on the economies of the EU and Russia, which in turn affects the world economy.

On the other hand, Japan is poised to become an enlightened nation that leads the way as a beacon for the rest of the world. This process begins with the shedding of certain traditions tied to the past. For one thing, the Japanese government discovers the proper way to express humility for acknowledged atrocities during World War II. For another thing, it is time for governments worldwide to stop using pride and politics to continue disputes with other nations, disputes that ultimately serve the politicians and stifle the voice of reason and cooperation of the Present.

Politicians take the money they want from the public in the form of taxes, and somehow that money ends up in coffers of their financial supporters. Politicians, justify their spending by pointing to threats of terrorism and war to maintain their *status quo* power. In this manner, countries across the globe keep their people in check. Insane! The ultimate healer is the change that is the Age of Light.

At the end of 2014 into 2015, the Sibly chart had Pluto start the transit of the Second House of banks, financial institutions, and national wealth. This positioning is going to bring financial difficulties for several years to come. While Pluto on its own doesn't bring sudden decline, Pluto is the harbinger of major change to the financial structure and *status quo* that starts to take place with its transit in Capricorn. Beginning in mid-2019, transiting Saturn in Capricorn conjunct transiting Pluto in Capricorn with the Sibly chart, and it brings a restructuring concerning the Second House of money, property, and resources. Saturn conjunct Pluto historically is a dangerous and foreboding period, and a war somewhere in the world is a real possibility. Or a cyber attack hacking into America's financial institutions by a foreign government is a possibility. Russia undeniably helped Donald J. Trump, win the 2016 presidential election. Americans cannot bring themselves to think that this was even possible; it is, and they did!

The United States rekindles its approach to manufacturing and starts to rival those countries that pride themselves on moving products of excellent quality. Made in America stands for excellence, that is the direction the United States is going.

Pluto transiting the astrological Second House in the Sibly chart represents wealth, property, home, trade, banks, and financial institutions. In many ways, this shake-up is a revolutionary portent for the United States. This transit certainly speaks for the potential of a major financial transition in the United States finding its financial foundation by 2032-34.

Of course, in a global economy uncertainties will not be restricted to the U.S. economy. Japan must come to grips with its tremendous debt ratio to GDP, which is hindering Japanese economic expansion, especially in terms of the high value of the yen. However, with the election of a female Prime Minister in 2020, a "third opening" may develop, presaging alternatives with which Japan can change its course as it travels beyond the Mayan Prediction. Japanese women are going to take their rightful place in politics for navigating the future of Japan.

The world is now experiencing the most dramatic spiritual energy shift in the history of humankind. For example, the first landing of the spacecraft rover Curiosity on the planet Mars took place in the summer of 2012. Explorations on the planet over the next several years will lead to the discovery of fossilized forms of microscopic life that existed there many millions, if not a billion, years ago. Such exciting scientific discoveries are changing the world forever.

This is a powerful new moment in Japan's history, and Japan is on the forefront of cutting-edge communication. Whoever owns the communication technology can attempt to rule the world. However, the truth is no one can ever rule the world. One cannot rule that which is beyond rule. It is futile.

In the beginning of 2016, due to the unexpected global stock market swings and the reduction of Chinese manufacturing demands, the stage was set for a potential worldwide recession (for several years to come). The recession didn't occur and the US stock market has been setting record highs by the end of 2017. The United States is going to shift gears and reprioritize to become a manufacturing country once again. The United States may enjoy some prosperity despite the dark overall astrological portents because of the booming Chinese demand for U.S. goods and products. However, this demand may be short-lived because the Chinese government is already claiming it may limit what Chinese consumers can buy from other countries. Eventually, China wants to increase its domestic markets for its own products. Due to a predictive slowdown of China's economy to 7% (or some speculate it could be even lower), the currency's official rate in August of 2015 became 6.4 renminbi (yuan) per dollar, which means it dropped to 4.4 percent in three days. The norm has been the renminbi rises or falls a small fraction of a percentage point per day. This raises concerns worldwide and has prompted many new questions concerning the stability of the Chinese economy and its ability to control its financial structure.

The United States, however, is in trouble due to the deeply divisive opinions of its citizens. As the Mayan Prediction unfolds, the United States will undergo a tremendous evolutionary process that will take many years to work itself out. In the meantime, rabble-rousers, evangelicals, the Tea Party, the Occupy Wall Street movement, leftist splinter groups and vociferous reactionaries of many other stripes will stretch the sociopolitical fabric out of recognizable shape. It may well take the United States sometime to find and secure its sociopolitical and socioeconomic footing once again, if we ever had it.

Back in 2001 and 2002, Saturn started its transit through the Seventh House and was above the horizon of the Sibly Chart. The years 2002-2016 were a time for taking a visible role for the U.S. public in world affairs. In this period, we had two wars that weren't paid for, tax breaks for the wealthiest, and the worst financial collapse since the Great Depression. With Saturn in 2016 starting its transit below the horizon of the Sibly Chart,

Chapter 5 United States, China, and Japan

the United States will be reevaluating from within its cultural psyche. This brings a deep introspection for the U.S. to look at who and what we are as a divided country. We will still be standing. It is all in the mind's eye—the good, the bad, the ugly politicians, the intelligent, the ignorant and the enlightened. Saturn takes away, and what it takes away, it replaces with growth and maturity. The lowering of the tax rates for corporations and tax cuts for the wealthiest in America by President Trump and the Republican Party is the catalyst for America's financial woes begin around 2022 - 2024.

> *We don't see things as they are, we see them the way we are.*
> ~ Anaïs Nin

In the Sibly chart, Saturn entering the First House assists or impels the people of the United States to look deeper into the financial problems we ourselves have created. We act as if we have no power over the system and the ensuing daily chaos that has become the *status quo* of capitalism. On the other side of the planet but also under Saturn's influence, India has the potential to have a booming economy and can become an important source of Japanese financial investment. Such investment support can stabilize Japan's economy as recovery efforts continue. In 2014, India experienced a financial slowdown, as sexual scandals and other events delay its entry into the Age of Light. However, in the Age of Light China is going to have the most lucrative consumer market, not only for Japan but also for the rest of the world. And don't forget Taiwan, small, formidable and on the move, and the difficult resolution between China and Taiwan is cause for great alarm for a revolution in the next several decades. It could take that long for a resolution to the unresolved separation between Taiwan and China. China has never recognized Taiwan as separate from China. China is waiting for Taiwan to recognize itself as one with China. In time, if necessary, China will take military action to ensure its sovereignty over Taiwan. This would be the last resort, but make no doubt about this, it could happen. And, the United States will be powerless to do anything about it.

Beginning in 2016, Japan is forging a transition from oil-based and nuclear energy-generating technologies to innovative renewable-energy economy away from nuclear power and embracing alternative energy such as tides, wind, solar and geothermal. In 2016, the Meiji chart has transiting Neptune (which speaks to the ocean and seas) entering the Tenth House of national prestige and government sources. Japan is slowly transitioning during this time and enters a period of disorientation. Confusion can be associated with this Neptune transit. Getting rid of nuclear and oil-generating sources in favor of the alternative energy-generating technologies of tomorrow will help Japan move forward during this time of uncertainty. There is the potential for the Japanese people to march in large numbers in the streets and demand the government listen to their concerns. They don't want a nuclear future. The roots of Shinto make themselves known.

Beginning in Tunisia and continuing in Egypt in 2011 and then across the world during the second decade of the 21st century, country after country is changing its political landscape. I've already stated the importance of the major square of Pluto in Capricorn Uranus in Aries from 2010 through most of the coming decade. It is this square that provides the astrological shift concerning advents of revolutions, and its effects will continue until the end of this decade and beyond. Both of these planets remind us of the change needed to heal corrupt governments in the world. This square is consistent with the changes brought about by the Arab Spring due to the history of Pluto square Uranus, which coincides with the upheaval in the Middle East.

The astrological shift associated with the revolutions of the second decade of the 21st century include Pluto entering Capricorn, Uranus entering Aries and Neptune entering Pisces in February 2012 (Neptune remains there until March 31, 2025). Pluto square Uranus in this decade provides the unexpected focus on governments reconsidering their priorities and actually listening to their citizens' concerns. A conscious awakening in the world helps us all realize everyone must have education, healthcare, shelter and employment. As humans, we can and should invest in one another for the sake of the planet. Give to one another to serve one another so we can heal the planet. All three planets remind us of the need to change and to end the confusion that consumes our lives and the world, which is the idea of consumption itself. The way we are headed presently is only going to destroy us, and the planet will carry on without us. This century is the point of no return for either flourishing or floundering. The world must experience a great upheaval before it is disinfected of its past ignorant ways of living in an unconscious world before evolving to the Age of Light.

Many upheavals took place in 2011-2012, including the civil war in Syria, the overthrow of the head of state in Yemen, the continuing confusion in Egypt and the behind-the-scenes political instability in Iran. As the Mayan astrologer-priests foretold, uncertainty is certain in our day and age. Beginning in 2017, terrorist attacks are becoming dramatic in their creative manner of the attacks, and they are becoming more frequent in Europe and the usual locations. These murderous attacks are often seen as desperate acts by desperate people, and terrorists don't care that the vast majority of the world population are against them.

Solving the core problem of the Middle East is quite simple: share the wealth from the oil in the Middle East with the people of the Middle East. Doing so could bring an end to all the revolutions in the Middle East, as well as provide greater opportunities for shelter, education, healthcare, and job training. Love and only love as forgiveness and by sharing the wealth is the approach that can finally bring peace to the Middle East. The Arabian government has undertaken such an approach in terms of wealth distribution for its countrymen, which was the purpose of staving off a revolution within its own country. As a consequence, Saudi Arabian politicians and royalty are ensuring the continuing existence of a stable and unified government backed by their people. Of course, Saudi Arabia is still living hundreds of years in the past when it comes to the treatment of women, but this behavior must change and will for the betterment of everyone. However, Saudi Arabia for many years has experienced terrorism hardly reported in the media. Information for public consumption is kept to a minimum.

★ ★ ★ ★ ★ ★ ★   ★ ★ ★ ★ ★ ★ ★   ★ ★ ★ ★ ★ ★ ★

Geologists and archeologists have shown how the Earth has changed over millennia. Change is the breath of the Universe, and we witness the change. We are all interrelated. It is part of the evolution of our awareness to be cooperative and considerate to one another, because it's not easy being human.

Chapter 5 United States, China, and Japan

From 2008 through 2013, the Pluto square Uranus provided a shift combined with Neptune entering Pieces in 2012 (for the first time in around 164 years). Generally speaking, this shift disturbs the *status quo* with revolutions until the end of this decade. Syria is a good example, with more refugees to come. In 2016 Europe is starting to react to the overwhelming refugee flood that is creating a negative backlash and a potential crisis in Europe. Both Pluto and Uranus signify the clearing out of a past that no longer works and the planting of seeds for eliminating the evils of terrorism, corruption and greed. This combination emphasizes the misuse of money and power by elite groups and individuals to further their own personal wants and needs. President Assad's regime in Syria is an example of this kind of misuse of power. It is the epic struggle between Dark and Light. Evil cannot hide from the Light. What is, is, and what is not, is not. The Present is all there is.

You = Light/Dark. The way to live an enlightened-aware life is to be the balance of these two energies and then allowing yourself to learn how to live outside opposites of which we are derivatives. It is a question of when the world evolves to serve each other, to cooperate with each other, and then a wondrous world develops in harmony with nature.

The Mayan Prediction is ushering in an era of awareness and planting the seeds for the Age of Aquarius that will affect social, psychological and political realms around the world for many years. For my part, I am doing what I can to help the world continue by choosing a lifestyle that is productive and not destructive. I consume as little as I can, and I live a simple life. I am happier and healthier because of the simple choices I have made. I attempt every day to live my life intelligently. Living a life without conflict is not easy and yet worth the effort and the understanding it takes. It is a beautiful way to live.

For its part, Japan should not allow its manufacturing industry to rely solely on shipping goods and automobiles overseas. The temptation for profits and cheap labor has a way of destroying the mightiest countries in the world, including the United States. However, the United States has a history of bringing itself back from the brink of disaster. It may take longer this time for the United States to recover due to the political gridlock freezing the body politic, but in time the country will regain a strong economic footing.

The rise of political reform is inevitable and must be addressed as it affects the way the United States relates to itself and the rest of the world. Since the presidential election of 2012, the United States has been attempting to correct its position on immigration reform and bring the American people a less-expensive healthcare system.

However, in the Sibly chart of the United States, Pluto entered the Second House of national wealth in 2014. The United States is going to have financial problems interrelated to the rest of the world as the next decade dawns. We live in a global economy, and one part of the world can and does affect the rest of the world. It is a delicate financial balance. A monster like capitalism has a mind of its own, meaning the world is being subjected to a system it cannot truly control or understand.

One problem is the people of the United States generally aren't very sophisticated when it comes to international politics, largely due to the self-absorbed nature of the American culture. According to the Sibly chart, the Sun sign of the United States is Cancer, and the

Sun sign of Cancer tends to be self-centered. Americans, it seems safe to say, have a self-aggrandized sense of their importance in relationship with the rest of the world.

However, it was not always so. The Watergate scandal of the early 1970s showcased the ability of the U.S. media, with the support of the American people, to report the truth that ultimately led to Richard Nixon's resignation as president. As America celebrated its bicentennial in 1976, the country became a unified nation for the first time since World War II—even if it was only for that one day! The United States tends to overlook its past to save itself the conscious humiliation of what we did to the Native Americans and participation in slavery. Japan, on the other hand, has a tradition like no other, and its loyal band of survivors will never abandon their tribe. Of course, Japan also has a past it would like to forget, a past involving its efforts to colonize Asia and the brutality inflicted on their captors.

A government that attempts to control the masses eventually encounters difficulties as the world moves into unknown territory. It is estimated the world's population could increase to 9.7 billion people by 2050 as the 21st century unfolds. The availability and distribution of water, energy, and natural resources will, to some extent, define and shape future events in terms of which countries thrive and which struggle. We are going to witness in this century famines responsible for the deaths of millions of people, due to lack of water, food, and poor health.

★ ★ ★ ★ ★ ★ ★   ★ ★ ★ ★ ★ ★ ★   ★ ★ ★ ★ ★ ★ ★

Sir Winston Churchill once said, "Many forms of Government have been tried and will be tried in this world of sin and woe. No one pretends that democracy is perfect or all-wise. Indeed, it has been said that democracy is the worst form of Government except for all those other forms that have been tried from time to time." Churchill's words certainly rang true for Japan after 3/11. For one thing, the Japanese people did not expect their government to allow such an outrageous catastrophe to occur in the first place.

In late May 2012, Prime Minister Naoto Kan indicated the Japanese government didn't receive enough information about the accident from Japan's nuclear safety agency and other sources at the time of the Fukushima Daiichi disaster.[123] Kan then asked a top Tokyo Electric Power Company (TEPCO) official why emergency venting of the reactor containment vessel was not carried out with rising pressure occurring on the inside. According to Kan, the TEPCO official replied he didn't know. This answer is inexcusable.

It seems the breakdown in communications occurred within the ranks of TEPCO. On NHK in 2012, it came to light the regulatory arm of the Japanese government had a close relationship with TEPCO, and the government had not been providing the kind of critical oversight and scrutiny the public had expected of them.[124]

For that matter, evidence suggests NHK was expected to broadcast favorable information about the government. Along those lines, NHK, considered by many to be Japan's

---

[123] Corrice, Leslie. *The Hiroshima Syndrome*, www.hiroshimasyndrome.com/fukushima-accident-updates/fukushima-33.html.

[124] Kay, Jonathan. "The Fukushima Report: A 'Made in Japan' Disaster with Policy Implications for All of Us." *National Post*, 9 July 2012, http://fullcomment.nationalpost.com/2012/07/09/jonathan-kay-on-the-fukushima-report-a-made-in-japan-disaster-with-policy-implications-for-all-of-us/.

most authoritative television and radio news source, has also seen its share of problems due to internal scandals. In February 2014, it was disclosed in *The New York Times* that a longtime commentator for NHK announced his resignation after being ordered not to criticize nuclear power because of an important upcoming election.

In early 2014, these kinds of controversies at NHK had caused a number of Japanese liberals to fear Prime Minister Abe and his ever-expanding rightwing agenda. As *The New York Times* reported, opposition lawmaker, Kazuhiro Haraguchi stated, "'What I am worried about is that NHK will become loyalist media, become the public relations department of the government. [NHK is] part of the infrastructure that forms the basis of our democracy.'"[125]

A parliamentary committee then called on Katsuto Momii, the new president of NHK, to clarify whether or not he had been told to support the government's views on foreign policy and not to criticize their actions. "'We cannot say left when the government says right,'" he said when asked whether NHK would present Japan's position on territorial and other disputes. He explained that it was 'only natural' for the network to follow the Japanese government's position." [126] These toe-the-line policies are not helping Japan's position in its power struggles with China and South Korea concerning wartime history and current territorial disputes.

Experts say the newest controversy hurts NHK's image at a time when one in four Japanese households refuses to pay its monthly viewing fee of $13 to $22 because of scandals, including one in 2004 when a producer used company funds to take a mistress to exotic destinations. The broadcaster has also faced widespread distrust for coverage of the 2011 Fukushima accident that some say complied with government efforts to hide the extent of radiation releases.

In the fall of 2013, Americans experienced one of the worst kinds of misuse of government by the very members of Congress who were voted to uphold the Constitution of the United States and represent the American people. In October 2013, Congress purposely shut down the government. Our government is bought and owned by large money interests, and we no longer have democracy in this country. When there are divisive issues in the news, you can bet whoever spends the most money controls public opinion.

The best action the United States could pursue now is to remove its military from the Middle East. The U.S. relationship with Israel is one of the main reasons behind the U.S. presence in the Middle East. Additionally, there is fear radicals could acquire an atomic bomb and overthrow Pakistan, along with the potential for war with Iran over nuclear weapons. Israel is, in fact, an extension of the American military. This is all the more reason for the United States to get out of the Middle East. In looking to the foreseeable Present, we are going to keep the American military in the Middle East, just in case.

The United States has criticized the Chinese corporate-government state of manipulating its currency, the renminbi, in order to steal U.S. manufacturing jobs through

---

125 Fackler, Martin. "News Giant in Japan Seen as Being Compromised." *The New York Times*, 2 February 2014, www.nytimes.com/2014/02/03/world/asia/news-giant-in-japan-seen-as-being-compromised.html?_r=0.
126 Ibid.

outsourcing. Chinese labor is attractive to U.S. companies because there are no minimum wages or unions to deal with. This means the United States can pay sweatshop wages to Chinese workers. As governments and corporations continue to vie for control of the world's markets, considerations like those unions and others have fought for in the United States since the early 20th century—such as a 40-hour work week, a living wage, and health benefits—often fall by the wayside. With China's corporate-government complex fueling its economic juggernaut, the rest of the world's governments have to adjust.

Considering the cheap labor and vast stockpiles of natural resources China is buying up, China could well become immune to economic fluctuations, enabling it to export products the world's market will have to purchase in the absence of others at a comparable (cheap) price. Will China come to dictate what the rest of the world will have to take or leave?

And how does Japan challenge China's reach for economic hegemony? One thing is certain, as the Mayan Prediction unfolds: Uncertainty means no preconceptions are allowed as we search for certainty!

As previously mentioned, the United States for several years now has criticized the Chinese corporate-government state for manipulating the yuan in order to steal U.S. manufacturing jobs. Similar patterns unfold around the world. Of course, in the case of the relationship between Japan and the United States, diplomatic rough patches can be smoothed over due to each country's need for the other as a trading partner. However, it is yet to be seen how the world responds to China's buildup of its military and naval prowess, especially in the seas surrounding China and East Asia. In the ocean around the disputed islands are known oil and natural resources, which is why the outcome surely involves a financial agreement. However, advances in science are going to change the energy landscape forever by 2032. The major effects of limitless energy-generating capabilities begin when Pluto is well established in Aquarius by around 2026.

The bigger China grows, the more energy they are going to use, which is affecting the cost of oil. China is lacking in oil reserves and has to rely on the usual suspects. Clearly, the cost of energy is going to go up in Japan as a result, which is all the more reason for the Japanese government to address their long-term prospects for energy use. This loss of nuclear energy for Japan creates tremendous problems that must be resolved as soon as possible. Necessity brings out the best in the human spirit. Wave energy collection technology, fuel cell cars, and solar panels help to alleviate the world energy crisis. The Sun is the source of our life. It is the current and future solution to the world's need for energy in the Age of Light.

Beginning in mid-2019, transiting Saturn in Capricorn conjunct transiting Pluto in Capricorn with the Sibly chart, and it occurs in the Second House of money, property, and resources. Transiting Saturn conjunct transiting Pluto until the end of 2020. Financial woes for the United States are on the table, and they are not going away anytime soon. The summer of 2020 is politically explosive with social unrest on a major scale, which has not been seen in many decades. In June 2016 Great Britain voted to leave the European community and starting in 2018-2019, I see this could be the beginning of a potential world recession. In the U.S. Sibly chart, Pluto and Saturn have a rendezvous to conjunct in

Chapter 5 United States, China, and Japan

Capricorn as they transit the Second House representing revenue. If the European Union starts to splinter, this will be one of many factors contributing to this economic downturn worldwide. There is going to be uncertainty for the United States with its first Pluto return concerning the inexplicable political landscape in America.

The soul of America is going to be in question. What are we now? What do over 300 million Americans want for the future of America? We have so much. We can do and accomplish anything our consciousness is capable of imagining. But only if we can look at each other and ask what we can each do to help America be a better, cleaner, and safer place to live on a healthy, beautiful planet; the only home we have.

From 2010 on, Japan pays closer attention to its relationships with other countries than heretofore. It may be best for Japan to treat the United States with friendly caution because of the countries' close economic ties. Like many countries, Japan wants a strong United States. With the Saturn transit of the U.S. Sibly horoscope in the coming years, Japan can rely on the United States as a solid partner. However, it is also important for Japan to assert a new sense of independence within that relationship. Japan is going to serve as an example for people living a spiritual, happy and healthy life. Japan begins its journey into the Age of Light by increasingly meeting its future energy needs through a unique combination of renewable energy and sacrifice by the Japanese tribe.

With regard to the Japanese tribe, there's a kind of national honor code they exemplify. If you lose your wallet in the subway, you can expect to find your wallet at the local police station or at the subway lost and found. Honesty is valued, which comes from the cohesion of a strong tribal awareness. The Great Eastern Japan Earthquake Disaster has put a spotlight on the relationship between business and the Japanese government. The Japanese government has been struggling to effectuate national recovery efforts, especially with the subsequent three near-meltdowns of the Fukushima Daiichi nuclear plant. However, the Japanese tribe has gotten the recovery under way, all while enduring many hardships with dignity and grace.

However, Japan's tight-knit social fabric can also lead to discrimination against those who don't seem to fit in. For example, ethnic Koreans who immigrate to Japan are often discriminated against. Indeed, after the terrible earthquake of 1923, Japanese people accused Koreans of attempting to overthrow the Japanese government. As a result, some 6,000 Koreans were slaughtered.[127] This sort of mob action is based on a tribal consciousness distorted by fear. Fortunately, the Japanese people have greatly evolved throughout the 20th century and into the 21st century. As the Age of Light unfolds, I foresee a continuing dissipation of prejudice as the true character of the Japanese tribal soul expresses itself.

Today, Japan's sense of community is evolving beyond its dark past. Nonetheless, crowd-think is, of course, seen the world over. In parts of the United States, discrimination towards others because of their race or sexual preference has led to hatred and violence. When all of the people of a nation are not valued and supported by society as a whole, everyone pays a price.

---

127 Hammer, Joshua. "The Great Japan Earthquake of 1923." *Smithsonian*, May 2011, www.smithsonianmag.com/history/the-great-japan-earthquake-of-1923-1764539/

Gaps between rich and poor are more modest in Japan than in other First World countries, and Japan's corporate leaders would be embarrassed by the flamboyant pay packages commonplace for executives in the United States. Even the poor areas of Japan, including *burakumin* neighborhoods, have excellent schools. Japan has come a long way since the early days of the last century. The relationship between the United States and Japan is strong, and I see it continuing to be strong in the future, especially as the Japanese people evolve into tribal awareness, which in turn will influence the American people.

In the Age of Light, with all its uncertainty and potential for chaotic disruption of tradition and long-established business practices, I think it would be wise for Japan to diversify its approach to marketing. That is, Japan needs to "re-tool" the way its marketers tell stories about how Japanese engineers are constantly pushing the frontiers of quality and innovation. A generation ago, Japanese carmakers were able to penetrate the vast U.S. market because of the quality of their cars. In today's much more competitive global marketplace and in the wake of massive recalls of defective products, Japan doesn't want to blow its own horn because it is considered bad form. The Japanese know the quality of the work should speak for itself, a philosophy that evolves as Japan begins to diversify its approach to exporting and marketing its products.

Perhaps a good start to helping consumers around the world understand Japan's commitment to quality and excellence would be to explain how tinkering for no particular reason has a deep connection with the Zen Buddhist outlook. Lexus set out to create the best steering wheel in the world, a steering wheel made of bamboo that would enable the driver to be one with the car with the steering wheel as the conduit. This kind of dedication needs to be more widely communicated in order to reveal to the world the mystical element underlying Japanese craftsmanship. As German composer Richard Wagner once said, "Joy is not in things, it is in us." Consider if you may, we see the world as we are, not as it is.

Close security ties between Japan and the United States bring many benefits to both nations. The alliance is seen as deterring potentially disruptive forces in the Asian region, and U.S. officials have stated the alliance has kept China's expansionist military power in check and provides a major peacekeeping buffer against the Democratic People's Republic of Korea. The United States continues to play a quiet but powerful behind-the-scenes role in support of Japan concerning Japan's territorial disputes with China and Russia over the next 15 years.

During the years leading up to 2020, increasing numbers of U.S. citizens are going to become homeless. A massive jobs program is instituted to put U.S. citizens back to work. The Occupy Wall Street movement that spread around the world represents the stirrings of dissatisfaction among the "99%" of ordinary citizens who are not members of the elite. This movement is going to pressure governments in new and unexpected ways. For example, in the United States many customers of large multinational banks have been withdrawing their funds and transferring them to community-based credit unions over the past several years.[128] I think it is safe to point out the parallels between the Tea Party (an ostensibly "grassroots" movement that actually represents the interests of its corporate and elite funders) on

---

128 Phillips, Demetrius. "Bankers, Take the Time to Educate Your Customers." *American Banker*, 16 January 2014, www.americanbanker.com/bankthink/bankers-take-the-time-to-educate-your-customers-1064944-1.html.

the right side of the political spectrum and the Occupy movement on the left side of the spectrum. Both have attempted to dominate political discourse in the United States.

When a reasonable political check-and-balance system is employed, then we can once again win the day and bring a governable process to Congress, the Supreme Court and the Presidency, which the Founding Fathers intended.

The United States started as a republic and thinks it's a democracy. Yet, its democracy gets all muddled up for its own protection against the majority who seem to be very much unconscious about matters that matter.

Beginning in October and by December 17, 2020, Saturn enters into the sign of Aquarius in the Sibly chart as it is transiting the Second House of National Wealth. Also, Saturn conjunct Sibly's Natal Pluto squaring transiting Uranus in Taurus in the Fifth House of speculation and preparing to enter the Sixth House of Health and National Service, and trade unions. The emphasis here is on bringing about necessary monetary changes in the healthcare industry.

Eventually, the cost of healthcare has to be regulated by the government, so it no longer continues to skyrocket in a rigged capitalistic system designed to take from the masses and give to the asses, the few who have most of the wealth at the expense of the 99% of the world who are, for all intents and purposes, disenfranchised. Terrorism is a symptom of our worldly economic inequities, which reside in the hands of the haves and have-nots with the percentages growing further apart every day.

 In February of 2022, the United States begins to experience the beginning of a rare Pluto return to the celestial position it originally occupied on the founding date of the Sibly chart—July 4, 1776. The Sibly chart has Pluto transiting the Second House of national wealth from 2014 until 2031. Pluto moves into a new astrology House from the Second into the Third House in late February 2031. This brings an astrological 'air- quake' bringing with it social upheaval and a national dialogue about what America rep- resents to itself and the world.

The decade starting in 2020 is going to be one of the more significant growth periods in the history of the United States. Events in this decade can be tantamount to a second American Revolution, only this time, women have a more significant voice in the revolution and subsequent events. When the Sibly chart experiences its first Pluto return highlights Pluto's influence, which represents death and rebirth to the subject of the chart. Secretive aspects of U.S. society are put in question, and the United States reawakens as a people who share basic fundamental rights, including freedom of speech, personal privacy and a free press, all of which are under attack at the beginning of the 21st century. (Unfortunately, "free" press has already been bought and sold by biased points of view representing the *status quo* rather than the need for reform and the elimination of the corruption concerning government and its ties to the political body.)

Just as Japan reinvented itself with the help of the United States at the end of World War II, the United States undergoes a similar transformation starting in 2022. This time, Japan leads the United States into the Light. Great growth is on its way for the United

States. U.S. citizens will be challenged to decide if they can live up to the Founding Fathers' vision regarding opportunities for life, liberty, and the pursuit of happiness. This Pluto return brings out the Libertarian approach to governance, where the natural proclivities and talents of ordinary people are recognized and fostered.

In the past 50 years, the American people had their power of representation taken away. e U.S. Constitution has become a quaint concept that no longer applies to the American reality. Once a First World country, the United States has become a Second World country. It is hard for Americans to accept they have been slipping into Darkness for some time. The United States has the greatest military capability in the world, and on many levels, for a First World, it has one of the most outdated infrastructures in the world.

The United States has 5 percent of the world's population and confines 25 percent of the world's pensioners. This is not the land of the free. Corporations are the hidden rulers, orchestrating the world in which we live. Those who have the gold rule. A small number of people have more money than most governments. Governments are welfare coffers for the wealthiest people in the world.

At the time of its founding in 1776, the United States was an isolationist and agrarian republic. At that time, ordinary American citizens harbored a deep suspicion of standing armies anywhere in the world. Such an outlook and stance would, I think, characterize the attitudes that prevailed in Japan before the Meiji Constitution in 1889.

Pluto represents the death and rebirth of the hidden and secretive aspects of any society, especially concerning its political and socioeconomic structure due to the influence of Capricorn. Pluto rules the shadow of the collective unconsciousness (though there are always a few conscious individuals assisting along the way). The Pluto Capricorn at 27° (during the Pluto return in 2022) will occur in the Second House of national wealth. These aspects signify economic recovery is going to be slow and uncertain for the United States and the global community during the decade that began in 2010 and moving into 2024. The key word is uncertainty for Britain's departure concerning the European Union in 2016, which has set the stage for financial adjustments on all fronts. One is the possibility Scotland and/or Northern Ireland may reconsider leaving Britain so they can stay with the European Union. Another possibility is other nations leaving the European Union, which would kick greater uncertainty further down the road. This could lead to a financial world recession.

On February 20, 2022, the Sun is in Pisces at 1°, Jupiter is in Pisces at 11° and Saturn is in Aquarius at 17° in the Third House of communication, which codifies concepts, ideas and a major railway accident can occur at this time. Neptune in Pisces 22° is transiting the Fourth House of land and the opposition party in government, emphasizing remembering and shedding of the past represented by Pisces. Uranus will be in Taurus at 11°, just entering the Sixth House of the working class, wages, employment and unemployment. And Pluto in Capricorn at 27° signals the first major shakeup in America since the marches across the country that took place against the Vietnam War decades ago. The march to Selma, along with many other marches of blood, sweat and suffering, will rekindle an authentic America, similar to the demonstration events of the 1960s. We yearn for equality among all genders, races and colors.

Chapter 5 United States, China, and Japan

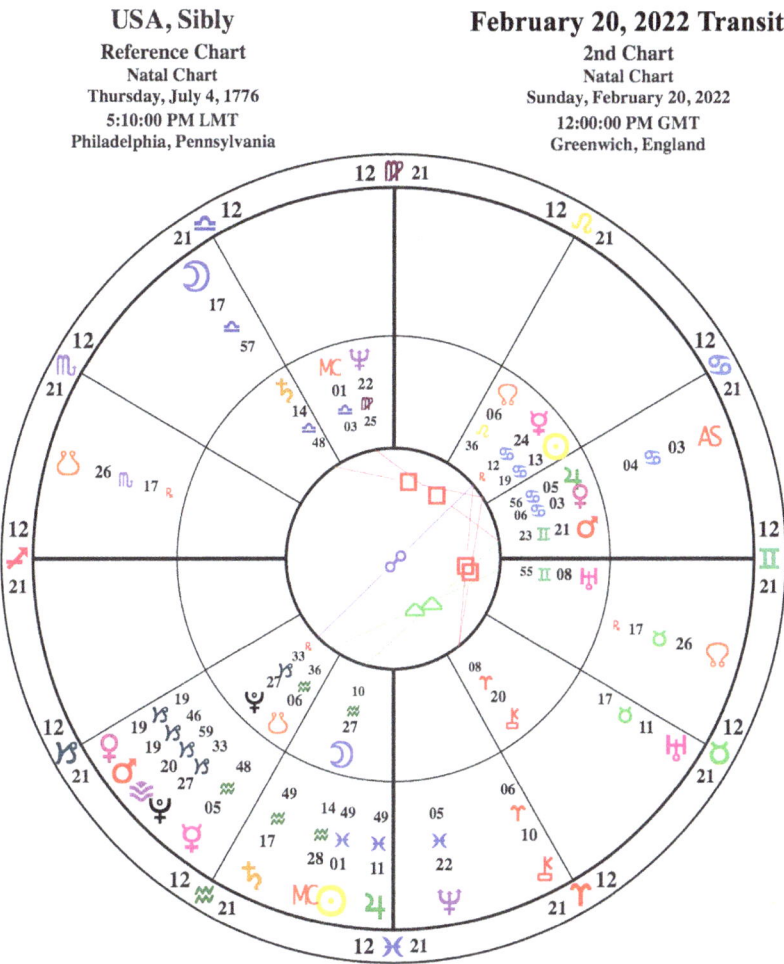

Neptune, the god of the sea, is known to rule Pisces. Neptune represents the subtle, human side of existence and tends to bring forth the artistic and sensitive side of individuals. Neptune is also associated with mysticism. However, escapism, deception, confusion and vagueness are also associated with Neptune. Neptune's influence could bring the United States into the turmoil of indecision due to the demands of the American people.

Saturn, the god of agriculture, was founded on the pretext of social order for civilization. Agriculture has been associated with family life through most of recorded history. Even today in some areas of the planet, it's the family that supplies the food source for the local community. In the United States, local farmers must face both climate change and large food corporations, which continue taking over the U.S. food supply.

Saturn is also associated with time, age, and society in general. It embodies the principles of stability and upheaval as well as disagreements. The principle of contraction is also related to Saturn—it transforms that which is vague and unformed and creates and manifests. These are some of the key astrological influences the United States will experience in 2020-2030, what I would call the decade of revolution. As the decade unfolds, transiting Saturn in Capricorn conjunct transiting Pluto and Sibly's Natal Pluto, and this speaks to unexpected acts against authority. This is going to be an explosive time. I suspect a national crisis occurs that has ties to terrorists, and the attack is aimed at our financial system. We are hit by cyber-attacks targeting our financial sector and tied to bombs exploding in the financial district of New York.

During this decade, the United States will redefine itself as a manufacturer of quality products. And like Japan, the United States is recognized as a quality manufacturer.

The U.S. government gives more autonomy to local officials in various regions in the country, because the American public is demanding more localized rule that strips the federal government of some of its local decision-making powers. Lao Tzu first formulated this self-sufficient form of village government many centuries ago. Now, amazingly, the young nation of the United States follows his political teachings, though most of its citizens remain unaware of his influence. Moreover, the United States' role as the food basket of the world depends on changing weather patterns. A lot depends on climate change. In the winter of 2014, the United States experienced some of the most extreme forms of weather in modern history (for example, the extreme drought in California, a state responsible for almost a third of the fruit and vegetable supply of the country). Thus, the United States has a major impact on the production and distribution of healthy food on a massive scale. As we know, food ultimately is more important than oil. Water is the ultimate resource we cannot live without, and it takes a great deal of water to produce food. It is estimated that 80% of California's water is used for agriculture. Food costs continue to increase steadily as the decade of uncertainty comes to a close.

Also on February 20, 2022, transiting Pluto conjunct Sibly Pluto in the Second House, and transiting Saturn in Aquarius demonstrates how a society can survive by shifting towards the Age of Light. The combination of Pluto and Saturn emphasize problems with banks with financial resources coming into question, material resources, wealth and economy are going to be in trouble. It also demonstrates security and insecurity in the collective. On a deeper level, it reflects society's values—that which society holds dear and no longer deems important. This is a dangerous time in America, and it's fermenting the change that's to become…

At this time, the United States branching out in many directions, much like that which occurred during the first "Hundred Days" of Franklin D. Roosevelt's first administration in 1933. There is a concerted effort by the spirit of America to bring the country together and to rebuild infrastructure so as to put millions of people in the United States back to work. A Newer New Deal means starting over again with a clean slate and reorganizing the financial infrastructure from top to bottom. The United States continues to maintain the most powerful military in the world.

The most upsetting aspect of the Pluto return at the exact degree and minute begins February 20-21, 2022 with a breakdown in the basic economic landscape of the United States. Growing business instabilities are going to spin out of human control, and the country will face great difficulties concerning money, borrowing, spending and growth.

Chapter 5 United States, China, and Japan

The infrastructure of the United States is in desperate need of repair. During this period, the United States is going to start to work its way out of the financial difficulties it has created for itself. During the decade of 2020-2030, by addressing problems head on, America grows into a stronger united country similar to the Marshall Plan. There is a spiritual and cultural growth of awakening that is an important component for this decade of evolution. Bob Dylan said it best, "The Times They Are A-Changin'."

The United States has become a combined form of plutocracy-oligarchy, which threatens the ideals upon which the country was founded. It seems a small elite group of people run the business of business in the United States, and this group tells the government what to do at the expense of the needs of taxpayers and voters. However, the world has a spirit of its own, which is another lesson the Age of Light is going to teach the elites of the world. The Age of Light prepares the world for the Age of Aquarius, which begins to shine brightly by 2150. This is a little over 120 years, less than the movement of a breath in Eternity.

> *Summa scientia nihil scire -*
> *The height of science is to know nothing.*
> Rosicrucian slogan

> *"To know that we know what we know, and to know that we do not know what we do not know, that is true knowledge."*
> ~ Nicolaus Copernicus, b. 19 February 1473

Japan Meiji-USA Sibly

Astrological Synastry Analysis

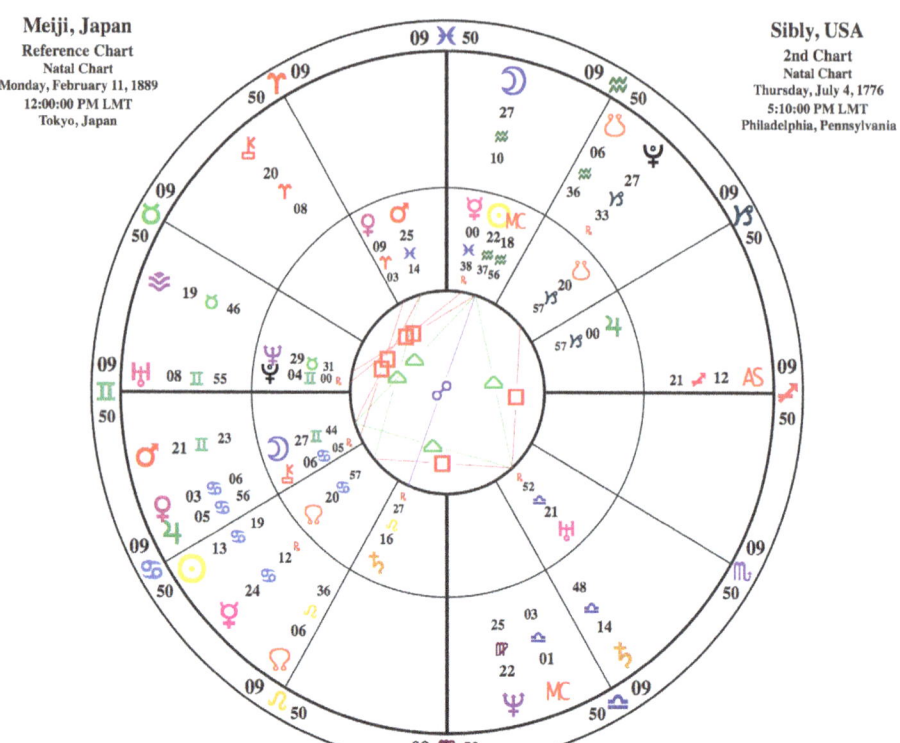

I n the figure above, Japan's Meiji chart is on the inside of the wheel, while the outer wheel shows the U.S. Sibly chart. The U.S. Sibly chart and Japan's Meiji chart are each a configuration for Synastry astrology. Synastry is an age-old practice of comparing two horoscopes, a technique that remains one of the most popular among astrologers. The word *synastry* is from the Latin meaning "together with the stars." In this case, it is the art of analyzing a relationship of two nations from which astrologers can gauge compatibility or incompatibility and areas of conflict or misunderstanding.

As I have stated, I have chosen the Sibly chart to represent the United States from a mundane astrological point of view.

The rising sign in the Sibly chart is 12° Sagittarius, and on September 11, 2001, transiting Saturn in Gemini at 14° had just entered the Seventh House of foreign relations and was opposite the Sagittarius rising sign of the Sibly chart, which represents the nation.

Transiting Pluto in Sagittarius at 12° was opposite Saturn at 14° Gemini, which represented the culmination of efforts that began 14 years earlier that triggered opposing forces and foreign enemies. In mundane astrology, Pluto represents disruption, decline, regeneration, death, and birth. Whereas Saturn represents authority, limitations, and deaths. This astrological opposition symbolizes the tragedy of 9/11.

On September 11, 2001, transiting Uranus was in Aquarius at 21° and conjunct the Sibly Moon in the Third House of communication, transportation, and diplomatic messages.

Transiting Mercury at 14° Libra was conjunct to the Sibly Saturn at 14° Libra in the Tenth House of national prestige, and Saturn in Libra speaks to tradition, the police, rules, and regulations in people employed by the state. In the course of this research, I became curious to see if there might have been some form of violence occurring on the same day in Tokyo, the city of my birth. So, I set aside the Sibly chart and consulted the Meiji chart. On September 11, 2001, the Meiji transiting chart had the conjunct of Uranus in Aquarius at 21° and the Sun in Aquarius at 22° occurring in the Ninth House of foreign lands, high seas, the airline industry, religion, and preachers and their beliefs. Transiting Saturn in Gemini 14° in the First House of the image of the nation in the Meiji chart was opposite transiting Pluto at 12° Sagittarius in the Seventh House of foreign relations (and/ or hostile activity with foreign countries) and workers. In addition, in the Seventh House transiting Mars in Capricorn at 1° conjuncts Meiji Jupiter in Capricorn at 00°. Consulting weather charts and the news, I noticed Typhoon Danes hit Tokyo with winds at 185 km/ hour on September 11, 2001. In other words, both nations experienced different forms of violence on September 11, 2001 (see the chart below).

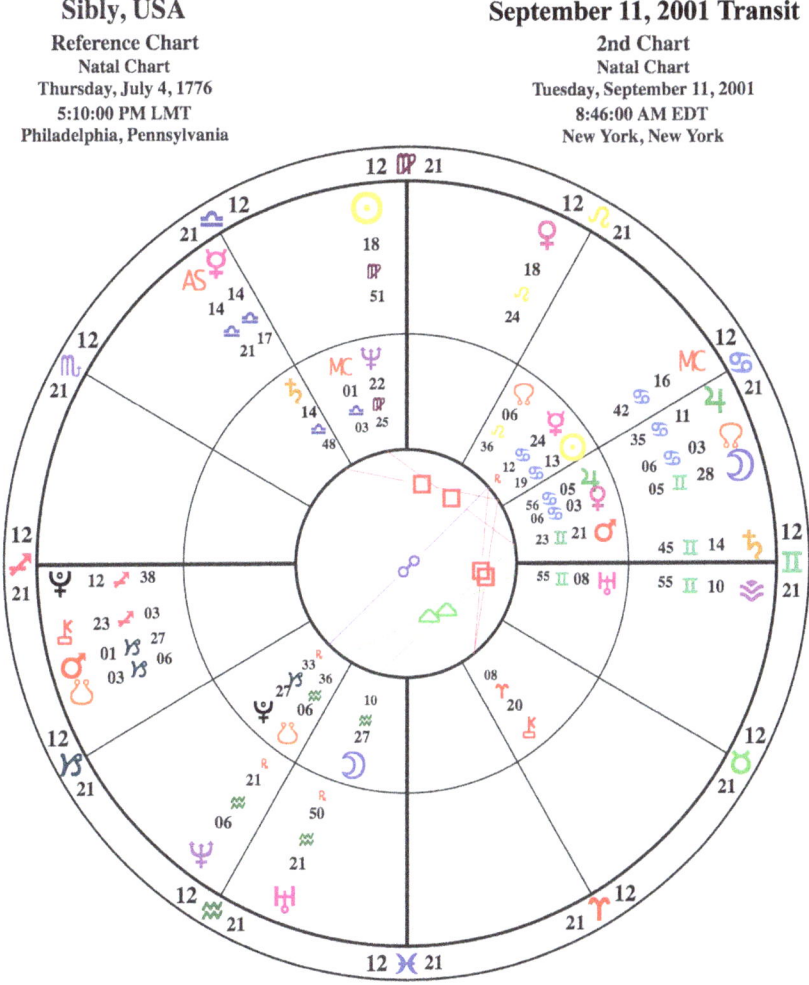

Below is the Synastry chart comparing the horoscopes of the United States and Japan. Looking at the placement of the Moon of both countries, I find they are both air signs and have a natural trine at the exact same degree, which is unusual. The trine signifies empathy, sympathy, and mutual support. With both nations, an emotional understanding comes between two charts with the Moon placement of the same element of energies. In this case, the air element leads the people of both countries to react emotionally in certain situations. The U.S. Moon in Aquarius speaks to the idealism embodied in the U.S. Constitution, whereas Japan has the Moon in Gemini, which speaks to the idealistic inclination toward intellectual concepts. Both countries have similar attitudes toward dealing with family and children. This shared aspect allows the two nations to be friendly and live in harmony.

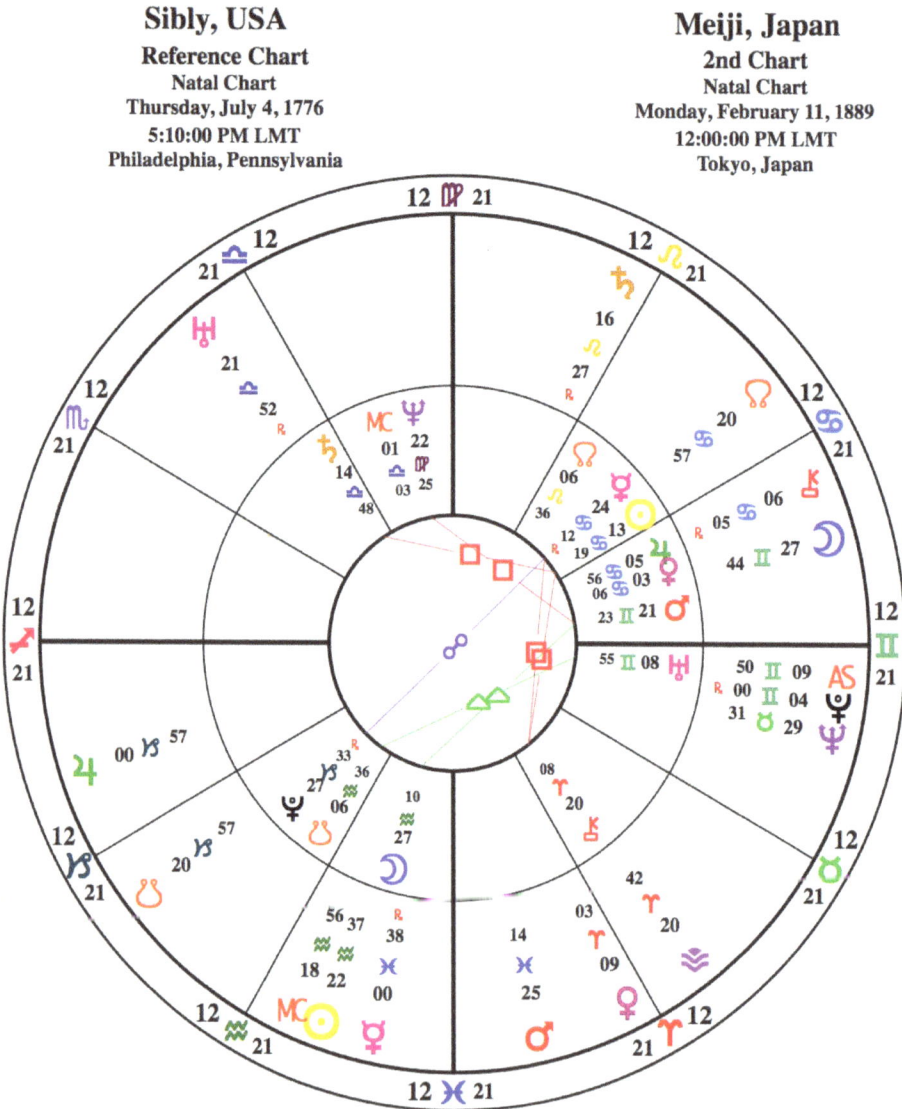

Astrological Predictions for The Age of Light ©2018

Chapter 6 Japan Meiji-USA Sibly

The Meiji chart of February 11, 1889 has Saturn in Leo at 16°, and the USA Sibly has Saturn in Libra at 14°. This close sextile between the two charts favors cooperation in business and organizational concerns, especially in activities that require stamina and discipline. When these two nations combine their resources and intellects, they become a formidable power, especially when there are only two degrees separating their relative sextile. There is also a real sense of responsibility and determination when it comes to working with each other, an idea supported by the Meiji Saturn and the Sibly Saturn in sextile to each other. The next remarkable thing about the two charts is their ascendants are opposite one another. This classic conjunction represents two elements that are mutually attracted and have a propensity for cooperation with each other. The Meiji chart has a Gemini rising at 9°; the Sibly chart has Sagittarius at 12° rising.

The Aquarius Sun of Japan, in Aquarius at 22°, is conjunct to the U.S. Moon, which is in Aquarius at 27°. Dr. Carl Jung, one of the founding fathers of psychology, studied relationships based on astrology charts. He indicated a harmonious relationship is associated with a receptive complement of the Moon and Sun like the one shared by Japan and the United States. This powerful connection means the two countries can work in tandem and get along.

Among other things, Jung is known for his experiments in synchronicity. He actually coined the word *synchronicity* to refer to the "meaningful coincidences" that occur in people's personal lives. He noted combinations of planets like the Sun in Aquarius and the Moon in Aquarius that shared the same sign or element. Japan's Sun in Aquarius is trine to the U.S. Mars in Gemini, which represents two partners who encourage each other. This aspect can allow Japan and the United States to challenge the other in very positive ways. I know a partnership for exploring outer space together is in the stars for both countries, a goal that should be pursued for their mutual benefit.

The placement of Japan's Mercury at 0° Pisces is trine to the Sibly placement of Venus in Cancer at 3°. This placement speaks to the idea of harmony when it comes to literature and all expressive forms of entertainment, film, music, and fashion. A trine indicates good communication when it comes to the emotions unless major negative aspects disturb the rest of the chart. In this case, stress areas between the two charts are minor. Because of the strong reciprocal, planets of the Sun and Moon in both charts may explain why U.S. soldiers after World War II married so many Japanese women.

The placement of Venus in Japan's chart is in Aries, and Uranus is in Gemini in the Sibly chart. This sextile encourages a great sense of friendship between the two countries. Another important point is each nation is giving the other the freedom to make this relationship as strong as possible as the two countries move together into the future.

In Japan's chart, Mars in Pisces is opposite the Sibly chart when it comes to the placement of Neptune in Virgo, which indicates to me the Japanese government may at times feel somewhat annoyed with the United States. The Japanese government is often discreet, respectful, and subdued in its expression of political dissatisfaction with the United States. An example is the Japanese people's desire to remove the U.S. military base in Okinawa. This debate has gone on for decades and long been a source of Japanese contention. The US has 90 military installations in mainland Japan and Okinawa including significant bases! So their work is cut out for them. (http://www.jca.apc.org/wsf_support/2004doc/WSFJapUSBaseRepoFinalAll.html#U.S._Military_Presence)

Japan's chart placement of Neptune in Taurus trines Sibyl's Pluto in Capricorn, which provides compatible views and convictions when it comes to deep-down reactions. The United States can appreciate the roots of the Japanese tribe go far back, making the United States seem like a child in comparison.

Japan and the United States do hold compatible views when it comes to the ideas of spirituality, religion, and psychology. Of all of the aspects examined above, only one might be considered somewhat problematic—the opposition of Mars and Neptune. Otherwise, the relationship between the two countries is very compatible and productive and has a solid partnership. As with all relationships, the two may have some differences, but the connection and bond between these countries remain strong through all trials and tribulations.

The lessons of the Age of Light are reinforcing the importance of self-reliance for both countries and teaching both countries they must stand on their own. Both nations can learn not to rely on anyone, anything, or any other country for their existence. Nonetheless, there is strong mutual interest in and support for their friendship. Furthermore, China will strongly influence the kind of relationship that will be developing between Japan and the United States over the next several decades.

How ironic that in an interdependent global economy each country and person has to learn to be self-reliant. Everyone in this new era is tested in terms of the way they behave. Individuals adopt lifestyles in harmony with the Earth's planetary vibrations and the community in which they live, or they perpetrate the destruction of the planet. Because the pressure to conform is immense in Japan, it might be difficult for the Japanese tribe to understand the importance of individuality. However, it is part of the lesson associated with having the Sun sign in Aquarius in the Meiji chart of Japan. The Japanese tendency toward assimilation may, of course, seem strange to Americans, who tend to pride themselves on their individuality.

The Aquarius Sun speaks to the idea of community, family, and interrelatedness. The Japanese learn to express their individuality. By pursuing your authentic self, you contribute to the rest of humanity and your community to enable a better way of life.

The Japanese do not fear anything or anyone. How apt that March 11, 2011 and September 11, 2001 have so much in common regarding the restructuring of both countries. Time stood still on March 11, 2011 and Japan will never be the same. However, a beneficial and prosperous outcome from the Great Eastern Japan Earthquake Disaster. It may take several decades, but the lessons learned are going to be invaluable for Japan and the rest of the world.

Living with nature instead of against it is the major challenge humanity and the planet will face. When I look at the Sibly chart of the United States from a Synastry point of view, the USA Sibly has an Aquarius Moon at 27° conjunct Mercury in Pisces at 00°. Likewise, the ideas and words of the Japanese people can have a powerful effect on U.S. citizens and the way they perceive Japan. The best way to further the relationship is to manage China and keep it within an equilibrium of understanding with the United States and Japan so as to avoid a war or any armed conflict, which would have untold ramifications on the world's financial markets. All three nations can find a peaceful way out of any conflict that may arise.

In the Sibly chart, Mercury at 24° in Cancer trines Mars in Pisces at 25° in the Japanese Meiji chart, which signals an intellectually stimulating relationship between both countries. Together they can create plans of great consequence and put those plans into action. Japan and the United States each have the ability to inspire one another.

The Sibly chart has Mercury in Cancer at 24° square the Japanese Meiji Uranus at 21° Libra, which provides a creative exchange of ideas with periodic misinterpretations and misunderstandings, which ultimately can lead to clarity. The field of medicine and the world of business seem to have a viable financial future, with the United States and Japan working together on research and products for the medical community. The U.S. Venus in Cancer at 5° is opposite Japan's Meiji chart of Jupiter at 0° Capricorn, which indicates a harmonious relationship of mutual admiration. The United States feels a genuine admiration for Japanese intellectual and cultural wisdom and knowledge. Both countries can broaden each other's cultural and educational aspects in order to evolve towards a better, more aware-conscious world.

The concern in this relationship is to discourage overindulgence and extravagance. There is a tendency for such waste to occur if these two countries don't pay closer attention to political issues that mutually concern them. These political issues are similar in essence to family rivalries (elements that bring out competition in relationships) and are associated with Mars at 21° Gemini, which is trine to Uranus at 21° Libra. This is a dynamic relationship that can have extreme results. Many astrological aspects speak to a mutual cultural and social attraction. Sibyl's Venus in Cancer in the Seventh House linked to foreign relations, business relationships, agreements, national marriage and divorce rates, and Japan's Jupiter in the First House signifying the nation and its people, national characteristics, and general conditions of prosperity, are good examples of opposites attracting. Many marriages between U.S. GIs and Japanese women occurred after World War II. To this day, there is a great deal of exchange between the two countries. The aspect between the Sibly Venus and Japan's Meiji Jupiter supports these kinds of connections. Rice is an important cultural symbol for Japan, and a growing number of Japanese have moved to California and Hawaii since World War II. Japanese influence on Californian agricultural interests has strengthened as a result.

Though they both need to stand alone to assert their own independence, both nations also have to take into consideration the fact the United States can and does provide Japan the energy boost and protection it will need in the future as China's economic power continues to grow. The USA Sibly has Uranus in Gemini conjuncts Japan's Gemini ascendant—they are separated by only 1°. When I examined the Japanese Meiji chart as dominant, I noticed a conjunct with Japan's Meiji Pluto at Gemini 4°. The Sibly

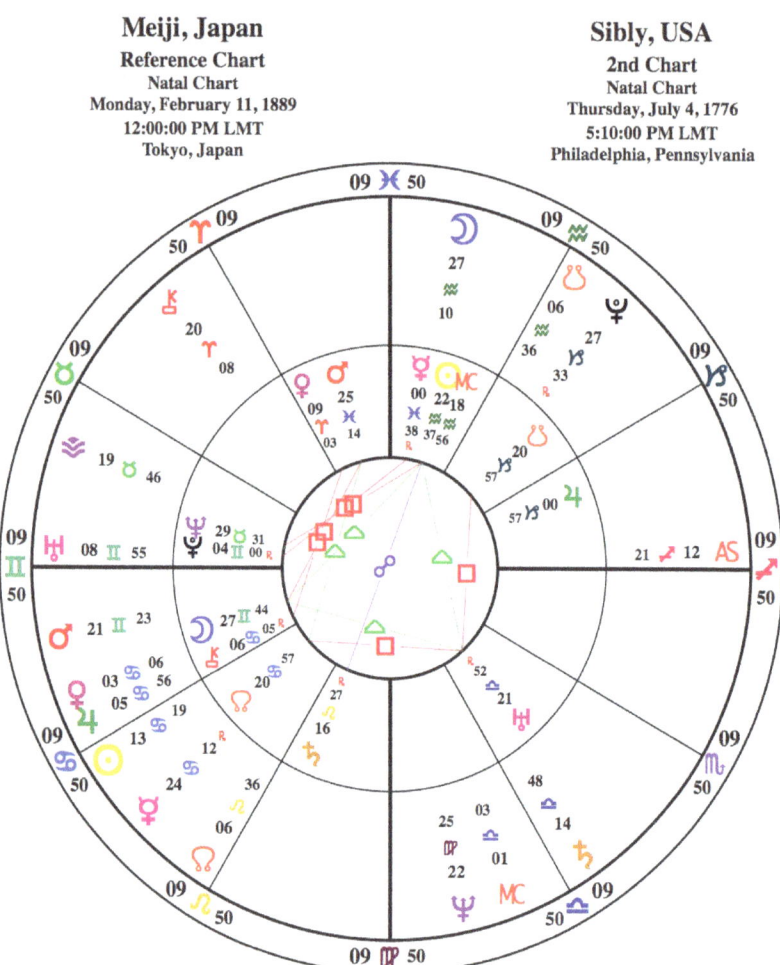

chart has Uranus at 8° just on the cusp of Japan's First House (see the chart below). The charts indicate there could be some instability with this relationship. It is important to make commitments that are solid and based on practical matters in order to forestall frustration.

In the Meiji and Sibly Synastry charts, Pluto in Capricorn is located in the Eighth House with an emphasis on financial relations with foreign countries and international finance. It is clear the United States has had a transformational impact on the people of Japan and vice versa since World War II.

Pluto in the Eighth House, representing financial relations with other nations, and foreign investment is naturally positioned; therefore, it intensifies the effects it will have on Japan. The defense alliance Japan has with the United States gives Japan an important buffer with China. In addition, ongoing discussions between the United States and Japan regarding location of the U.S. Marine base have strained the treaty relationship. Resolving the issue of the Okinawa Marine base does enable Japan to become a more decisive, self-sufficient

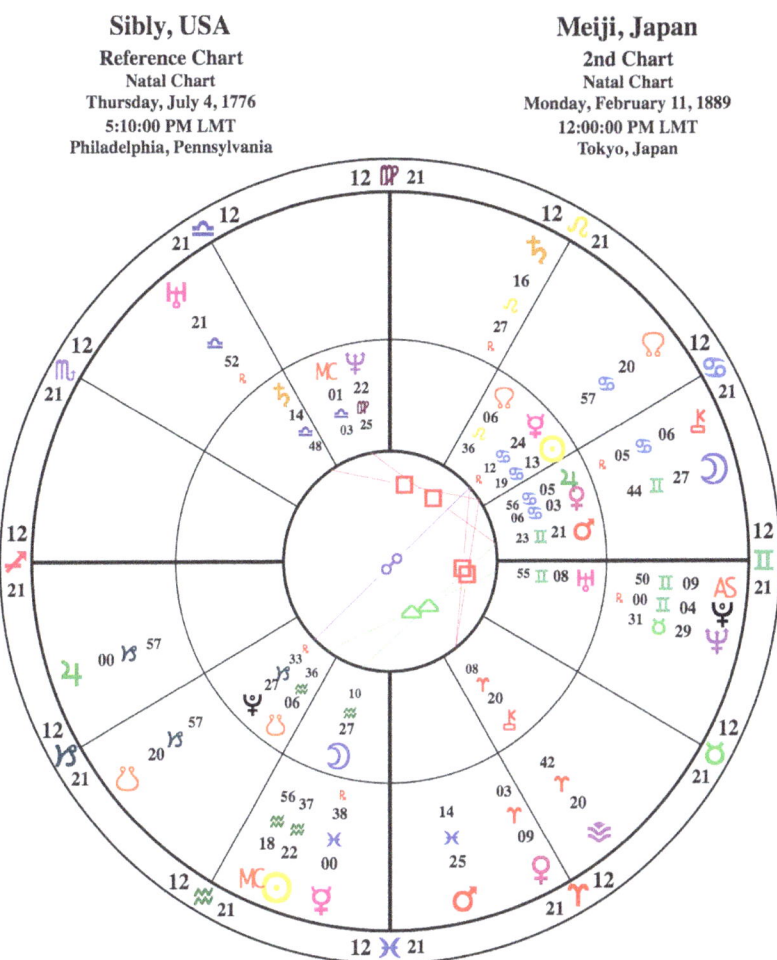

player in the region. In 2016 a delicate negotiation continued after several years. Then, most recently, the United States returned a 4-hectare strip of land back to the central government. However, this has not solved all the tension within the region and among the countries regarding this issue.[129]

The United States comprises a huge market for many Japanese products and services. It is estimated Japanese-affiliated companies employ about 700,000 people in the United States. I see this number getting larger due to the uncertainty of the trading relationship between Japan and China. In addition, the huge number of American/Japanese families created through intermarriage over the years continues to help both nations achieve stronger mutual understanding as we enter the Age of Light. Japan has a great deal to teach the United States about spiritual awareness, religion, philosophy and the importance of living in harmony with nature. Any power struggles between the two will not have as much consequence in the future as they have had in the past.

129 Kyodo, Jiji. "U.S. Returns Small Strip of Land at Futenma Air Base." *Japan Times*, 31 July 2017, www.japantimes.co.jp/news/2017/07/31/national/politics-diplomacy/u-s-returns-japan-small-strip-land-contentious-futenma-air-base/#.WeqXM62ZNsM

When I look at the Ascendant of the Sibly chart (see above), and I overlay the Meiji chart on the Sibly chart, planets Neptune and Pluto both fall into the Sixth House of public health, health workers and national service—the police, civil service and issues concerning national defense. Japan has the ability to inspire the United States in regard to taking healthcare as the first line of national defense for the nation. However, the planet Neptune speaks to the idea unrealistic expectations should not be projected in these two areas. Instead, America can strive for the practical, because the Present is where it has to happen. In this Synastry chart, the U.S. Sibly chart is ascendant at 12° Sagittarius. The Meiji Pluto is retrograde in Gemini at 4°, and Neptune is in Taurus at 29° and has a loose conjunct with Uranus in Gemini at 8° in its Sixth House, that speaks to the health of the nation for good or ill in the Sibly chart. Japan is going to influence the U.S. healthcare industry, especially in the field of geriatrics research. After all, Japan has some of the healthiest older people in the world. Japan's success in addressing the challenges of diet and exercise and in finding new methods for elder healthcare is having a positive effect on both economies. Americans can learn from the Japanese tribe about the importance of fitness and a nutritious diet. Japanese women are among the healthiest women in the world. As *Health Magazine* noted in 2012, "Okinawa, a Japanese island region, is known to have the highest concentration of centenarians (people aged 100 or older) in the world. Compared to Americans, they have an 80% lower rate of breast cancer death and less than half the rate of ovarian or colon cancer deaths. They also have much lower rates of dementia and a lower risk of heart disease."[130] The sense of social support, connection, and community in Japan also contributes to longevity. I clearly see Japan's influence on the United States is going to be more profound than the other way around.

One way or another, the relationship between the United States and Japan has already changed the way we eat in the United States (think, for example, of the introduction of sushi into our diets). The Japanese have also influenced the kinds of cars Americans drive (higher gas mileage and smaller cars are largely the result of Japanese influence).

Change is not easy, and the people of the United States have much to learn from the Japanese tribe. Working together as a cohesive nation toward one unified goal has occurred only a few times in the history of the United States (and usually only during moments of attack or crisis). The United States can learn from Japan how to resolve the differences that divide the population.

In the Age of Light, the Japanese discover their unique individuality like the Samurai of the past. This individuality becomes more evident as the Japanese become an enlightened nation leading the way for rest of the world.

★ ★ ★ ★ ★ ★ ★   ★ ★ ★ ★ ★ ★ ★   ★ ★ ★ ★ ★ ★ ★

---

130 Frankely, Valerie. "World'sHealthiestWomen." *Health Magazine*, 13 January 2012, *www.cnn.com/2012/01/13/health/secrets-worlds-healthiest-women/*.

Chapter 6 Japan Meiji-USA Sibly

In 1924 Professor W. H. Williams, who was a specialist in the field of relativity, wrote and presented a parody of "The Walrus and the Carpenter" called "The Einstein and the Eddington" at a dinner party in honor of Albert Einstein. Here is a part of that presentation. This appears to be pertinent to the Age of Light.

"And space, it has dimensions four,
Instead of only three.
The square on the hypotenuse
Ain't what it used to be.
It grieves me sore, the things you've done
To plane geometry.

You hold that time is badly warped,
That even light is bent;
I think I get the idea there,
If this is what you meant;
The mail the postman brings today,
Tomorrow will be sent.

The shortest line, Einstein replied,
Is not the one that's straight;
It curves around upon itself,
Much like a figure eight,
And if you go too rapidly
You will arrive too late."

Einstein
The Life and Times
By Ronald W. Clark
Published by Avon Books

Chapter 7

Japan Understanding China

Neighbors for life

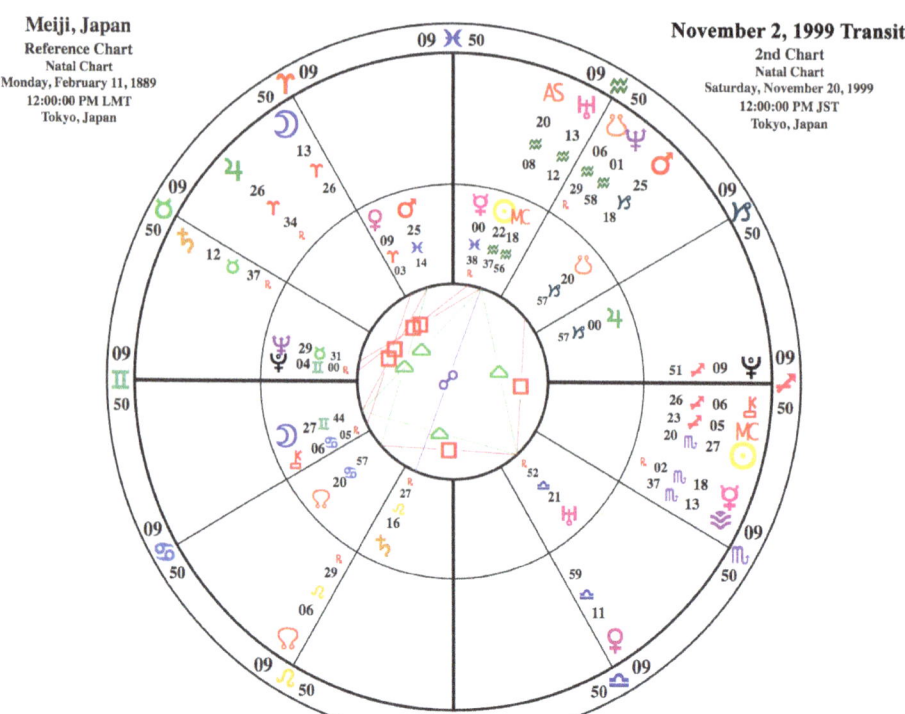

Before we look to the future, let us examine the past. On November 20, 1999 the planet Pluto, in the sign of Sagittarius, entered the Seventh House of foreign relationships and all kinds of relationships that deal with business in the Meiji chart (Japan's mundane chart). Transiting Pluto was in Sagittarius at 9° and opposite Meiji Pluto in Gemini in the Twelfth House, which represents institutions of any kind, especially secret groups or hidden enemies within governments or other institutions.

Concomitant with these transits of Pluto, Japan was bound to have difficulties concerning relationships and partnerships with other countries. For example, in 2009 and 2010, Japanese manufacturers were forced to recall defective autos in the United States.[131] Toyota ultimately recalled 10 million cars because they were defective.[132] In 2015, the Department of Transportation announced it could levy a fine to the Japanese manufacturer, Takata, of up to $200 million for failure to recall faulty airbags that killed seven people and injured dozens of drivers.[133] When Pluto makes itself felt, unprecedented disruptions of this sort occur.

Pluto in Capricorn was on the cusp of the Eighth House of death and financial relations with foreign countries on October 29, 2013. A planet like Pluto, traveling from one

---

131 Vlasic, Bill and Matt Apuzzo. "Toyota Is Fined $1.2 Billion for Concealing Safety Defects." *The New York Times*, 19 March 2014, www.nytimes.com/2014/03/20/business/toyota-reaches-1-2-billion-settlement-in-criminal-inquiry.html?_r=0.
132 Ibid.
133 Chappell, Bill. U.S. Fines Takata Up To $200 Million Over Defective Airbags." *NPR*, 3 November 2015, www.npr.org/sections/thetwo-way/2015/11/03/454330217/u-s-fines-takata-200-million-over-defective-airbags.

Astrological House to another or from one sign to another, is generally associated with shifts of major political or financial significance somewhere on Earth. This is what I call an 'air-quake'. For example, on November 4, 1995, seven days before Pluto entered Sagittarius, Israeli Prime Minister Yitzhak Rabin was assassinated. Though his death did not occur on the exact day of Pluto's transit, it occurred close enough to be associated with this event of vast political importance. Pluto moves very slowly and its influence was made known.

Pluto in Capricorn at 9° entered the Eighth House on November 19, 2013. Uranus was at 8° conjunct Natal Venus. This square combined conjunct of Venus brings sudden and unexpected change, perhaps instability when it comes to international finance and dealings with multinational corporations. Changes heralded by Pluto are deep-seated. They are the outcome of a long process of revolution. By contrast, Uranus brings the sudden unexpected change that sweeps away the old and allows space for new Japanese evolutionary growth. At that time in Japan, Prime Minister Abe's government had changed its fiscal policy towards increasing inflation to stabilize and manipulate the value of the yen.[134]

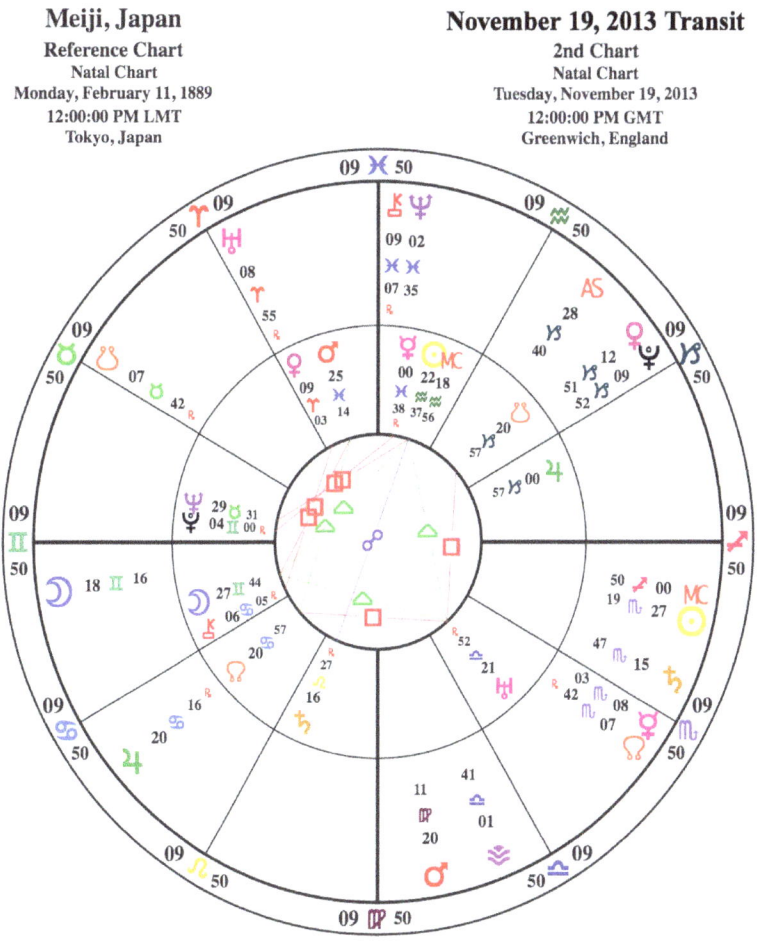

[134] Boesler, Matthew. "The Truth About Abenomics-The Japanese Economic Experiment That's Capitivating the World." *Business Insider*, 16 March 2013, www.businessinsider.com/what-is-abenomics-2013-3.

However, as Pluto moved from the Seventh House to the Eighth House, the shift for Japan was towards even more fundamental transformation, another 'air-quake'. Thus, in this time frame, it was of the utmost importance Japan avoid futile power struggles with potential trading partners and prevent unnecessary economic losses. In addition, Japan must be aware other countries, especially China, may not be as forthright with information during negotiations as they could be. In other words, quicksand is the foundation at this time.

During this transit, the government of Japan suffered from espionage and cyber-hacking. Perhaps Japan was tested by a rival country simply to gauge the efficacy of its reaction. As with any dispute, both parties bear responsibility in terms of provocation and response. Ever since the end of World War II, for example, Japan and Russia have not signed a peace treaty, and as of 2016 Russia still occupies Japan's former territory known as the Kuril Islands.[135] It will take many more years of negotiations for Japan to regain this territory. After economic negotiations with Japan, President Putin of Russia will return the Kuril Islands by the end of this decade, so he can demonstrate how reasonable he can be. If Russia doesn't turn over the Kuril Islands to Japan, Russia will (if it hasn't already) set up a listening station to tap into the intelligence of the surrounding countries, which is the real purpose of occupation.

Japan must take care not to act with prejudice. Japanese politicians must also take care not to speak or act based on mistaken assumptions. Russia has a history of taking over land for its political interests, which it did after World War II.

September 12, 2007, Prime Minister Shinzo Abe announces his resignation. On October 29, 2007, there was an opposition of transiting Pluto to the Meiji Gemini Moon Square to Meiji Pisces Mars. These celestial events ushered in an emotionally trying period for Japan, as it prepared for its leadership role in the Age of Light.

In early 2008, Pluto was opposite the Moon and square to Mars, a position focused specifically on opportunities in recognizing women for their contributions to and significance in Japanese life as it evolves to the Light. The knowledge, wisdom and experience of the women of Japan must be acknowledged in order for Japan to evolve.

On November 27, 2008, Pluto entered Capricorn in conjunction with Japan's Meiji chart Jupiter. A gestalt and overall tonal shift took place at this time in Japan. Sudden change occurred as power shifted in the Japanese government for the first time in 50 years. Pluto's transit took place in the Seventh House of business relationships, public relations and alliances. Thus, Japan's political influence and financial status began to be challenged around the world as never before.

During that same period, transiting Neptune was conjunct to the Meiji Sun of Japan in Aquarius. Saturn in Virgo was opposite Uranus in Pisces at that time as well. All of these celestial events, but the opposition in particular, heralded a unique moment in time. Japan in 2012 started to see the way to truly distinguishing itself in the eyes of the world.

---

135 Rich, Motoko. "Meeting Between Japan and Russia Ends with Stalemate on Disputed Islands." *The New York Times*, 16 December 2016, www.nytimes.com/2016/12/16/world/asia/japan-russia-abe-putin.html.

Chapter 7 Japan Understanding China

Japan began a pivotal shift economically and spiritually in 2008, culminating with the Great Eastern Japan Earthquake Disaster. From this point on, preparation for the year 2012 and the vibrational shift of the Mayan Prediction began. Each year has included new lessons for the Japanese tribe to learn on their way to an enlightened awareness.

On April 2, 2008, Pluto went retrograde to reemphasize the opposition of the Moon and the square to Mars that occurred on October 29, 2007. This retrograde lasted until September 9, 2008, after which Pluto went direct, meaning the planets in our solar system appeared to be moving in a forward direction. From 2007 to 2012, transiting planets in the Meiji chart brought forth the preparation for Japan's new shift to an enlightened way of life.

For readers who, for financial or other reasons, want to know how events shaped up, we will now examine astrological aspects that transpired before December 21, 2012.

Let me begin by stating that, in the interests of accurately analyzing the contours of future developments in and for Japan, I cannot address all of the many and varied events that will occur between 2012 and 2024. It would be impractical to attempt to do so. I have instead chosen some of the major aspects that transit the Meiji chart. ese particular aspects provide a wealth of pertinent information, and in analyzing them, I present the basic astrological concepts, rhythms, and patterns that can and will affect Japan and the world.

Financial interests and politics are, of course, integral to the Japanese character. My analysis integrates these subject areas within the framework of the transit interpretation that follows.

In the Meiji chart from October 29, 2009 through March 31, 2010, Saturn in Libra transited the Fourth House of agriculture, farming, real estate and weather, which is the foundation of society and its traditions. Saturn was also square to transiting Pluto in Capricorn in the Seventh House, which represents foreign relations, disputes, treaties and business relationships, as well as being conjunct to Meiji Jupiter in Capricorn in the Seventh House. This was a frustrating time for Japan in terms of finances and business stability. These placements indicate there may have been a temptation to struggle to make things different (better or more stable), when, in fact, things are (and always have been) outside of human control. The Japanese tribe may want to continue being patient, listening carefully and acting slowly and deliberately in accordance with what they learn.

On September 2, 2010, China and Japan experienced a major sudden confrontation in the East China Sea just off of Taiwan near several uninhabited islands known as Senkaku in Japan and Diaoyu in China. This incident became a test of Japan's ability to remain focused on a future goal instead of fixating on the context of an immediate conflict.

On September 7, 2010, Agence France-Presse reported the incident started when the Japanese patrol boat *Yonakuni* ordered a Chinese trawler to stop fishing in the disputed waters:

> *The Chinese boat's bow... hit the Yonakuni's stern and also collided with another Japanese patrol boat, the Mizuki, some 40 minutes later; Kyodo [News Agency] reported citing the coast guard. Three Japanese patrol boats then chased the Chinese vessel, and 22 Japanese personnel boarded the ship to question the Chinese crew on suspicion of violating the fisheries law, Kyodo reported. The Japanese Coast Guard later arrested the captain of the Chinese ship on suspicion of obstructing public duties [a senior government official was quoted as saying on condition of anonymity].*[136]

Japan, China, and Taiwan all claim the disputed Senkaku Islands, claims that frequently cause tensions among the three countries. China, for example, told Agence France-Presse its claim to the islands dates back, "to ancient times." [137] Regarding the *Yonakuni* incident, Japan could have made much more of the issue and declared China was invading its fishing grounds. Instead, the Japanese Coast Guard showed excellent restraint and refused to react violently, even when the Chinese vessel rammed the Yonakuni. As Agence France-Presse reported, Japan later asked, "the Chinese government to help prevent a recurrence of the incident and give thorough instructions to Chinese shing boats.[138] These calm and logical diplomatic efforts certainly saved lives and resources, a strategy that will serve Japan well as the Age of Light unfolds. The positive outcome of this incident with China will also help Japan's diplomats increase their sensitivity to the long and conflicted history of their dealings with China.

During this period in late 2010 and soon after the Senkaku incident was resolved, economists declared China had officially grown its economy larger than Japan's to become the world's second-largest economy.

It is important Japan remain cautious and manage its dealings with China carefully. As with a lawyer cross-examining a hostile witness in court, Japan should never ask questions to which it doesn't already know the answers. The Japanese government should carefully craft a relationship with China based on mutual cooperation and benefit.

China, in turn, will be in a transitional phase as it seeks to deal with the unexpected consequences of capitalism. It will soon face problems stemming from its aging population and rapidly growing economy. With a burgeoning over-65 population of more than 250 million people, healthcare costs are going to rise steeply in China. Generally speaking, this Chinese economic stress is why it would be wise for Japan to adopt a balanced trade policy with China.

Competition continues between the two countries, exacerbated by small but controllable disputes like the Senkaku incident. Therefore, Japan should limit its investments in China as much as possible and shift its trading emphasis to exports to China by finding cheaper labor elsewhere.

Concerning the Meiji chart, the date of the Senkaku incident, September 7, 2010, was significant. I found Uranus and Jupiter conjunct to the Meiji Mars in Pisces. Pisces represents water, and Mars is associated with the military. The Sun had just entered the Fourth House,

---

136 "High Seas Collisions Trigger Japan China Spat." *Agence France Presse,* 7 September 2010.
137 Ibid.
138 Ibid.

which represents weather, agriculture, and other monikers. The planet Mercury was in a conjunct to the Sun. Saturn in Libra was also in the Fourth House of the opposition party in government. The planet Saturn emphasizes limitations and the importance of relationships. At an angle, Uranus to Mars can be an accident-producing event. Uranus in Pisces tends to involve water. Transiting Pluto was conjunct to the Meiji Jupiter in the Seventh House of foreign relations and business relationships including agreements. Transiting Neptune in Aquarius in the Ninth House is in a loose conjunct with the Meiji Sun in Aquarius and Mercury at 00° Pisces. This provided a better understanding between China and Japan when it came to disputes over resources, sea traffic, and shipping.

On September 2, 2010, transiting Mars conjunct Venus, an aspect that deals with speculative interests in the Fifth House, which indicates the stock exchange. In fact, Mars and Venus were very close, only three to four degrees away from each other, heightening the power of the conjunct. At the same time, transiting Pluto in Capricorn conjunct Jupiter in Capricorn in the Meiji Seventh House—this major conjunction concerns disputes, foreign relations and situations of overt aggression. Further, expansion can take extreme forms, including revolution and confrontation. The key to this flare-up in Chinese-Japanese relations is the loose square that transiting Pluto had with Japan's Meiji Mars. This square heightened confrontational tensions. Aggression and change create a stress level that has to be addressed and hopefully resolved. Regardless, uneasy relations between the two countries will continue for many years to come as the Age of Light unfolds.

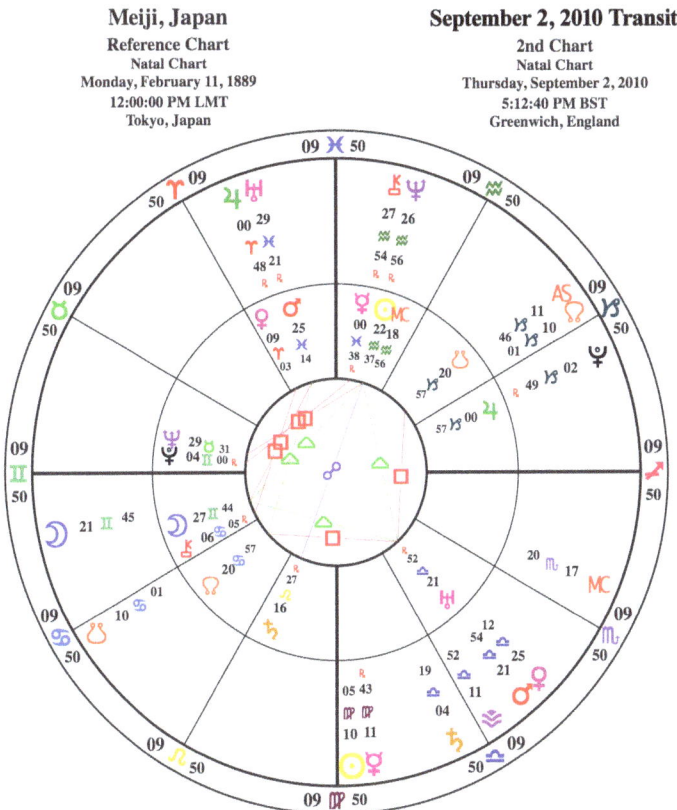

The role of Neptune concerns ideals, reform and the arts. It represents covert plots, fraud, loss and illicit activities. Consider the planet Neptune as a symbol of Japan's future relationship with China—undefined and fluid. Neptune was transiting the Ninth House of foreign lands and the high seas at the time of the Senkaku incident. Transiting Neptune was at 26° Aquarius and was square to Japan's Meiji Neptune at 29° Taurus. A square of this proximity is very powerful. Astrologically, this square of transiting Neptune and Neptune in the Meiji chart signals a crisis point. In connection with the Senkaku incident, astrological indications further suggest it would be in Japan's best interest to reexamine its goals regarding its future relationship with China. As the Mayan Prediction unfolds, the Japanese tribe examines the ideals according to which they set their goals. The question then is this: Are these ideals ultimately to Japan's benefit? In this astrological context, I would say it is time for Japan to consider implementing self-sustaining energy strategies and shifting its energy-generation infrastructure away from nuclear reactors.

September 2010 was a dangerous time for Japan, and Japan is to be congratulated for the prudence with which it avoided extreme behavior in dealing with China's straying fishing boat. Perhaps Japan could broaden the scope of its relationship with China by attempting to enact longer-term strategies? Historically, the two countries have had a complex yet mutually beneficial relationship, and they have influenced each other in the fields of religion and philosophy. The solution then is to allow the truth to reveal itself, whatever it may be, without falling back on preconceived notions and expectations. Let time pass so that truth can come forth. Perseverance and patience are the keys to awareness.

It would be well for Japan to remember, from a Chinese point of view, Japan's behavior in the past has not necessarily inspired trust. To this day, China has not forgotten nor forgiven Japan's invasion of China prior to World War II.

As the Age of Light unfolds, it will become increasingly important for all nations to realize, while the sins of the past cannot be ignored, the past can nonetheless be forgiven. It takes great strength and compassion for a culture to integrate forgiveness. Forgiveness is a tall order, but it can bring China and the Japanese tribe into Present awareness if honestly implemented from the heart. And, such forgiveness will be necessary as Japan leads the world into a sustainable future through its examples of self-sufficiency and self-responsibility.

Moreover, it is in the Japanese government's best interests to speak clearly and honestly in negotiations. With transiting Neptune in the Ninth House of Japan's Meiji chart, it may be possible for illusion to cloud the truly essential issues being negotiated. Neptune transiting the Ninth House represents foreign relations and secret plots. Meanwhile, China has Neptune transiting its First House. As a result, saving face is highlighted as being very important in terms of China gaining respect as a new superpower on the world stage. The First House is linked to the image of the nation. Due to Neptune's influence, any statements the Chinese may have issued to Japan from 2010 until August 2016 could have been confusing and difficult to understand. The need for open and accessible negotiations among countries around the world is one of the major lessons the Chinese and Japanese governments are going to have to learn as we all matriculate into the Age of Light. Governments are no longer going to be able to hide information from the public as easily as they have in the past. This fact alone is going to dramatically change politics in the world to come.

WikiLeaks (and the controversy this international organization has engendered) is a good example of how people around the world are making efforts (baby steps, really) to adopt a less-destructive paradigm in the future by leaking government secrets. Here's an ancient idea to consider: Within the matrix of life, there exists an intrinsic aspect of human nature to want to live in a peaceful world. People who go about their lives peacefully every day overwhelmingly outnumber those who act out violently. In the sensation-seeking media, of course, the Earth can come across as a planet of functionally insane people. Established power always has believed and assumed its own way must prevail, but the end of time predicted by the Maya is beginning to change the reality upon which that assumption is based.

Thus, we have the Snowden effect, where individuals blow the whistle on their governments and insiders leak government secrets to protect human rights and fundamental freedoms, while also informing the public about what is happening with their tax dollars in the name of national security.

History and astrology teach us the importance of cyclical events and how people keep repeating their mistakes without learning from them. We are coming to the moment when we can no longer afford to repeat the past. The conditions and circumstances the Mayans predicted are ushering us in a unique new direction, historically speaking—to a place of Peace.

Those who cannot remember the past are condemned to repeat it.
~ George Santayana

On September 2, 2010, Uranus in Pisces was transiting the Tenth House and was conjunct to Meiji Mars in Pisces in the Tenth House, which represents national prestige, the government and people in authority, national reputation and trade. Uranus conjunct Mars can be an disruptive-producing transit, especially at an angle. In Pisces it signifies water. The Senkaku boat collision incident occurred on September 7, 2010. Transiting Uranus in Pisces in the Tenth House was square to transiting Pluto in Capricorn in the Seventh House, which was conjunct to Jupiter also in Capricorn in the Seventh House, which deals with relationships related to business and trade balance issues. When two planets like Pluto and Jupiter come together, their energies blend to demonstrate a unique potential. This conjunct highlighted this house of foreign relations, agreements, negotiations and treaties. Jupiter generally represents expansion and contributions to benefit the nation. The emphasis with this aspect of Jupiter and Pluto conjunct speaks to replacing old attitudes with a new beneficial approach.

Pluto represents the principles of revolution, death, and regeneration. When Pluto is combined with the energy archetype of transiting Uranus, there is a tendency for sudden, unexpected changes to occur for good or ill. Japan's role is to represent the best the planet has to offer. Japan can serve as an example, leading the world into the Age of Light as the future unfolds based on my analysis of Japan's Meiji chart regarding the Age of Aquarius.

The emphasis on experiencing revolutions around the world will continue while Pluto is in Capricorn. This means until the end of 2024, Pluto's vibration will help the world to evolve, as the Hopi would say, from the Fourth to Fifth World. The past, of course, has an important impact on Japan's current situation with China. The Senkaku Islands incident, for example, has more to do with the past than it does with the Present. If Japan can handle events like these with consistent restraint and awareness, it could be a real game changer in terms of how Japan does business with China.

Another factor working to Japan's advantage as the Age of Light unfolds is its command of and innovative ability to effectively use communications technology. For example, a video on YouTube revealed the Chinese fishing boat did indeed ram the Japanese coast guard vessel. In the spirit of WikiLeaks, a member of the Japanese military released this video. Revelations via WikiLeaks have also caused large-scale embarrassing problems for governments around the world. This is the beginning of more revelations exposing people in positions of authority who violate the dignity of the human spirit. These revelations come via various media, such as Twitter, Facebook and YouTube. As a result, governments are forced to change, especially when the revelations are dangerous. Continued revolutions could ensue, as has happened in Myanmar, Libya, Syria, Egypt, Yemen and Ukraine. And, South America is on the verge of imploding into chaos and revolutions. Turkey is in danger of major instability with its continued corrupt government.

Of course, innovative communications technology and social media have helped activists and citizens spread word of the Arab Spring revolutions around the Middle East. During the period of Pluto transiting Capricorn, revolutions continue to spread in other countries as well.

Pluto, a very slow-moving planet, is a harbinger of coming revolution. As with the French Revolution, for example, a seemingly sudden explosion may have in fact been a long-simmering evolutionary process. Under the influence of Pluto, deep psychological forces can be released by slow-moving, virtually indiscernible evolutionary shifts. Depending on the context, however, Pluto's ultimate influence can be quite explosive indeed, as was the case on 9/11.

As far as letting go of the past, Pluto's transit represents a period of change in the way international finance is conducted. This transit reveals true spiritual intuitive values expressed with awareness and compassion are the best way to rule and govern. The Japanese tribe is starting to have a greater sense and understanding of its power and influence in the world. It is reevaluating how to position itself on the world stage as the Age of Light unfolds. This Pluto transit is going to affect a whole generation around the world, especially in Japan. The way in which Japan is viewed by other nations could change radically as the Mayan Prediction unfolds. As one generation (and its way of thinking and doing business) passes away, a new one takes its place. Thus, the cycle of life evolves towards the Age of Light, which illuminates the Age of Aquarius.

According to the Meiji chart, on October 17, 2010 Saturn entered the Fifth House of entertainment and stock exchange activity. Saturn brought an emphasis on limitations the Japanese tribe feels concerning creativity, especially in terms of dealing with the stock exchange and the economy as sudden changes and political influences lead to unexpected consequences. For Japan, a sense of limitation in relation to creativity was due to the square of Saturn in Libra, with transiting Pluto in Capricorn in the Seventh House, which was conjunct to Jupiter in terms of foreign relation and business relationships. These celestial events reflect a tension between Japan and diplomatic or trade relations it has with neighboring countries. The recent dispute over the Senkaku Islands between China and Japan is a good example of this aspect in relation to the evolving nature and character of Japan as a whole.

There is further evidence of the changes on the way for Japan. Late in 2010, a Full Moon lunar eclipse occurred on the winter solstice. The last time humanity witnessed a Full Moon lunar eclipse was way back in 1638, and such an event will not happen again until 2094. Historical accounts from 1635 record Japanese citizens were forbidden to travel abroad at that time. Will the recent high seas altercation with China have a similar effect on Japan? Will members of the Japanese tribe think twice before they invest in or travel to China? Possibly. However, strong economic ties between the two countries mean the relationship will probably remain fundamentally unaffected. The Full Moon lunar eclipse in late 2010 speaks to the exposure of the dark and hidden in Japan's society and brings to light the truth that cannot be denied the light of day. The media reporting on corporations will highlight revelations about Japanese authority figures who act with little regard for the public and commit acts of corruption.

Japan is now the third-largest economy in the world. The disruption concerning energy loss in 2011 could enable Brazil or India to take Japan's place as the world's third-largest economy sometime within the next ten years. The Japan of the future preserves and enhances its reputation for being one of the leading manufacturing countries in the world when it comes to quality. Much depends on how Japan solves its energy conundrum. Japan responds to the occasion as the Japanese tribe adapts, using self-sustaining energy resources to lead the way into the future.

In my analysis of the transiting chart of Japan, I note the ascendant sign is in Gemini, which can be interpreted as signifying Japan (as philosopher Alan Watts might say) is a nervous culture with divergent needs and wants. Finding a dependable and sustainable energy source to ensure Japan's independence from world energy markets will help alleviate this "nervousness." The Moon in Gemini at 27° is in the late stages of Gemini and moving towards the watery side of Cancer and into the First House, which emphasizes the image of the nation and its people's general conditions. An ascendant in Gemini gives Japan an intense need for discovery, information and creativity as a foundation.

The duality of Gemini is now expressed as polarization within the Japanese tribe in terms of how to proceed. Debate will ensue over the question of nuclear power use. Should it be used or should alternatives be found?

The outcome of this debate will be crucial to the direction in which Japan leads the world as the Mayan Prediction manifests.

The tensions engendered by the Japanese tribe's polarization indicate emotion overrides rational thinking in the debate over World War II and the Senkaku Islands.

In Japan's mundane chart, Saturn in Leo is opposite Aquarius, which is ruled by Saturn. As a tribe, egotism and desire for power is examined more closely than they have been in the past. Astrologically, Saturn evinces a profound interest in education and business, speculative investments and the field of entertainment. Saturn in the Third House representing forms of transportation and communication in the Meiji chart indicates discontent and elements of evil as associated with this planet House connection. As a nation, the demonstration of mental discipline and application of practical ideas can help Japan express its true character as the Age of Light unfolds.

Japan continues to experience the potential for difficulties with neighboring nations because of this position of Saturn in the Third House connected to affairs and diplomatic messages. Saturn demands clear communication to avoid any misunderstandings. However, problems with neighbors can be resolved if Japan adopts an honest and straightforward approach, as it did with China during the Senkaku incident. It almost goes without saying the members of the Japanese tribe are capable of working hard and acquiring the training to achieve whatever goals they need to pursue. It is important for Japan to recognize and accept its past and its past aggression. By learning from and forgiving past mistakes, the Japanese tribe can become an exploring light for the rest of the world to follow as a prelude to the Age of Aquarius.

As the year 2011 began to unfold, Japan experienced such terrible tragedies and internal tensions time seemed to stand still for the Japanese people. It was almost as if a foreshadowing of the Mayan Prediction had transpired. It was the first wake-up call signaling the dawn of the Mayan threshold.

As mentioned earlier, Uranus is associated with the unexpected. I have often observed when a major planet moves from one sign to another, it is like an astrological 'air-quake'. So when on March 12, 2011, a day after Uranus entered Aries, financial difficulties were bound to occur in wake of the day of the Great Eastern Japan Earthquake Disaster.

Squares in the Meiji chart herald a series of unexpected events that give the Japanese tribe the ability to strengthen relationships around the world. It is through the overcoming of difficulties resolutions emerge and evolve, especially concerning the disputes over the Senkaku Islands between Japan and China.

As this century unfolds, the world is not going to be able to continue business as usual as in the past. My astrological analysis indicates by 2032-2033 the world financial markets will find a new footing for a new global economy to be established due to the many changes taking place during this decade. In 2015 we saw a slowdown of the Chinese economy and the uncertainty of the Chinese stock market. There are major questions the

Chinese government is going to face in the second decade of the 21st century, and freedom of speech is the most important of all!

China comes to understand the true value of the concept of communism, which at the core of its ideologue teaches cooperation, not exclusion by fear. Let people naturally commune. Let governments relinquish control and simply assist and provide a safe environment for freedom of expression in a caring world.

It is essential the government of Japan does not take the Japanese people for granted, and that the government recognizes the importance the Japanese people play in the political process. The Age of Light is a time for open minds and hearts—a time to receive the wisdom of the ages from within.

At the end of 2011, Saturn was in Libra, transiting the Fifth House of speculative interest and the stock market. This transit did not and does not speak well for Japan's finances. For the country as a whole, this is a time for austerity and for embracing the idea the simple things in life bring the greatest joy. Saturn reinforces and supports the institution of the family and loving relationships within it. Saturn can seed opportunities that, if properly nurtured, bring the heart to an ideal state. It's not what you own but what you do that is important! The value of life comes from doing what you love to do!

Finally, Japan continues to have a strong and mutually supportive relationship with the United States. The Senkaku Islands/East China Sea diplomatic crisis had larger territorial ramifications—it was a wake-up call for Japan and many other nations within the East Asian region as a whole. However, Japan can continue to rely on the United States for support, and this relationship provides a firewall against future Chinese threats, whatever form they may take. In recent decades it has been established that the East China Sea is rich in oil and gas reserves, and China's energy demand is multiplying, while Japan's reserves are limited. Moreover, the Senkaku Islands can continue to be a point of contention throughout this decade. The resolution is unknown, yet I see a financial agreement with mutually beneficial rights--- rare minerals, oil, and gas.

The way China has presented themselves by building islands, claiming ocean territories, and creating disputes with Burma, Laos, Northern India, Vietnam, Nepal, Bhutan, Thailand, Malaysia, Singapore, the Ryukyu Islands—also known in Japanese as the Nansei Islands, 300 islands of the South China, East China and Yellow Seas—as well as Kyrgyzstan, Mongolia, Taiwan, South Kazakhstan, the Afghan province of Bahdashan, Transbaikalia, and the Far East to South Okhotsk.

China could create the equivalent circumstances we find in the Middle East, and that can become known as the Asian Middle East due to the ongoing conflicts and disputes with violent clashes and incidents over territories with these surrounding countries.

We are stardust floating at the
speed of living light.
~Clint Cochran, Mystic

Chapter 8

Japan's Relationship with China

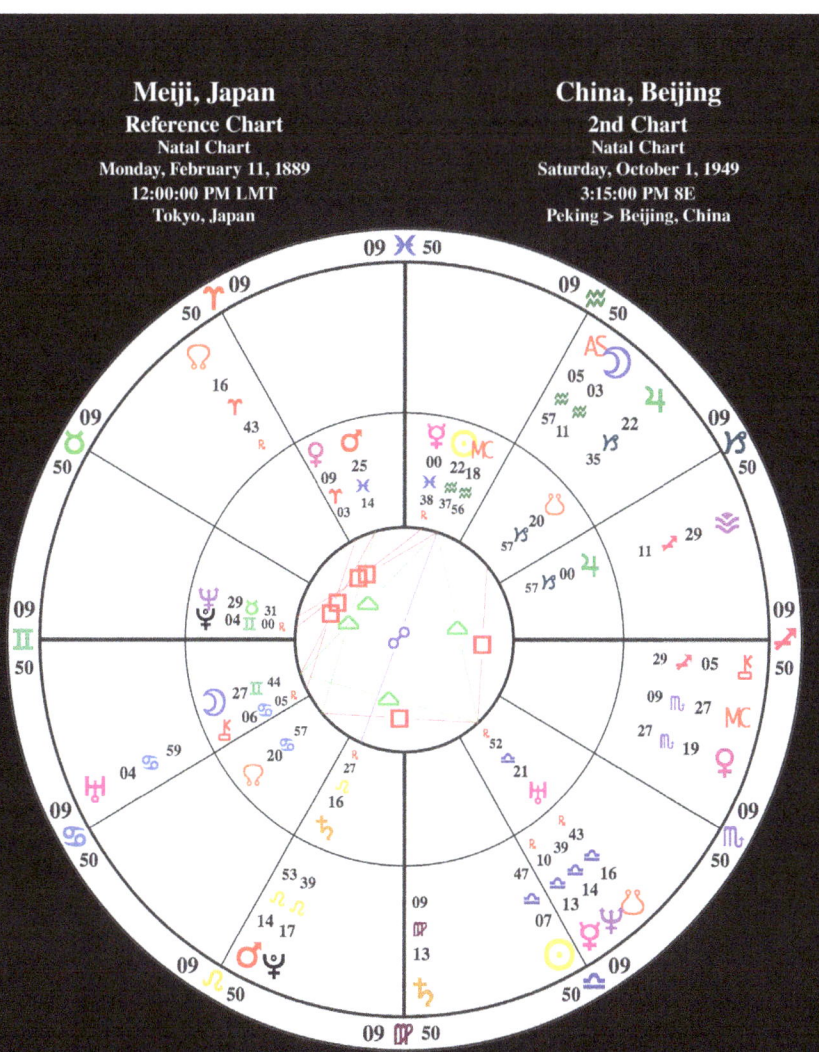

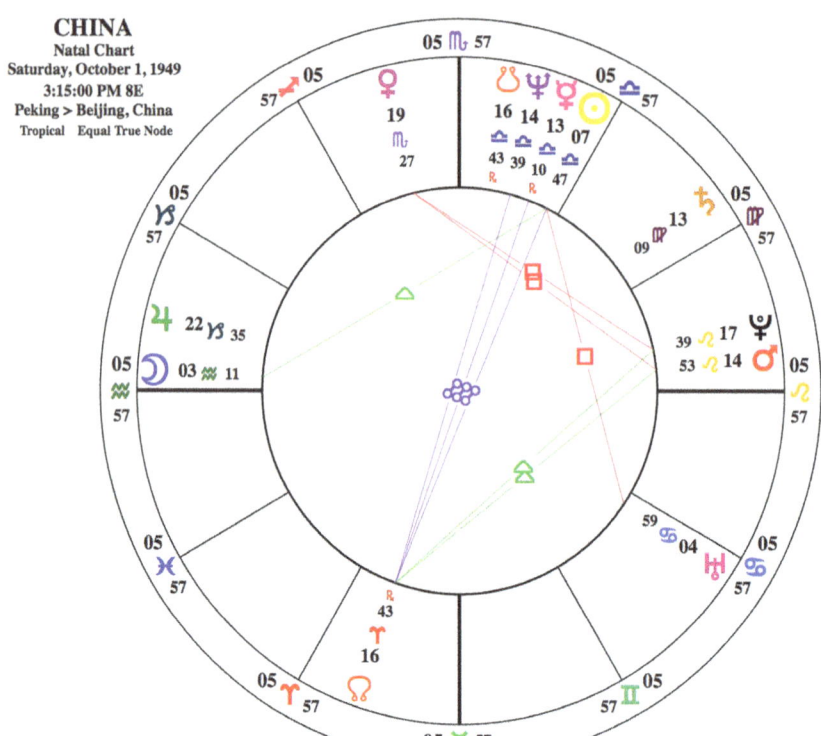

Japan knows China cannot be ignored because of its newfound economic influence and history. Consider Napoleon's statement about China: "Let China sleep, for when the Dragon awakes, the world will shake."

In 2011, trade between Japan and China totaled $345 billion. This economic partnership is in jeopardy unless a solution arises to allow both countries to save face with their respective constituents.

> *"According to analysis on Japan-China trade in 2015, based on import data from "Trade Statistics of Japan" by the Ministry of Finance and the "China Customs Statistics," total trade decreased by 11.8% to $303.3 billion, a double-digit fall for the first time in six years (since 2009)"*
> https://www.jetro.go.jp/en/news/releases/2016/c52b1f3efe0aa231.html

In September 2012, Japan appointed Ambassador Shinichi Nishimiya to China. Nishimiya died within the week of the Senkaku dispute, which by then was already growing out of control.

The Senkaku Islands incident in September 2012 is an example of the Chinese tendency to act first and talk later, rather than communicating and exhibiting restraint from the start of a disagreement. The war-waging chants from a handful of Chinese did not likely lead to any military exchange with Japan. What is a concern for Japan, however, are the potential problematic trade issues that underlie this dispute. I stated in my Synastry astrology chart analysis that financial trade agreements can ultimately help resolve other unforeseen disagreements. China can be a great market for Japan, and Japan can be a partner in innovation with each other when it comes to clean air and water pollution.

Responding in an aggressive manner is China's signature method for handling disagreements. It's a device used to manipulate public opinion while giving the appearance of strength. Made-up crises can be used to cover up and divert attention away from internal problems.

Ironically, Japan tends to reinvest its profits back into China, which creates cheap labor for Japan and needed jobs for the Chinese. Indeed, some financial analysts do not consider Japan and China financial rivals, instead viewing their economies as complementary. If Japan can consider patience in its dealings with China and respond from a position of strength, China will respect that strength as the only worthwhile currency. For the near future, Japan needs to be cautious with further investments in China. At this time, China is an unreliable investment source for Japan, though China can still be a lucrative market since the Chinese need Japan's technology and investments. This century, China's new religion for freedom is MONEY!

Until 2026-2028, the tendency is for China to be led by its ego and demand respect because China lacks the balance expected from most governments. China has a problem with finding and then maintaining the balance that comes with strength, largely due to having Neptune, Mercury and the Sun in Libra. This combination highlights the indecision endemic to the Chinese government and its complex bureaucracy. If it continues to be aggressive, China can't help but discover its economy will suffer because nations and corporations will limit future investment.

In September 2012, China accused Japan of stealing the Senkaku Islands in the South China Sea, setting a bad tone that has extended beyond the Mayan date of December 21, 2012. It is important for Japan to be realistic because in 2012, confusion resulted from unrealistic expectations concerning business in China. Aggressive speculations are to be avoided. Japan should stick to the facts and let awareness guide their business dealings. China is in a state of great change, and it would be best to let the country evolve before making too many more large-scale investments in such a potentially hostile neighbor. A fundamental psychological change is occurring in Japan, as evidenced by the unusual weekly street demonstrations in 2012. In 2016, demonstrations against reinterpreting Japan's constitution are not as surprising as they used to be, and the continued issue of the Okinawa Marine Base relocation is also questioned. To further complicate matters, Taiwan also sent a flotilla of ships to the region to stake its claims to the Senkaku Islands.

To tie in these ideas astrologically, China's chart on September 11, 2012 had transiting Pluto in Capricorn 6° square Uranus in Aries 7°, transiting Pluto square China's Sun in Libra at 7° and transiting Pluto in Capricorn 6° opposite China's Uranus at 4° Cancer. Transiting Mars in Scorpio at 12° is at the crown of China's chart, which demonstrates aggressive, subversive behavior due to the placement of China's mundane Mars in Scorpio square Mars at 14° Leo and Pluto at Leo 17° in the Seventh House of foreign relations, business relations, agreements, treaties and/or disputes. The combination of these squares and their opposition demonstrates the unexpected by Uranus,

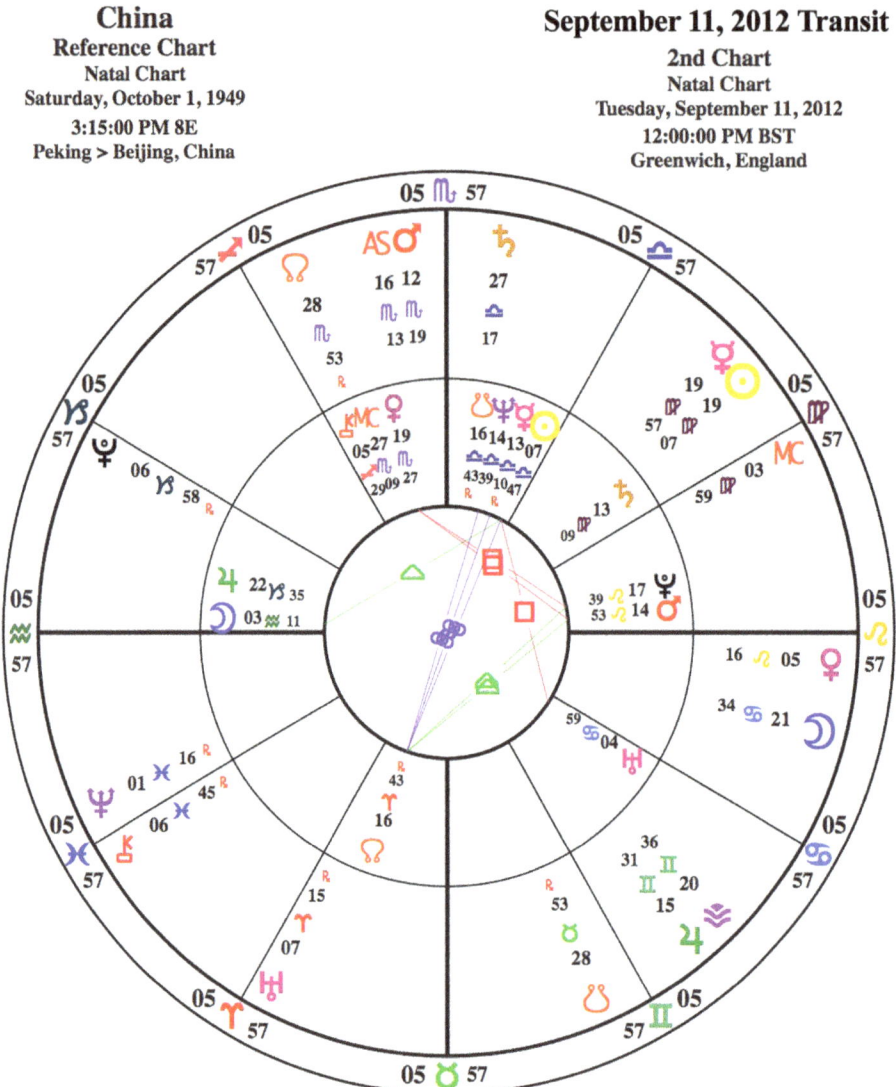

while the intensity of Mars in Scorpio represents the aggression and deceptive qualities experienced by Japan and China during the September 2012 Senkaku Island dispute.

The story of the Senkaku Island dispute goes like this. A rightwing group of Tokyo residents wanted to develop the islands, potentially making problems worse with China, which has a rich history of revolutions and political infighting. The decision by the Japanese government to buy the islands was thus intended to promote peace and stability by preventing this group from staking a claim. China, in turn, flatly stated the Senkaku Islands have historically been its territory and fishing grounds. However, Japan has been in control of the islands for almost 100 years now, making relevant the old adage that possession is nine-tenths of the law. Perhaps, needless to say, Japan would do well to remain very wary of China, as the China of today will not be the China of tomorrow.

Chapter 8 Japan's Relationship with China

Political analyst Li Weidong stated the official tactic of the Chinese government is to use protest to achieve its foreign-policy goals. In a communiqué sent to associates, Mr. Weidong compared the recent protests with the Boxers, a religious group the Qing dynasty used to drive foreigners from China: "Beijing dare not to fight, but it's unable to talk it over either. So it has to employ Boxers, using product boycott to press Japan."[139]

When the 18th Chinese Congress convened in November 2012, members installed a new set of Communist leaders, and the power shifted at the highest levels after 10 years of rule by China's leader Hu Jintao. The West knows very little concerning these new leaders. I predict further easing of monetary policies by China, a change that will be closely watched for its influence due to global dissatisfaction with the slowing world economy.

There is a strong possibility the Chinese government staged the Senkaku Island dispute so the government could demonstrate to the Chinese public they won't be pushed around, especially by Japan. It is in China's interest to point to enemies outside of China rather than dealing with the enemies from within. China cannot afford to be seen as backing down from Japan, and it is in Japan's interest to demonstrate a cool resolve. The Senkaku Island dispute had market repercussions as well, prompting China to withhold rare minerals used for cellular technology from Japan. But in time China will understand actions on the world stage will affect its financial status with other countries. No matter how big the financial market is in China, corporations will not want to do business with an unpredictable, aggressive Dragon. However, sometimes protests can grow out of control, and even governments can't stop a mob.

Japan's election in 2012 was a critical moment for Japan. Regarding the Senkaku Islands friction with China, former Prime Minister Noda stated, "Creating a vacuum in the political responses to these issues must be avoided at any cost." [140] Prime Minister Noda was undoubtedly counting on this idea for his reelection. However, actions by the Japanese government created the dispute with the Senkaku Islands and, combined with the ensuing financial costs to Japan, cost Noda the election in 2013. Severe austerity is the wrong path for Japan to take leading up to 2020. A balance must be found in order to achieve slow, sustainable growth.

Energy generation and consumption is an important debate among the Japanese, and reducing greenhouse gases is one of the lessons of the Age of Light. Japan is motivated by a sense of long-term goals—rightly so for the Age of Light. In 2012 the former Democratic Party of Japan (DPJ) leader Ichiro Ozawa, challenged his new political party by announcing the idea of eliminating nuclear power in Japan within 10 years. This is going to be a difficult transition to switch its energy away from nuclear due to financial considerations. Japan will need to transition gradually from the use of old technology to innovative green technology so businesses are not denied the energy needed during the transition. As they add to the collective wisdom, the Japanese people are learning about themselves along the way.

---

139 Johnson, Ian and Thom Shanker. "Beijing Mixes Messages Over Anti-Japan Protests." *The New York Times*, 16 September 2012, Li Weidong quoted, *www.nytimes.com/2012/09/17/world/asia/anti-japanese-pro-tests-over-disputed-islands-continue-in-china.html*.

140 "Noda to Seek Reelection as DPJ Leader." *Daily Yomiuri Online*, 8 September 2012, *www.yomiuri.co.jp/dy/national/T120907004331.htm*.

Astrologically connected to September 11, 2012, the Japanese felt a sense of restriction, which was inflicted by an aggressive external force (China). This sense relates to the transiting planet Mars in Scorpio at 12°, which is in the Sixth House associated with the navy, including public healthcare. Transiting Neptune retrograde at 1° Pisces was also conjunct to Japan's mundane Mercury retrograde in Pisces at 0° in the Ninth House of shipping, sea traffic, law courts and scientific institutions. Furthermore, what caught my eye in Japan's transit mundane chart was Pluto in Capricorn at 6° and its exact opposite, the asteroid Chiron retrograde at 6° Cancer in the First House concerning general conditions of prosperity and health. Chiron is an asteroid known for being the wounded healer, and at times it plays an important role. This conflict between Japan and China clearly speaks to the idea of past wounds that are hopefully in the healing process. I do think eventually these two countries reach a resolution based on financial cooperation concerning the energy reserves of gas and oil that lie at the bottom of the sea surrounding the Senkaku Islands.

As previously mentioned, this current dispute began when the Japanese government bought three of the islands from a private Japanese citizen. This action prompted the Chinese government to send naval vessels to the islands, only escalating the tension. This resolution eventually takes the form of a financial agreement, but the process is going to take some time before it is finalized. In May and June 2014 there was a powerful and transformative square between Pluto and Uranus, which marked an important change in the stirrings of a revolutionary environment in the world. The forces driving these revolutions around the world have been simmering for many years and bring further disruption to world economies. These forces speak to the potential breakup of the Eurozone. I see an economic problem that will ferment further revolutions in fragile countries around the world. With Britain leaving the Eurozone in 2016, it only adds to the potential unraveling of the European Union.

On September 11, 2012, the tension between Japan and China escalated, which was not surprising since both China and Japan were having an 'air-quake'. Japan had Pluto in Capricorn at 6° moving into the Eighth House of international and transnational corporations, signifying international finance with multinational corporations. China had experienced a mild 'air-quake' at the beginning of 2011, when Pluto entered the Twelfth House and went retrograde. In July and November of 2011, Pluto retrograded back and forth over the Eleventh House representing friends, allies, hopes of the nation, and the Twelfth House border, which caused another 'air-quake'. In China's transit chart of September 11, 2012, Pluto was in the wake of an 'air-quake'. In December 2012, Pluto entered the Twelfth House and remains there until February 22, 2027, when Pluto enters the Meiji First House. The Twelfth House represents secret groups, places of confinement, institutions and enemies from within, and manipulations behind the scenes. It is around 2026-2028 a revolution takes place in China. The Chinese Dragon awakens and "shakes the world" with its cultural internal self-confrontation about who it is, what it has been, and what it wants to become. Cultural biases of the past have minority groups resenting the Chinese and rejecting its political mandates. Minorities are finally going to demand their regional rights from Beijing. Tibet is an example of the absence of consciousness of the Chinese government, which invaded and brutally destroyed a beautiful culture of peaceful people. Revolution and violence is no stranger to China. It would be likely the Chinese to envelope

Chapter 8 Japan's Relationship with China

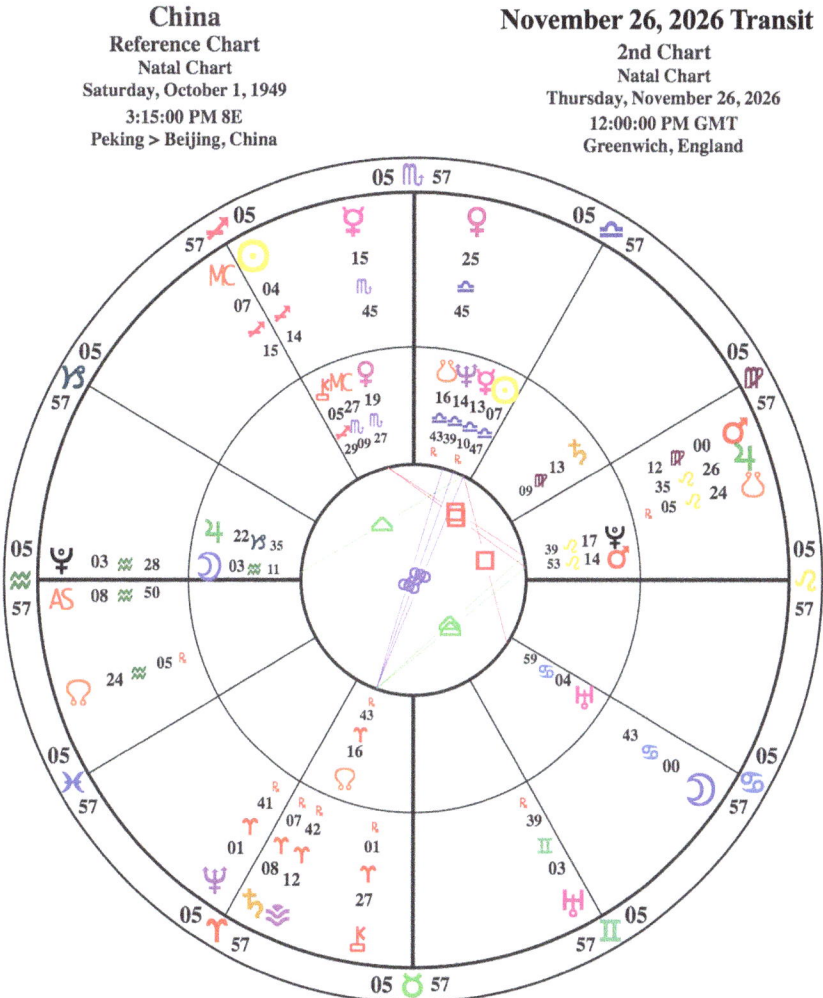

North Korea as part of China and Korea become one of many regions for the New China that it comes to resemble. This would remove the growing nuclear tension and eliminate the confrontation.

By 2026, Pluto touches the First House, which for China highlights secrecy and deception behind the political curtain. (Of course, in astrology the outer planets move slowly, and their effects are not always felt right at any given moment.) In addition, Japan will experience increased internet hacking of its military, business and government infrastructures in the next 12 years. As Ted Koppel writes in his book *Lights Out: A Cyberattack, A Nation Unprepared, Surviving the Aftermath*, the new field of war for terrorism is the internet.[141] This means the energy infrastructures of nations can be shutdown, or even worse, nuclear energy plants can be taken over and converted into bombs by way of the internet.

---
141 Koppel, Ted. *Lights Out: A Cyberattack, A Nation Unprepared, Surviving the Aftermath*. Crown, 2015.

Looking forward to November 2026, transiting Pluto in Aquarius will be conjunct China's Moon in Aquarius at 3°. In 2026-2028, after China's revolution, they create geographical areas that become a union of regional provinces. This revolutionary approach creates the People's Regional Republics of China. This Eastern/Western style approach will be a new beginning for China. Mutual respect is central for Japan and China's peaceful coexistence, as they recognize what is at stake, if they want to get along instead of indulging in regional disputes and animosity.

I've written about the positions of Uranus in Aries, located in the same sign at approximately the same degree it was in the 1930s, which was then associated with the Great Depression. Countries around the world experience a recession or a slowdown in their economic outlooks, and countries around the world are going to struggle to secure their financial footing. India, in the decades to come, experiences millions of deaths from the lack of clean water. Due to the lack of sewage-waste management, contaminated water in India has the potential to set back the country for several decades. We have taken clean water for granted far too long. The scarcity of clean water is a world crisis waiting to happen, and it *is* going to happen. For the next several decades, the world continues to experience financial swings and an uncertain economic approach for its future. Political and financial corruption, combined with distribution of wealth, is often the yoke of revolution. Japan is not immune to this trend. Because of their sense of duty and honor, the tribe will pull together and make the best of this challenging situation. The outcome of these dark years is to become the Age of Light, which illuminates awareness as the century unfolds.

Japan can no longer rely on a "business as usual" mentality because the vibrational shift the Mayan astrologer-priests predicted is finally coming to the world. Human attitudes are going to shift regarding the ideas of money and the amount of wealth being kept by so few and kept from so many. World governments have to solve the problems of health, education, and poverty, so violent revolutions will finally cease. These governments will have no choice but to reexamine the past and create a new paradigm for a brighter future. President Trumps 2017 tax cut for corporation's and for the wealthiest in America is a good example of the wrong approach for the Age of Light.

The years ahead are going to be difficult ones with widespread instability around the world, affecting the economic balance of world financial conditions around the globe. The vibrational shift in attitudes is marked by an event concerning quantum physics, a turning point of great historical significance, not unlike that felt when Copernicus revealed the Earth orbits around the sun. For example, the discovery of water on Mars in 2015 is just the beginning of the changes science is going to reveal. New scientific discoveries at Hadron Collider are going to reshape the world and our view of the Universe based on physics and new sources of energy, even though it will take decades for this new energy to become consumer ready. Scientific discoveries will change governments around the world, as technology brings greater transparency and a new consciousness regarding the way we treat the Earth and each other. The last frontier humankind has to discover and conquer is true world peace, which becomes our only destination driving humanity's fate.

More than any other country, Japan creates for itself a sense of well-being. Politics in Japan reflect the tribal voices within. After all, it's the people who fund the government. I also cannot stress enough the importance of women becoming more involved in politics and running governments on equal terms with their male counterparts worldwide. This responsibility is squarely on the shoulders of Japanese women who need to stop being passive in the political realm. Japanese women must be involved if Japan is to evolve. In 2020, the first female prime minister in Japan is elected. This monumental event will reflect the dramatic shift underway in Japan.

Since Japan is an island nation, it faces many challenges with regard to climate change. Scientists predict the upper world jet stream will shift to the northern hemisphere, which can create large, unstable swings as jet streams dip down to lower latitudes, breaking temperature records around the world. This in turn creates greater droughts, larger floods and greater storms of all kinds, as well as increasing the melting speed of the largest glaciers. Projecting future rates of the sea level rising is challenging. If carbon dioxide emissions in this century remain at their current rate, by the year 2100 the sea level encroachment could be around 3.3 feet.[142] Our climate is changing; that is a fact. The Mayan Predictions are coming true in regards to extreme weather.

The future brings major changes to the atmosphere around the globe. These changes are going to bring problems for Japan, including rising water levels and more frequent large typhoons. More troublesome still is the idea the northern jet stream may undulate, making it even harder to predict world weather patterns.

Japan's commercial success of the future transforms current ways of doing business and reprioritizes the values of the past. Japan is a leader in the public health arena in coming years. As just one example, Olympus and Sony are forming a company that is going to develop innovative technology to help meet future medical needs. Along the way, in 2012 Olympus received $640 million in investments from Sony as they prepare for the future needs of humankind.

In 2013, the Japanese people increasingly demonstrated against government policies concerning nuclear energy and tax hikes. Japanese citizens will continue to demonstrate in the streets, asking their government to listen to their concerns. The Japanese government is asking trade unions to make financial concessions for the good of the country. The Japanese are going to demonstrate the tremendous creativity needed to overcome any hardships.

In September 2012, the Bank of Japan made a move to support the Japanese economy when it offered $128 billion in bonds, which is also known as printing money. More money will increase investment, thus helping to create more spending. With revenue loss in China due to the rioting in September 2012, it was prudent of Japan to offer bonds and look toward the future.

---

142 Plumer, Brad. "An ocean mystery: How high did sea levels rise in the 20th century?" *Vox*, 15 January 2015, www.vox.com/2015/1/15/7552539/sea-level-20th-century.

In Japan, inflation did pick up in 2011, but the economy slid back into a recession. The current economic state in Japan cannot be sustained and therefore results in drastic cutbacks, which could translate into a lower quality of life. Unfortunately, higher taxes are just the beginning of what is needed to overcome the obstacles Japan faces. The advice the Japanese must heed is what Akio Morita, the founder of Sony stated years ago, "Don't be afraid to make a mistake. But make sure you don't make the same mistake twice." A significant challenge for Japan is to reconcile the future with the past. The Japanese people have always been motivated by long-term goals. At a fundamental level, Japan understands the value of allowing people to discover their own way. The most important ongoing debates among the Japanese concern progress toward more sustainable practices in energy generation and consumption. This debate continues for years to come.

At the end of 2012, Japan was on a financial cliff, and the Japanese government would have run out of money if it had not raised taxes and issued bonds to raise revenue. Japan and the United States have the largest First World deficits. Furthermore, both countries have dysfunctional political landscapes, which is the core problem that requires attention. The returning recession in late 2012 has created the pressure needed to force businesses and the government to implement necessary economic changes. In this new world economy, change is not as predictable as it used to be. The Japanese economy rebounded from the previous contraction and tax hike of 2014. I do see the possibility of a major earthquake hitting Tokyo in 2018 or 2023, and this delays Japan's financial recovery.

It seems clear to me that pollution could be China's downfall economically. It is the most important trauma China will experience in the Mayan era As *The New York Times* reported, "Public health is reeling. Pollution has made cancer China's leading cause of death…Ambient air pollution alone is blamed for hundreds of thousands of deaths each year. Nearly 500 million people lack access to safe drinking water. Chinese cities often seem wrapped in a toxic gray shroud." [143] The air pollution flowing from China in turn contaminates Japanese air quality, which has to be addressed by both countries.

Japan and China by 2050 finally become better neighbors. Asia has a bright future, however, it does not occur by confrontation, rather by cooperation.

In the Mayan era, Japan survives beautifully, making it a great example of what a cohesive, loving tribe can accomplish. As Thich Nhat Hanh once said, "Our own life is the instrument with which we experiment with truth."

> *When all the trees have been cut down,*
> *when all the animals have been hunted,*
> *when all the waters are polluted,*
> *when all the air is unsafe to breathe,*
> *only then will you discover*
> *you cannot eat money.*
> ~ Native American Prophecy

---

143 Kahn, Joseph and Jim Yardley. "As China Roars, Pollution Reaches Deadly Extremes." *The New York Times*, 26 August 2007, *www.nytimes.com/2007/08/26/world/asia/26china.html?pagewanted=all.*

Chapter 9

Transit Chart of Tokyo

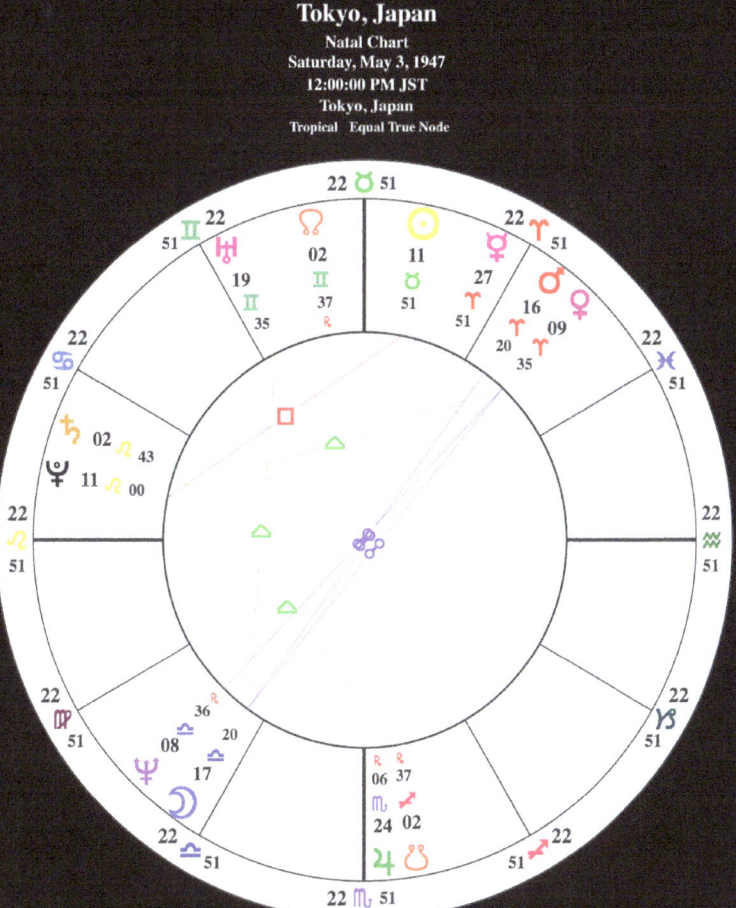

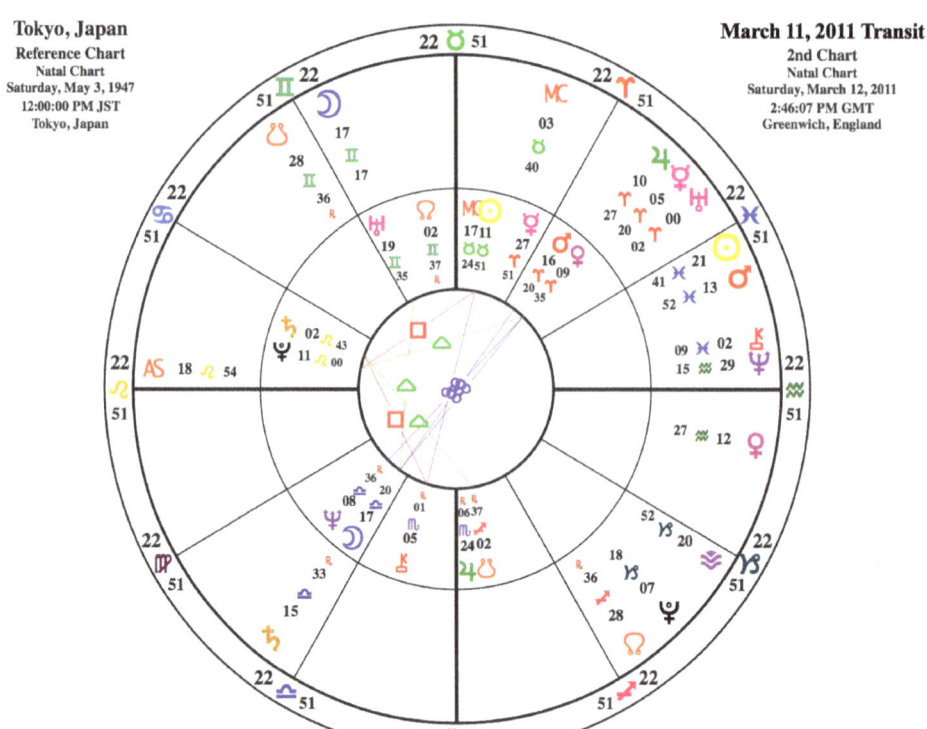

The Great Eastern Japan Earthquake Disaster coincided with two unusual celestial events. On March 11, 2011, the day of the disaster, the planet Uranus entered Aries for the first time in 84 years. Then a little more than a week later on March 19, the moon appeared in the sky over Tokyo as what astrologers refer to as a "Supermoon." A Supermoon occurs only when there is a full or new moon and when the moon makes its closest physical approach to Earth on its orbit. This particular Supermoon came closer to Earth than any other Supermoon had since 1993.

It will take the Japanese people many years to recover from the Great Eastern Japan Earthquake Disaster.

★ ★ ★ ★ ★ ★ ★   ★ ★ ★ ★ ★ ★ ★   ★ ★ ★ ★ ★ ★ ★

My approach to understanding the fate of Japan is based on the discipline of Mundane Astrology, which means the choice of a "founding date" is critical. As a mundane astrologer, I am interested in casting the most accurate horoscope for Japan. Therefore, I consulted *The Book of World Horoscopes* by eminent astrologer Nicholas Campion. This reference work is found on the desk of any reputable astrologer interested in the horoscopes of places and events around the world throughout history. In fact, it is the only book of its kind."

When there are several choices of potential founding dates and times for a city or a country, then the mundane astrologer ultimately looks for historical events that coincide with astrological data. Intuition plays a role, too. For what I shall refer to as the "Tokyo chart," I considered several founding dates.

What I came to realize, however, is transits on the 1457 chart did not correlate with historic earthquakes. Furthermore, Tokyo was a very different city back in 1457. Nearly five centuries ago, the habitation now known as Tokyo was a small medieval fishing village called Edo ruled under a feudal system. The Tokyo of today is a world-class megalopolis and center of technological innovation. Tokyo has been reborn.

Eventually, I had to acknowledge this centuries-old chart did not provide me with the information necessary to offer proper warning of impending disasters that could impact the Japanese islands from now through the 2030s.

At first, April 12, 1457 was a real contender. After researching and eliminating many possible founding dates for Japan, only May 3, 1947 remained. For all intents and purposes, this date turns out to be the most relevant to the casting of mundane horoscopes for Present and future because it marks in many ways the rebirth of postwar Tokyo. On this day, Emperor Hirohito presented the new postwar democratic constitution to the Diet of Japan at Nagatachō, Chiyoda, Tokyo.

I chose the constitutional presentation date of May 3, 1947 at 12 p.m. as the basis of my astrological inquiry into the fate of Tokyo.

I see this date as the rebirth of Tokyo as we know it today, the city becoming a self-sustaining light in a world of darkness as the Mayan Prediction unfolds. Even though some other astrologers assert the constitutional presentation Tokyo chart as representing the entire nation of Japan, I perceive it as solely marking the rebirth of Tokyo. Though the characters of Tokyo and Japan are inextricably intertwined, Tokyo's destiny is unique and in many ways separate.

The Great Kantō Earthquake that struck Tokyo on September 1, 1923 bore striking astrological similarities to the Great Eastern Japan Earthquake Disaster of March 11, 2011.

Transiting Saturn was at 17° Libra on the day of the 1923 quake. I was astounded to discover on March 11, 2011 transiting Saturn was at 15° Libra, a difference of a mere 2° out of the 360° zodiacal total. That both earthquake charts have the same transiting planet with only a 2° difference between the 1923 and 2011 positions in Libra (the sign of balance) is quite extraordinary. The connection between Saturn in Libra and the Tokyo earthquakes seems like a powerful omen.

During both earthquakes, Saturn was transiting the Second House representing conditions of supply and demand. The significance here is Saturn challenges the House it transits, and the Second House represents home, trade, money markets, banks, financial institutions, and national wealth. Saturn takes away the old to make way for new growth.

In 2000 while attending Kepler College of Astrology in Seattle, Washington, I was privileged to attend a very informative class in Mundane Astrology taught by Nicholas

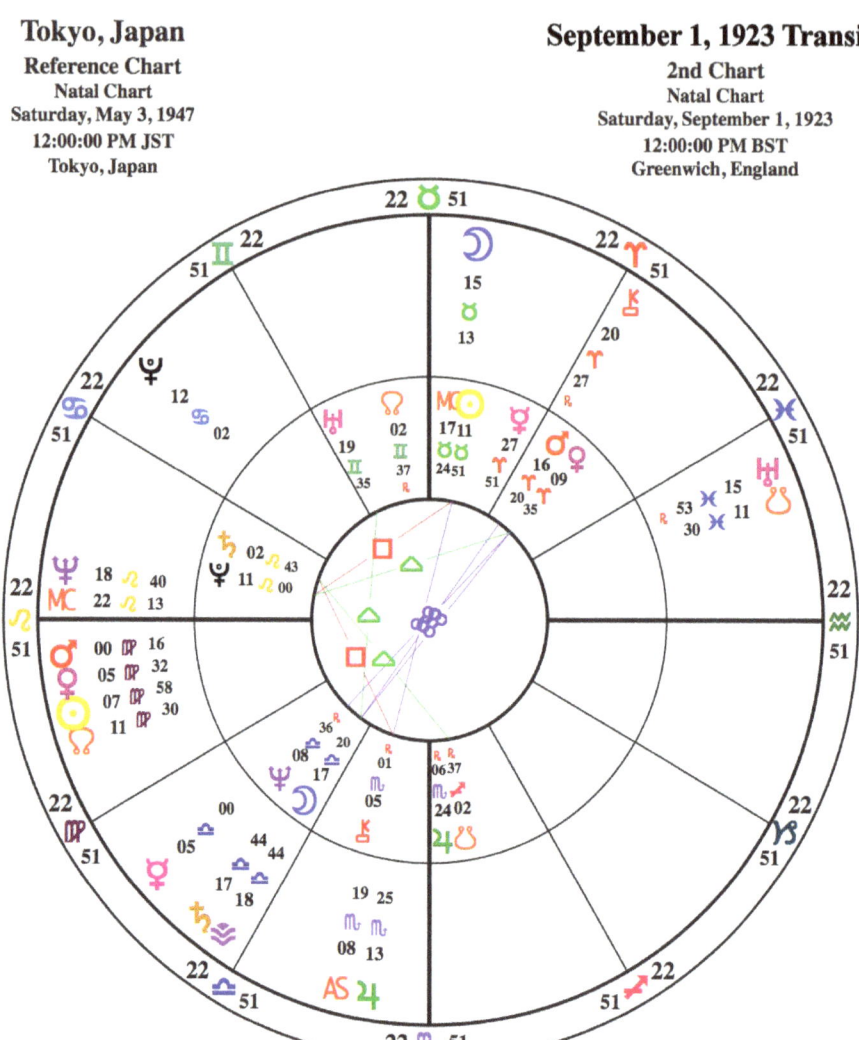

Campion. Kepler College was founded that year as the first institution in the West devoted to the academic study of astrology since the time of the Renaissance. In the class, Campion alluded to research he had conducted concerning national (as opposed to personal) horoscopes. With reference to national horoscopes, Campion encouraged his students to, "Experiment with the charts. Make predictions. And, yes, prediction remains a perfectly valid exercise: one successful prediction reveals more about the nature of the Universe than a hundred retrospective studies. Just as the individual is contained within the collective, so natal astrology can be seen as contained within mundane astrology." [144]

Supermoons: Portents of Disaster?

The Moon is normally 238,855 miles from Earth. On March 11, 2011 the Moon was around 221,567 miles from Earth, and the full moon in Virgo on March 19, 2011 became a Supermoon; an Extreme Supermoon, to be precise.

---

144 Campion, Nicholas. Mundane Astrology, Kepler College, Seattle, WA. Class lecture.

Mercury entered Aries on March 9, 2011, and Uranus entered Aries on March 11, 2011 in the West and March 12, 2011 in Japan. The International Date Line accounts for this.

Through my mundane astrological analysis, I attempt to bring to light periods when Tokyo is vulnerable to earthquakes. Supermoons, especially Extreme Supermoons, appear to be associated with previous earthquakes. Through calculating various astrological aspects, I think future earthquakes can be anticipated by charting the Supermoons that historically have been connected with earthquakes. In my analysis, Supermoons appear to trigger earthquakes rather than astrological aspects. And, there is correspondence with the synchronicity of astrological aspect and Supermoons on occasion, which can be enough to make us take notice.

We are all constantly changing, as is the Earth. Analyzing historic Supermoons is an astrological experiment that may help predict earthquakes based on certain oppositions, conjuncts, or squares created by the slower-moving planets, including Mars, Jupiter, Saturn, Uranus, Neptune, and Pluto, along with the Supermoons themselves.

Astrologer Richard Nolle has discoursed extensively on the concept of the Supermoons and was kind enough to send me the following article:[145]

SUPERMOON – Impact and Implications
What It Is, What It Means by Richard Nolle

> Clearly there's a lot of confusion about what's really a Supermoon. I know because I created and defined the term in an article published over 30 years ago. When I see people misrepresenting the idea, not really understanding it at all, I feel impelled—not compelled—to try and set the record straight. Words mean things, after all. For example, referring to the date of the last Supermoon as 18 years ago—as several media reports are doing lately—is completely wrong. There are 4-6 Supermoons a year on average. The one on March 19, 2011 is, in fact, the closest Supermoon of the year, but it's not by any means the first one in 18 years, nor even the first Extreme Supermoon in 18 years. The truth is, March 19 will be the second Supermoon this year, and we only have to go back to January 30, 2010 to find the last example of an Extreme Supermoon, as revealed in my tables published in the last century. Supermoons are noteworthy for their close association with extreme tidal forces working in what astrologers of old used to call the sublunary world: the atmosphere, crust, and oceans of our home planet—including ourselves, of course. From powerful coastal tides to severe storms to impactful earthquakes and volcanic eruptions, the entire natural world surges and spasms under the sway of the Supermoon alignment—within three days either way of the exact syzygy, as a general rule. Supermoon solar eclipses tend to have a wider sphere of impact, extending roughly a week before and after the actual event.

---

145 Richard Nolle holds a Professional Certificate of Proficiency in Natal Astrology from the American Federation of Astrologers. For more information, visit *www.astropro.com*

A Supermoon that approached Earth in April 2011 presaged the disaster that followed. On May 23, 2011 a volcano in Greenland erupted. In the United States, more than 1,000 tornadoes wreaked havoc throughout April and May 2011, the greatest number of tornadoes over any two-month period in recorded history.

Even though Supermoons don't occur every month, time periods before or after a Supermoon do seem to presage or coincide with weather-related disasters. In June 2011, devastating forest fires in Arizona spread into New Mexico, burning tens of thousands of hectares and thousands of homes.

SuperMoons also seem to affect other forms of intense weather due to their effect on the Earth's gravitational field. Everything is interrelated and connected, and the Present is the wholeality of the infinite oceanic energy of creation.

In combination with global warming, drastic weather is manifesting more often in all corners of the globe. This trend continues for the foreseeable future. Ash clouds erupting from volcanoes on occasion in the next decade continue to interfere with air travel. Torrential floods in China and Thailand hit record levels in 2015 with more to come. In 2011, floods in the United States broke all records throughout the Midwest from North Dakota all the way along the Mississippi down to New Orleans. In 2014 and 2015 in various parts of the United States, floods continued to break records. In 2017, due to the destruction of hurricane Harvey and hurricane Maria in Puerto Rico, these communities are going to be rebuilding for several years to come. Due to heavy snowfalls in Canada, the runoff was more than the tributaries could contain. New Zealand, with its earthquake of February 22, 2011, is another example of the changes happening around the world. A month later Japan, situated on the "Ring of Fire," suffered the Great Eastern Japan Earthquake Disaster.

What we do here on Earth affects our environment. Everything is interrelated, especially considering the growth projected in this century. Could the building of megacities be changing weather patterns on the planet? It seems so. China's megacities, for example, are having a tremendous impact on the environment. The air quality in Beijing is the worst in the world and getting worse. And yet, prospects for the future are ours to determine. Humankind can choose to change.

After the Great Eastern Japan Earthquake Disaster, it occurred to me to examine and add astrological analysis of the Supermoon parallels with historic earthquakes, specifically with reference to the disasters affecting Japan. Simply put, Supermoons, especially Extreme Supermoons, tend to occur a few weeks prior or subsequent to earthquakes. Indeed, these Supermoons seem to foster unusual weather.

I started writing this book in the spring of 2010. When the events of March 11, 2011 transpired, I felt vindicated in extending my astrological inquiry beyond economic and political affairs to also take into account the forces of nature. The interrelation of human and natural affairs is evidenced by the slow recovery from the Great Eastern Japan Earthquake Disaster and its detrimental effects on the economy—effects I had, in fact, foreseen. However, I wasn't sure why that was going to be the case. When the Fukushima earthquake occurred, then it became clear why the economy was going to have a downturn and a slow recovery in this decade.

Extreme Supermoons: A Few Recent Examples

January 10, 2005 – Full Moon – Supermoon in Capricorn. An earthquake cracked the Indian Ocean floor off the coast of Sumatra on December 26, 2004. It was an earthquake of magnitude 9.3 on the Richter scale, the strongest felt in the area in 40 years. The earthquake also triggered a massive tsunami.

Then on March 28, 2005, a major earthquake occurred killing roughly 1,300 people, mostly on the island of Nias (on the west coast of Sumatra) causing widespread panic. It was the third most powerful earthquake since 1965 in Indonesia.

December 12, 2008 – Full Moon – Supermoon in Gemini. On November 16, 2008, a magnitude 7.3 earthquake struck off the coast of Indonesia. During this period, the Japanese economy also posted consecutive second-quarter contractions for the first time since 2001. Japan was officially in a recession. Severe flooding in southern Brazil caused 45 deaths and the evacuation of 20,000 people. In December on the full moon, a massive ice storm hit the U.S. state of Massachusetts, and hundreds of thousands of homes were without electricity for days.

January 30, 2010 – Full Moon – Supermoon in Leo. A severe magnitude 7.0 earthquake struck Haiti on January 12, 2010, and a tsunami washed across the Caribbean. Large numbers of structures in Port-au-Prince were damaged or destroyed. Haiti's government estimated the death toll at 230,000.

On January 3, 2010, an earthquake of magnitude 5.1 left 20,000 people homeless in eastern Tajikistan. That same day, a magnitude 7.1 earthquake also struck the Solomon Islands in the South Pacific, resulting in a tsunami measuring 10 feet in some parts of the islands. As many as 1,000 people were left homeless after the earthquake, and the tsunami destroyed approximately 200 homes.

In addition, prior to the Supermoon, a horrific mudslide left many homeless in Brazil due to extreme rain. At approximately the same time, a volcano erupted in Colombia, forcing the evacuation of 8,000 people.

In January 2010, extreme weather across Europe also caused dozens of deaths, including 122 in Poland and 79 in Switzerland after an avalanche. A magnitude 6.5 earthquake also struck about 33 miles off the shore of Eureka, California, on January 9, 2010, leading to minor injuries, minor damage and an area-wide electrical power outage.

March 19, 2011 – Full Moon – Supermoon in Virgo. March 11, 2011 was the day of the Great Eastern Japan Earthquake Disaster, one of the five most powerful earthquakes since 1900. The earthquake measured 9.0 on the Richter scale and struck approximately 42 miles off the eastern shore of Japan, triggering extremely destructive tsunami waves reaching up to 128 feet. Waves were recorded as traveling up to 6 miles inland. Over 15,000 people were killed, and thousands of people were missing. It was estimated the costs to Japan could exceed $300 billion.

After the tsunami damaged the Fukushima Daiichi reactor, radioactivity levels surged in Japan, and the Japanese government raised the radioactive threat level to VII, the highest level possible on the international scale. This radioactive danger was equivalent to that which resulted from the Chernobyl nuclear disaster.

The Fukushima Daiichi nuclear plant cleanup and recovery can take at least 40-60 years, and the ripple effects of the disaster will take many years to accurately identify. The ramifications of the damage to ocean ecosystems off the coast of Japan are going to take decades to fully evaluate and mitigate. Further information about the radioactive leaks into the ocean thus far being withheld from the public will be revealed. More specifically, information about radioactivity contaminating the ocean in disturbing amounts highlights the true damage to the fishing industry and to the health of the ocean around Japan. News reports of continued leaks of radioactive water being stored in large storage tanks only adds to the uncertain future of nuclear energy use in Japan. The courageous men working in the cleanup of Fukushima have succeeded in filtering most of the 620,000 tons of toxic water stored at the site.[146] As of 2016, several thousand people who lost their homes were still living in temporary housing.[147]

In June 2011, another earthquake at magnitude 6.7 occurred in Japan, again in the Honshu vicinity in the north of Japan. No deaths or major damages were recorded. A Supermoon occurred April 7, 2016. On April 16, Japan had a magnitude 7.0 earthquake, which hit in the area of Kumamoto Prefecture, and 32 people were reported dead. is gives us further information to show the correlation between Supermoons and earthquakes.

★ ★ ★ ★ ★ ★   ★ ★ ★ ★ ★ ★   ★ ★ ★ ★ ★ ★

Tokyo Earthquake Forecast – The Most Important Potential Dates and Year
2018 and 2023 stand out years for earthquake disasters.

2018

January 2, 2018 – Full Moon – Supermoon at 11° Cancer of the most extreme. This Supermoon signifies added problems Tokyo may encounter through early 2018, especially in terms of a major earthquake. January may have an earthquake or major landslides, and heavy snowfalls right into February, along with a winter flu epidemic. Tokyo is on the brink of a major transformation. Tokyo's revolution in consciousness becomes a beacon for the people of the world as the Mayan Prediction unfolds. During this Full Moon – Supermoon, the transiting aspects will not be as intense as during the November 14, 2016 Supermoon. I can see potential for a strong earthquake but not one with destructive power.

February 10 - April 5, 2018. In Tokyo's Natal chart, transiting Jupiter in Scorpio is in an 'air-quake' position which has recently entered the Fourth House, which indicates weather conditions, the people versus the government and signifies the party not in power. Jupiter is stationed on March 9th and then goes retrograde. Transiting Jupiter conjunct

---

146 "Tepco says all radioactive water in Fukushima No. 1 tanks filtered ". *Japan Times*, 27 May 2015, www.japantimes. co.jp/news/2015/05/27/national/tepco-says-radioactive-water-fukushima-1-tanks-filtered/#.We0lm62ZNsM.

147 Hu, Elise. "5 Years After Japan Disasters, 'Temporary' Housing Is Feeling Permanent." *NPR*, 11 March 2016, www.npr.org/sections/parallels/2016/03/11/469857023/5-years-after-japan-disasters-temporary-housing-is-feeling-permanent.

Tokyo's Jupiter is a positive time for expansion as the people of Tokyo contemplate their actions. This is an opportunity for Tokyo to come together as a community and become a beacon of light for megacities around the globe.

February 19 - June 17, 2018. Transiting Saturn in Capricorn in the Fifth House of Speculative interests squares Tokyo's Neptune in Libra in the Second House of national wealth. This Saturn square is exact on March 22 and May 14. Tokyo is in the news and recognized as a city on the move as it prepares for the 2020 Summer Olympics. If an earthquake occurs before the Tokyo Olympics, it is not clear how this will disrupt the Olympics in Tokyo.

July 12, 2018 – New Moon – Supermoon at 20° Cancer. This should be a quiet, hot summer. Setsuden (energy saving) will be imperative; otherwise, the weather will be dangerous for tribal elders. Tokyo uses solar panel power, productive rooftop gardens and other environmentally friendly ideas to make a strong energy sustainability statement to the world. Urban gardens come into their own. Works of art contribute to better lives for all. By the end of this century, Tokyo is the first world-class city to use over 50% of their energy consumption using solar panels.

August 11, 2018 – New Moon – Supermoon at 18° Leo. The transit of Uranus occurs in Aries along the Ninth House of philosophical and scientific institutions, long distance or international communications and shipping in traffic. Uranus in Aries square to Tokyo's Saturn in Leo in the Twelfth House of secret groups from May 29 through October 20. Uranus is stationed on August 7 and goes retrograde. This positioning speaks to letting go of the past and embracing the future. The Zen quality of Tokyo is making itself known. Tokyo is recognized as a model community when it comes to large megacity evolution. Tokyo shines its light on a self-responsible sustainable future in all Presents to be Present.

November 19 - December 25, 2018. Transiting Saturn in Capricorn in the Fifth House of speculation is square to Tokyo's Neptune in Libra in the Second House. Saturn square is exact on December 7. There is political debate regarding the future of Tokyo and how to proceed when it comes to energy consumption. People become suspicious of the government and demand honest answers to their questions. The patriarchal system of Japan continues to change and evolve. Women are going to be the newly discovered power of this new century as it evolves into the Light.

2023

January 21, 2023 – Full Moon – Supermoon at 1° Aquarius. This is a Supermoon of the utmost intensity—the last of the most Extreme Supermoons. Transiting Saturn in Aquarius in the Seventh House of foreign affairs, treaties, and alliances squares Tokyo's Jupiter in Scorpio in the Fourth House of housing and living conditions. The Saturn square takes place from December 22, 2022 through February 3, 2023. The Saturn square is exact on January 16. During this period, I do not see many major aspects related to earthquakes. I meditate nothing harmful ever comes to my beloved Tokyo. However, events occur whether we like them or not, and what really matters is how we respond to what happens. Our wisdom and response to life events determine the quality and understanding of our living.

If Tokyo experiences a tremendous natural disaster, then the city and people of Tokyo will rise and rebuild their lives and their city. The 2011 Great Eastern Japan Earthquake Disaster occurred after an Extreme Supermoon, one similar in terms of its proximity to Earth as this one. As long as humankind is determined to live near the ocean and atop sensitive, earthquake-prone land, then losses of life and property are inevitable. It's a question of when and where, as well as a question of how the character of the Japanese tribe is to be tested.

February 20, 2023 – Supermoon – New Moon at 1° Pisces. Either a major earthquake or continued aftershocks from the potential January earthquake may occur. The first two months of the year 2023 will be astrologically the most vulnerable in terms of earthquakes that I have seen for some time. Neptune in Pisces in the Eighth House of death, losses, and financial relationships with other countries is poised for this ominous period of time. Uranus in Taurus is in a loose square to Pluto in Leo in the Twelfth House of terrorist activities, hostage situations, and behind-the-scenes manipulation. Uranus in Taurus speaks to the Earth moving suddenly and unexpectedly.

July 10 through October 18, 2023. Transiting Uranus in Taurus in the Ninth House of science publications, shipping, and sea traffic is opposite Tokyo's Jupiter in Scorpio in the Fourth House of land, houses, real estate, and the opposition party in government. The Uranus opposition is stationary on August 29 and goes retrograde. In the middle of this opposition on August 1 a Supermoon – full moon takes place at 9° Aquarius. This period is a time for caution and preparation for disaster, not a time for speculation or risk-taking. During this period, the omens counsel conservation with expenditures and preparation for significant changes to arrive unexpectedly, especially for those who live in Tokyo. This counsel carries on through the end of the year. Typhoons can be a potential problem in August.

August 31, 2023 – Full Moon – Supermoon at 7° Pisces. There is added need for caution, as the potential for unexpected occurrences extending into October and November. This is a time for spiritual growth and awareness and for a revival of interest concerning the traditional religious ways of Japan. Zen Buddhism is evident as the mystical, healing quality that has always resided in these wondrous islands. Like the mist rolling away from the mountains, the unseen becomes known.

This forecast has been an attempt to assist in understanding the correlations between Supermoons, astrology, and weather-related disasters. I look forward to returning to my homeland.

> *There is surely nothing other than the single purpose of the Present moment. A man's whole life is a succession of moment after moment. If one fully understands the Present moment, there will be nothing else to do, and nothing else to pursue.*
> ~ Yamamoto Tsunetomo, Hagakure, The Book of the Samurai

Adopted 26 September, 1924, League of Nations

Geneva Declaration of the Rights of the Child

1924 | Geneva

Five-Point Plan

By the present Declaration of the Rights of the Child, commonly known as the "Declaration of Geneva," men and women of all nations, recognizing that mankind owes to the child the best that it has to give, declare and accept it as their duty that, beyond and above all considerations of race, nationality, or creed:

The child must be given the means requisite for its normal development, both materially and spiritually;

The child that is hungry must be fed; the child that is sick must be nursed; the child that is backward must be helped; the delinquent child must be reclaimed; and the orphan and the waif must be sheltered and succored;

The child must be the first to receive relief in times of distress;

The child must be put in a position to earn a livelihood, and must be protected against every form of exploitation;

The child must be brought up in the consciousness that its talents must be devoted to the service of fellow men.

Epilogue

All Is Light

"Forgiveness is the Fragrance the Violet Sheds on the Heel that has Crushed It."

~ Mark Twain

The four great moral challenges of the 21st century are the struggle for gender equality, race relations, terrorism, and climate change. As Nicholas Kristof of *The New York Times*, "The global statistics on the abuse of girls are numbing. It appears more girls and women are now missing from the planet, precisely because they are female, than men were killed on the battle field in all the wars of the 20th century." [148]

In 2014, the European Union Agency for Fundamental Rights revealed disturbing information concerning violence against women in the European Union: one in every twenty women in Europe has been raped, and one in three has experienced physical or sexual violence.[149] Such violence is unacceptable in a part of the world considered culturally advanced.

Such violence is unacceptable anywhere and everywhere in the Age of Light. The Age of Light will expose and eliminate ignorance by enlightening the Dark.

As Euclid pointed out some 2,000 years ago, "Things which are equal to the same thing are equal to each other." Let's apply this rule of mathematical reasoning to gender. If women are people and men are people, then women and men are equal.

---

[148] Kristof, Nicholas D. and Sheryl WuDunn. "The Woman's Crusade." *The New York Times*, 17 August 17, www.nytimes.com/2009/08/23/magazine/23Women-t.html?pagewanted=all.

[149] "Violence Against Women: Every Day and Everywhere." *European Union Agency for Fundamental Rights*, 5 March 2014, http://fra.europa.eu/en/press-release/2014/violence-against-women-every-day-and-everywhere.

Epilogue All Is Light

From the beginning, terrorism has been a part of civilization in different forms. However, one thing is clear: poverty on all levels is one of the main elements at the root of terrorism. Poverty comes in many disguises: terrorism as poverty of the spirit and of the soul; poverty as lacking the opportunity of a proper education. Poverty, like a virus or disease, can and will spread if not checked. Because of the sensationalism of international terrorism, domestic terrorism tends to be overlooked. Race relations in some form or another relate to terrorism and the way we treat women. The treatment of women as second-class citizens has been a form of terrorism. I think it's safe to say terrorism is committed by spiritually ill individuals who are out of touch with reality and themselves. Such violence is unacceptable anywhere and everywhere in the Age of Light. The Age of Light completely exposes, and for the most part, eliminates, ignorance and poverty. This exposure occurs by the Dark being overcome and growing into the Light. Death is the most loving way creation takes care of evil. Death is the healer of the Dark, which is put to sleep by Light. We are on the edge of a new frontier for an enlightened planet and an enlightened age. Truth hides not, but is recognized by few.

For me, the Internet is an example of the Age of Light. Electronic media delivers Light as information. The American people receive the government they vote for and deserve. Instead of complaining about our beloved America, let's work to fix it. In my opinion, Congress is the main source of the continued problems we experience in the United States of America.

The frequency of awareness concerning the planet is changing, and cultures around the world are never going to be the same. History repeats itself by changing everything and remaining similar in a different manner. A Renaissance of Light Consciousness brings a fresh, unique view and witnesses Creation for what it is and not for what we want it to be. Truth as love inherits the earth.

As predicted by the Mayans, a fundamental level of awakening is occurring, and it continues to increase as the Present witnesses the decades to come. An awakening of the conscious mind is in full swing, and the swing is getting lighter. People are waking up around the world. Ignorance is being exposed. Corruption is being illuminated. Financial structures worldwide are being exposed for their empty value. Instead of living as we do today, destroying the planet, the Age of Light liberates, facilitates, and after much rumination, the world learns to love for a living (one human breath at a time). The world will adapt to live for a living and not consume for a living.

Recently, the U.S. Supreme Court ruled a corporation has some of the same rights as a person. In the historic January 2010 U.S. constitutional law case *Citizens United v. Federal Election Commission*, the U.S. Supreme Court held the First Amendment prohibits the government from restricting independent political expenditures by corporations, associations and labor unions. This destructive law must be reversed.

Corrupt money ("legal" bribes) has been cleverly disguised as political contributions around the world. This disturbing and parasitical development has brought the world economy to a point of financial implosion.

In response to this Supreme Court decision, President Barack Obama made the following statement:

> *"With its ruling today, the Supreme Court has given a green light to a new stampede of special interest money in our politics. It is a major victory for big oil, Wall Street banks, health insurance companies and the other powerful interests that marshal their power every day in Washington to drown out the voices of everyday Americans. This ruling gives the special interests and their lobbyists even more power in Washington—while undermining the influence of average Americans who make small contributions to support their preferred candidates. That's why I am instructing my Administration to get to work immediately with Congress on this issue. We are going to talk with bipartisan Congressional leaders to develop a forceful response to this decision. The public interest requires nothing less."* [150]

The Supreme Court is treating the American people like commodities that can be used by the corporations to do their bidding. The ruling is accelerating the decline of the American Dream as we know it. As governments increasingly make corruption the law of the land, it's no wonder people are starting to rise up against governments around the world. The American Dream may be alive, but it is slowly turning into a nightmare.

The American Revolution came about in large part because the colonists felt they should not be taxed without political representation. Returning to its roots of inception, the United States' Sibly chart starting in 2020 has Pluto in Capricorn with its first ever close conjunct concerning its Pluto return, and the idea of No Taxation Without Representation returns people to the streets. A wide range of dissatisfied Americans are marching and demonstrating with demands to be heard, much like Americans did in the 1960s and early 1970s. If a small yet significant percentage of Americans boycott their jobs for an extended period, it could have the potential of shutting down various businesses in the country, forcing the establishment to relinquish political power back to people. It isn't going to be easy; it never is.

The majority of corporations are concerned with one thing: selling more so they can make more money for their shareholders. Profit is the name of the game, and on and on it goes at the expense of our natural resources and our spiritual responsibility for taking care of our fellow men and women and our Mother Earth.

Governments the world over have become nothing more than puppets of capitalist global corporations. With their inscrutable agendas, governments do not seem to place a high priority on serving the interests of ordinary people. The wealthiest run the world by proxy, and they, too, know there is a force called the Universe... and no one controls anything, except their personal choices in life.

---

150 "Statement from the President on Today's Supreme Court Decision." *The White House*, 21 January 2010, www.whitehouse.gov/the-press-office/statement-president-todays-supreme-court-decision-0.

All governments like that in Russia grow into corruption steering the way. Putin openly runs the government and controls the media. In countries like Russia, which exist to maintain control, intimidation and violence are used to silence oppositional voices. Circumstances like this have to change worldwide if we are to live in peace and harmony. The world looked the other way when China seized Tibet, which was populated by some of the most loving and peaceful people in the world. The history of humankind makes it all too clear, anything is possible with the inhumanity to humanity.

Pollution and political ignorance will destroy China from within before it is ever defeated from without. China is on the edge of an abyss. It can either break up into various regions like the former Soviet Union or become the largest democracy in the world. China has a peaceful uprising or a bloody revolution or, as often seen in history, a bit of both by 2026-2028. For China, this "change" is a major turning point for letting go of the past to flow into the Age of Light.

Let us remember both the United States and China came into being because of revolutions. Revolution is part of the American heritage; it's in our blood and theirs.

A financial crisis in Japan can occur in 2019, which can forge a pivotal political move to satisfy financial markets around the world. In 2020 Japan elects its first female Prime Minister, and it's a symbolic shift for Japan and the world. This event signals a turning point, not only for the Japanese but also for the world, as the world is awakening with each day.

The United States must stop waging war in an attempt to impose its will on others. The U.S. Founding Fathers would be horrified to see what has happened in their country. Today, money rules America, and the American people no longer rule themselves. When the United States accuses Russia of imposing its political will on Ukraine, the words ring hollow. Just think back to the military actions of President George W. Bush in the Middle East.

In 2014, President Obama went to Japan and reconfirmed the military alliance between Japan and the United States, sending a message to the region and China. In response to this relationship, China has been preparing to strengthen its own influence in South America to balance out the influence the United States has in that area. In 2017, the first head of state to visit the newly elected President Trump was Prime Minister Abe of Japan, which reinforced the importance of the United States and Japanese alliance.

Unlike the Chinese people, the Japanese people see themselves as harmonious members of the same tribe. Japan is the guide for the people of every nation, showing how to demonstrate real respect for the world in which we live.

These two ancient cultures have ancient-Present issues. Russia, the wildcard, is creating greater ties with China in an attempt to o set the power of the United States. The Age of Light arrives as great cultures resolve their differences. There are always exceptions to the rule, and this is part of nature's mystery in a conciliatory manner. Instead of being the solution, in recent times politics has been a tool for creating problems (wars) for financial gain. It's an old story that has to end for a peaceful Present. Meanwhile, as we attempt to destroy each other with war, we are "burning down the house."

What the Chinese government did to the people of Tibet is horrific, and not unlike what the United States government did to the American Indians.

It is darkest before the Age of Light illuminates the human condition. This century is the turning point of no return to the past and a questionable future if the people of the world do not consciously choose to make a change in the Present. If our current willful destruction of the planet does not come to an end in this century, we will be responsible for bringing extinction to millions of living creatures and perhaps ourselves. The people of the world have been at war with each other since the beginning. Ever since the Big Bang, the Universe has been exploding with infinite finite energy configured beyond our imagination and comprehension. We are an example, the inexplicable unknown energy that we want to call God. We are who we are searching for. After all, we need God more than God needs us!

Climate change and social instability can have an effect on our food supply. Further, we are losing landmass due to the melting of the ice in the Arctic and Antarctic. The ocean is not only getting warmer, but it is also growing more acidic. Higher levels of carbon dioxide in the atmosphere are eventually absorbed into the ocean, which is damaging the coral reefs that feed the fish that feed humans. The world continues to live in the Dark Ages of unconsciousness.

The world is threatened by pollution, and the ocean has become the waste dump for the world. Garbage in the ocean provides innumerable hazards to marine life—and to life itself. As writer Jacob Silverman notes, "Of the more than 200 billion pounds of plastic the world produces each year, about 10 percent ends up in the ocean. Seventy percent of that eventually sinks, damaging life on the ocean floor." [151]

California is responsible for providing almost half of the food for the United States. 2015 marked the fourth year of a drought for California; its worst drought seen in more than 100 years. The world's major supply of food and water is in danger for future generations.

Climate change is the most important health issue for humankind and Earth. By 2020, evidence will show various kinds of environmental air and ground pollution in California are far worse than anyone thought it would be.

We have the technology to save the planet, just as we have the technology to destroy it. It is estimated by around the year 2045 there could be 70 to 80 million more vehicles on America's highways in inner cities. A smart city experiment in Columbus, Ohio, will be a technological and transportation laboratory for the sole purpose of establishing a set of guidelines so any city in America can adapt and utilize it. Our congested transportation system is inadequate and out of date because Congress has refused to act for too long to fix America's transportation infrastructure problem. All governments and corporations are made up of individuals who make decisions usually based on profits and not the spiritual, loving communal choice. Every Present moment, every individual choice and every decision affects every one of us. If there is evil, then it is us. If there is love, it is us. We decide!

---

[151] Silverman, Jacob. "Why Is the World's Biggest Landfill in the Pacific Ocean?" *HowStuffWorks.com*, 19 September 2007, http://science.howstuffworks.com/environmental/earth/oceanography/great-pacific-garbage-patch.htm.

In 2015, the gravitational ripple we heard concerning two black holes colliding a billion light years ago will redefine astronomy as we know it. There is evidence we know very little about where we are, who we are, and what we are. We live in an ocean of energy in which (through consciousness, awareness, hearing, seeing, and feeling), we are still learning to measure what we don't understand: ourselves!

I was born in the sign of Aquarius, and my yoga practice shows me how to live for a living, and the power of now is teaching me how to love for a living. As a sorcerer living in the mystic, I accept every prediction I make will not manifest or be accurate. In my astrological approach I employ non-judgmental observation, and I listen with my Present awareness to what the astrology charts indicate to me by way of my own personal experience. I see life beyond the constant finite and infinite state of opposites—yin/yang, alpha/omega—which manifests as the Present, imploding and expanding as a living organic Universe. For me, there is no inside and no outside, only love as Present Bliss.

Truth is all there is as love! Dark is Light; Light is Dark. Movement provides experience of the unknown. This reminds me of an old Zen proverb I made up, "If you learn to do nothing, you can do anything."

TimeSpace

Creation

KnowWhere

Transparent Mirror

Liquid Stardust

Eternal Consciousness

Age of Light

Acknowledgments

Genesis

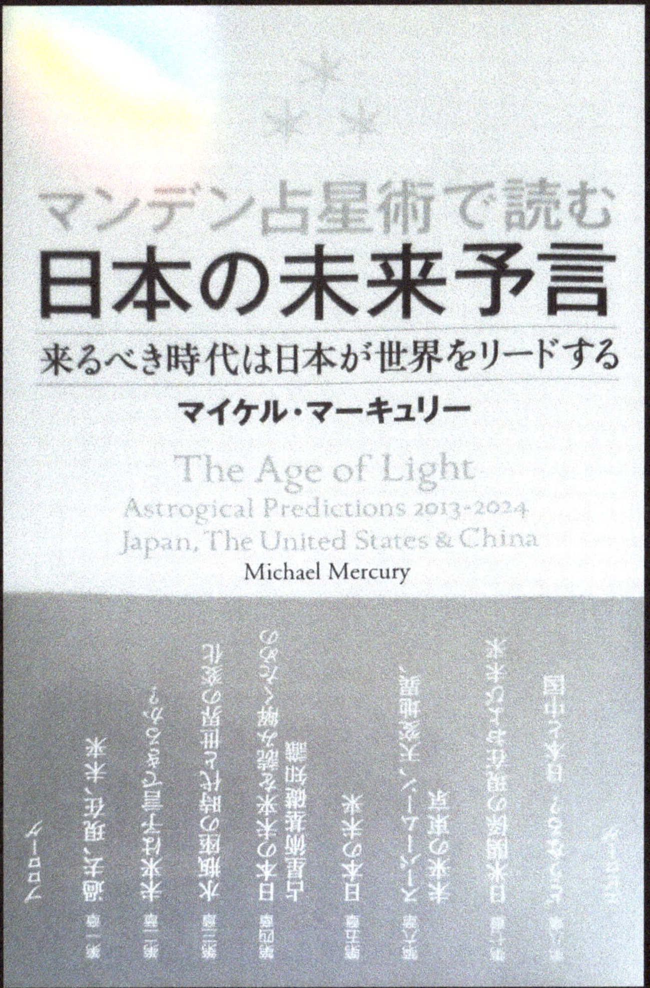

マンデン占星術で読む
日本の未来予言
来るべき時代は日本が世界をリードする
マイケル・マーキュリー

The Age of Light
Astrogical Predictions 2013-2024
Japan, The United States & China
Michael Mercury

- 第一章 日本のこれから、日本と中国
- 第二章 日本の関係性が改善、米国の軍隊
- 第三章 ジャパン・パワーの台頭
- 第四章 日本と米国の軍事的な結びつき
- 第五章 早すぎる復活の苦難対策
- 第六章 米米米米 台頭する星々のささやき
- 第七章 アメリカ、衰退へ…

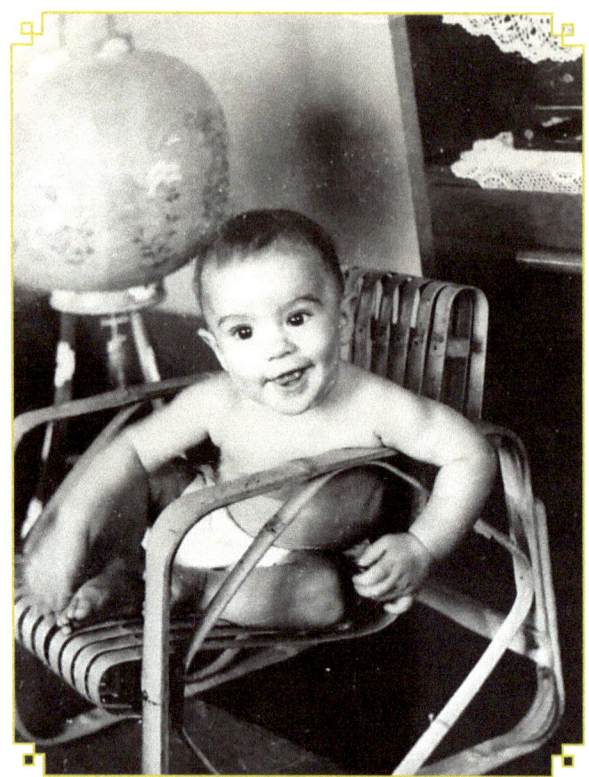

The genesis for this book came about after I gave an astrology reading for Sadaaki Hayashi at the home of Fumiko Takatsu. I don't believe in God; I understand God is all there is!

The subsequent conversation over dinner turned to speculation about the Mayan Prediction and its possible effects on Japan from an astrological perspective. Intrigued with this idea, I began to wonder if a book on this subject could be brought to life. After Sadaaki returned to Japan, we corresponded for several months, sharing thoughts, and from those discussions, the book was born. The living language of astrology led me to a Japanese publishing company in the spring of 2010. This book was completed in September 2012, translated into Japanese and published in April 2013 in Tokyo, Japan.

With love and humility, I wish to thank the many people who touched the original book and to those who have been an important part of my life:

My publisher, Sadaaki Hayashi, for planting the seed of an idea, and for his Japanese translation and publication of the resulting book.

I want to acknowledge and thank my mentors, and these are only a few: Ardyth E. Cochran, Carmen T. Cochran, Bill Rase of Sacramento, The Tao Te Ching, I Ching, J. Krishnamurti, Joseph Campbell, Alan Watts, Lao-Tzu, the Buddha, D.T., Suzuki, Jesus Christ, the Dead Sea Scrolls and many more have shown me how to follow my bliss. Thanks to the many who have been, and still are, smoke signals for a new awareness, which for me has pulled back the cosmic curtain to reveal the Age of Light is dawning in this century.

Acknowledgments

Here are only a few friends and people who have made a difference in my life:

Jack Koulbanis, good friend, for his wisdom and insight from the beginning of this project through its completion. His guidance has been invaluable. He is one of the wisest men I know.

Fumiko Takatsu, Henry Calanchini, and beautiful Nina, dear friends, for their love and kindness.

Shauni Mills DeVeaux, my muse and flying mermaid from the stars, for reminding me that unconditional love is the only love.

Dave and Mary Taormino, my oldest friends, who have blessed me with love and kindness when I needed it most.

Tom Hsieh, my best long-time friend, for his loyal support over the years.

All the many students I had the privilege to guide in their yoga practice at Yoga Loka, Pipeworks, and Asha Yoga studio, all located in Sacramento.

Brian Elsasser, editor, thank you for the journalistic skills and edits in the original draft of this book.

Maria Mateus, colleague, for her astrological expertise and clarity, and for writing the Preface to this book. Thank you for your invaluable editing when I needed it the most.

Tem Tarriktar, and Kate Sholly the co-founders of the Mountain Astrologer, you changed my life in a beautiful way. I want to thank the staff for the most comprehensive astrology magazine on the planet.

Kurt Booker, my friend and webmaster for many years, for his technological skills and his generous gift of time.

Mahnaz Westerberg and Manuel Hoffman, for showing me what a loving couple can be. I am grateful for the love and abiding friendship we have.

Sara Judson, you are light and love. I cherish having you and your mother in my life.

Mark and Shannon Borge, and beautiful Sophie, I am overjoyed with your love.

Bill and Sandy McCauley, good friends and founders of Yoga Loka, for their generous love and trust.

Robert Turner and Nicole for their love. Robert, we are bothers from our American Indians past lives, many moons of eternity ago.

Eddie Harris and Les McCann, for teaching me so much... "Compare to What" indeed!

In memoriam, Don Barbeau: for his patience and friendship, which is love.

David Carey, Peter Brown, and Julie Partansky for all the wild gatherings at the white house barn at 7th and D street in Davis.

Charlie and Pat Metz, for their wisdom and love they shared.

www.MichaelMercury.com

Ken Kemmerling and Rod Macdonald and Mora Metz, R. Crumb, Phil Gross, and Public Access TV in Davis, where I created the Davis Channel. Davis has been very, very, good to me. In 1992, Cafe Cinema, was a thrill to create with the wonderful Toye Richter.

The UCD Theatre Department that allowed me to awaken in my own way.

Kristine Clark, my yogini roommate, who is like a sister, brings love, support, friendship, great laughter, and humor.

Kayla Simas, my true friend and colleague for her great presence and magical energy. She is fun, happy and wise from the beyond.

Alex de Rafols and Robin in Davis, for their love and support for my new website: *Increation.com*

Safeway Goya, and his wife Anja for their love and support all these many years. And what wonderful children you raised that became beautiful, magnificent human beings, Staik, Alex Paris, and Lisa.

Asaad Kaddourah, and Helena Bergstrand, I can't thank you enough for helping me and for your genuine friendship and eternal kindness.

Barbara Torza and Barbara Burgum, the true value of friends are those who make a difference in our lives.

Anja and Chad Brey, organic friends, for their support and demonstrating what true love is. I will never forget your wedding on a sailing boat under the Golden Gate bridge.

Jody Leidecker and Faith Peel and Liz Peel for the support and friendship we have shared in life.

Bill and Shirley Rase, Kip, Ester, I am so grateful for all the fun we had at Bill Rase Studios in Sacaramento.

Herb Lightman, Hollywood director, in memoriam for his love and teaching me about what is important in life.

Shecky Green, for his humor and sacrifices.

Julie Marciel and Stella, new friends whom I have shared so much in eternity.

Anna Skacel, for her contribution to my growth, and awareness. We are good friends that learn from each other.

Jean Lochkart, astrologer, artist, in memoriam and my biggest fan who kept me grounded when I needed it. Thank you!

Julie Mumma, who inspires me and one of the amazing mindful spirits on the planet.

Lu Ann Sloan for your friendship and support over the years.

Dr. Dan Beilin, OMD, L.Ac., thank you for your long-time friendship and contribution to my radio programs over the years.

Peter Richter, for his wisdom and friendship. What fun it is to laugh and sing with the light.

Acknowledgments

Ray Grelecki, one of the founding members of The Office of Strategic Services (OSS), a United States intelligence agency formed during World War II. I miss you and thank you for your love and service.

Gore Vidal and William Buckley for their contributions to the political landscape.

Elmer Bartley, long time good friend, for his financial support, love and friendship of many years.

Kurt Vonnegut, for sharing a cigarette with me, and for his encouragement. "I want to stand as close to the edge as I can without going over. Out on the edge you see all kinds of things you can't see from the center."

Michael and Julie Rosen, and their angel Mia, for demonstrating to me how to create heaven on Earth, with love and kindness as a way of life.

Riverside Military Academy in Gainesville, GA. Thank you. For whatever mysterious reason, I chose you as my boarding school, which introduced me to Eternity. What a great thrill in hindsight, and I want to thank all the professors and classmates who are a part of this mystery.

Robert Zoller, the amazing astrologer, my spiritual brother, for his friendship, love, inspiration, and wisdom.

Kepler College in Seattle was an amazing, illuminating experience that altered the course of my life, and I'm deeply grateful.

Robert Hand, I want to thank you for your wisdom and truly one of the great astrologers of the world. What a pleasure it was to be able to study Astrology with you at Kepler College.

A.T. Mann, I appreciate your support with your appearances on my radio program over the years. Tad, you inspired me toward the light when I was in a dark place.

Mary Jane Pop, I want to thank you for your love and support for my passion ever since we met back at Channel 31 in Sacramento.

Bruce Lee for all the wisdom, beauty, and spirit that you demonstrated and taught without teaching by being.

Krista Campbell, it's fun and always a surprise to share love when you least expect it.

Werner and Barbara Bosshard, my time in Switzerland were some of my most cherished times in my life and thank you for making it happened for me. I miss and love you both.

Mike Oddino, Grant Napear, we had so much fun with so little to work with at UC Davis and doing what had never been done before. Your two of the best in the broadcast business and I am grateful for our time together.

Stan Atkinson for his friendship and support over the years in the broadcast business.

Mary Ann Grant, we have known each other for eternity and thank you for your love and the wonderful times we had in Hawaii.

Michael Kinsey, I am grateful for your support and the passion for your due diligence that you bring to my yoga practice. Also, to the students at Yoga Loka, I love being with you. To my fellow yogini colleagues, Kally, Kahlil, Kristine, Kayla, and Mireya, thank you for your friendship.

Bob Hope, thank you for the memory of interviewing you. Also I had the most unusual day of my life the last time I was in New York City. Clearly, this was a long time ago. I meet Joan Rivers after her talk show on a local program in New York City. We had coffee and she was generous with her time and advice. Within a half hour of meeting with Joan Rivers, walking down a street in New York, I walked into Muhammad Ali and spent over a half hour talking with him about the Vietnam war and his thoughts on life. Within five minutes there must have been one hundred people surrounding us as we continued our conversation.

Lenny Bruce for his courage and truth.

Nicolas Campion, the extraordinary astrologer, for his kindness and contribution to the astrological community.

Lee Lehman, for her wonderful energy and encouragement towards my astrological studies.

Don Imus, who I met in Sacramento in the late 60's before anyone knew who he was. Imus in the morning has been an inspiration for my radio program over the years.

Dick Cavett, thank you for your genius and the pleasure of hearing a kindred spirit.

Ram Das, for our illuminating conversations on 'forgiveness,' and our many unexpected and joyful encounters over the years.

Louis S. Bostwick, founder of the Berkeley Psychic Institute, for his love, kindness, and support in teaching me how to read auras, energy fields, and assisting my awakening.

Glenn Waters, one of my students who is an inspiration to me and many others who is practicing Bikram yoga at 87 years young.

Richard Nolle, I appreciate your insights and contribution to clarifying Supermoons.

Elizabeth Valentina, an amazing lady, thank you for your support, love, and helping me get this book published.

Mort Sahl, my first rebel of shining light with his wit, intelligence, observations, and insight. A true mystic in our midst.

Johnny Carson for his wit and his positive contribution to the United States culture.

Charlotte Tighe, what innocent fun we had. You were my first significant connection with another.

Nina Vafa, our love in Tehran, Iran, was the most profound and life-altering experience of my life. I do miss you.

Van Morrison, who lights the way with his spirit and music.

Rick Caesar, for his friendship at UC Davis and all the great stories about his father Sid Caesar.

Acknowledgments

Clint Cochran, my spiritual guide, for his patience, friendship and love.

Thank you Uncle Albert Einstein, you lead me to this book not so long ago.

Stevie Wonder, my spiritual brother, who saved my life with his music and love.

I also want to thank all the people involved in this expanded and updated version of the original book:

Robynn Mccann, you are not just my publisher, you have become a good friend and without you this book would not have happened in the way it was intended.

Rebecca Woolston, thank you for all the last minute editing. I am very grateful to you.

Frieda Kodl, as my editor whose expertise brought this book altogether.

Carolyn Daughters, Linda Martin for their editing contributions and formatting guidance.

Ahrynn McCann and Julie Rosen, for their contribution to the cover design.

Thom Vallance, formatting this book was a heroic effort on your part. Thank you for your *parent-like* patience with me.

Lyn Birkbeck, astrologer, I want to thank you for your contribution to the astrology community.

Stephen Mathews, of the United Kingdom for his work on the Kindle digital formatting.

Resolution from California State Legislature, Sept 2012: Ascend was awarded a Resolution from California State Legislature setting forth that it "be commended for the outstanding contribution it has made to lowering recidivism and increasing public safety."
    Toni White, Christine Morse, co-founders of Ascend.
    Law Offices of Toni White, a Professional Law Corporation
    11930 Heritage Oak Place, Suite 6, Auburn, CA 95603
    Tel 530.885.6244, Fax 530.344.9298

About the Author

Michael Mercury was born in Tokyo, Japan, and has lived in many countries throughout the world. His exposure to different cultures has influenced the development of his approach to astrology.

His knowledge of ancient wisdom is insightful and illuminating. By using his intuition, quick wit and prescient awareness, Mercury delivers a positive message his readers and listeners have come to love.

Mercury is a seasoned radio and television commentator. His astrological call-in radio show is his passion. You can hear him streaming on KUBU 96.5 FM in Sacramento, California. You can also check his website mercuryminute.com for weekly audio updates.

Mercury resides in Sacramento, California, where he teaches a unique style of Astro Yoga with Kayla Simas. He has a Master's Degree in Fine Arts from the University of California at Davis.

www.ingramcontent.com/pod-product-compliance
Lightning Source LLC
Chambersburg PA
CBHW051559010526
44118CB00023B/2747